Criminal Law, Feminism and Emotions

This book critically engages criminal law issues relating to sexuality and violence in order to argue that an attention to emotions can produce a more nuanced – and more adequate – feminist account of legal subjectivity.

Although the relationship between law and feminism has resulted in a vast body of work, the issue of emotions has not been foregrounded in feminist legal scholarship in India. Indeed, many feminists have argued that reason and not emotion must provide the foundational basis for all laws and legal reforms – an argument that has led to a division of the legal and the psychic or the emotional into separate and distinct zones. Challenging this separation, the book engages a range of recent criminal law cases and legislations in India in order to advocate for a 'feminine' law that embraces its inherent cracks and contradictions. Drawing on psychoanalytic theory, the book takes up a range of issues surrounding sexuality and violence in order to propose a shift from viewing law as reason to seeing law as the terrain of messy and contradictory emotional continuums; where legal subjects are viewed in their psychic dimensions, and where law itself is opened up to its own unconscious desires. This volume argues that foregrounding emotions in this way can offer new insights into the operation of criminal law, as well as new orientations for feminist ways of responding to – and engaging with – it.

This book will be of interest to scholars and students working in the areas of criminal law, legal feminism and gender studies.

Latika Vashist is Associate Professor at Dr. B.R. Ambedkar University Delhi, India.

Criminal Law, Feminism and Emotions

Thinking through the Legal Unconscious

Latika Vashist

Routledge
Taylor & Francis Group
LONDON AND NEW YORK

First published 2025
by Routledge
4 Park Square, Milton Park, Abingdon, Oxon OX14 4RN

and by Routledge
605 Third Avenue, New York, NY 10158

Routledge is an imprint of the Taylor & Francis Group, an informa business

British Library Cataloguing-in-Publication Data
A catalogue record for this book is available from the British Library

Library of Congress Cataloging-in-Publication Data
A catalog record has been requested for this book

ISBN: 978-1-032-46926-3 (hbk)
ISBN: 978-1-032-48104-3 (pbk)
ISBN: 978-1-003-38741-1 (ebk)

DOI: 10.4324/9781003387411

Typeset in Sabon
by Taylor & Francis Books

Contents

Acknowledgements

This book is a gift for my teachers, who taught me how to struggle to arrive at 'thinking': Anand Prakash (AP Sir) gave me the first, very difficult, lessons in feminism; B.B. Pande, M.P. Singh, Ved Kumari and Alka Chawla taught me how read the spectrum of colours in the black letter of law; Kamala Sankaran, Jyoti Dogra Sood, P. Puneeth (and Amit Bindal) helped me realise my dream of becoming a teacher.

Anup Dhar, my thesis supervisor, let me fly with fledgling wings and was there to hear every question, clarify every doubt. He believed in this project and my capacity to give it words when I was on the verge of giving up. I cannot thank him enough.

Ratna Kapur opened the world of feminism for me. During the six months when I was her research assistant, she pushed me out of my comfort zone and changed the trajectory of my academic life.

Ashley Tellis first blinded me with his sheer brilliance and then held my ideas and words with extraordinary empathy; this book, the reader must know, got written because Ashley spoke, dreamt, wrote and fought. All the ideas that could undo my own (middle-class) conception of law, are his. This book owes him immensely.

Usha Ramanathan taught me the value of slow and steady academic labour and is my favourite feminist.

Upendra Baxi and Kalpana Kannabiran raised many difficult questions and gave insightful comments on my thesis.

Shiv Visvanathan paved the way for the much-needed indiscipline of interdisciplinarity, taught me to not conform, to not give up. He opened his house and library to all lost academics like me and embraced all of us, never forgetting to remind us how boring we are all becoming!

Manoj Kumar Sinha's support and encouragement made the Indian Law Institute the most productive space for my work. Lawrence Liang and Anushka Singh shielded me from the woes of administrative work at Ambedkar University Delhi; Lawrence shared fascinating books, comics and stories which I am yet to read.

Oh Friends, there *are* friends.

I thank Jyoti Dogra Sood for all those days when I could just huddle up in her office, where she let me think, sulk, weep; for making me finish the PhD (and feeding me forcibly).

Pooja Satyogi was that friend with whom conversations and feelings reached the deepest abyss, only to come afloat, I basked in her love of reading and listening.

I thank Avantika Tiwari for appearing like a genie whenever I wished for her presence and for getting things done real fast; also, for being my best student ever.

Deepti Sachdev and Anshumita Pandey were my co-travellers in those dark days, when the PhD was just not happening! That was also the time when Rukmini Sen and Bindu K.C. displayed how ethics of care translate into pedagogy.

Rakesh Ankit showed me the mirror all the time and reminded me how academic work needs to be done without any ambition.

Jibraan Mansoor enters the skin of one's prose and excavates the hidden and unarticulated affects. He has been that loving reader and critic whom any writer would die for.

Kaushik M. helped me with the citations and referencing style.

The Teachers of Aarambh Waldorf offered their courage and conviction and are rocks for hopeless mothers like me. Mamta Devi ensured that the house and food was in order, so that we could read and write.

Payal Vashist was a support as I was growing up; Sameera Vashist showed me how one can be hopeful and love life, despite everything.

Vijay Bindal was that person in the family who can be relied on completely; her care and patience helped us recover from terrible times.

Usha Bindal showed hope and remarkable strength; Rajeev Bindal offered his support and encouragement. Payal Mangla was a reassuring presence in the family when things just weren't going right.

My mother, Kamlesh Vashist, is my world; her laughter and her scoldings, her wit and her despair, her courage and love and giving that know no limits shape my being. I once saw tears trickle down from her eyes while she was reading a novel. That was the day I learnt how to read a text.

My father, Om Datt Vashist, made me love social sciences; he gave me a dream and made it happen. He did not lose patience with my six-year-old scared self on the slide in children's park; even as the world was mocking me, he waited for an eternity for me to gather the courage to slide down. I am grateful for his silent presence.

Dhruv, my brother, lives in the most vulnerable part of my heart and continues to love me despite my bossiness. Divya has become the thread that weaves our fragile worlds together. Dev came into our lives and brought so much joy.

Amit, let me say 'thank you' for bearing, holding, loving me; for creating a world for our son that I could never have; for holding my home, for being my home. And, of course, for being the most passionate teacher, for all the reading sessions, discussions, debates, fights, with his characteristic 'oh my God' and 'WTF' moments; for giving me hope in 'superhumanities'; for reading everything I write, multiple times over, for giving me a hand and lifting me up from the rubble of citations. *This* book happened, because *that* one is pending; for not letting me feel the weight of this fact.

Kabir Kaivalya, my baby, I love the way you love me and the way I love you. Kabir, I hate this book for all the time that it kept me lost in my thoughts and I did not hear you. Now it is over. Now we will play.

*

[Chapter 1 previously appeared as: Emotions and Criminal Law: Limits of Martha Nussbaum's "Evaluative Conception". *Journal of the Indian Law Institute,* 63(3), 298–324 (2021). A shorter version of Chapter 6 appeared as: Age of consent and the impossibility of child sexuality. *Seminar,* 721 (2019)].

Introduction

In recent years, it has been claimed that feminism wields immense power in the legal arena. In both domestic and international law, feminist ideas are institutionalised, there is a proliferation of women-related laws, gender-mainstreaming is a primary agenda and women have now come to occupy public and political spaces as never before. Feminists, it is claimed, walk 'in the corridors of power', their ideas have found a strong foothold within state institutions, and they are now 'a crucial part of the lawmaking process' (Kotiswaran, 2017, p. 78; Halley et al., 2018; Rottenberg, 2018; Halley, 2006). This is one narrative.

The other narrative is not so certain about either feminism or its effects on the law (Menon, 2019; Kapur, 2013; Otto, 2009). Despite the decades-long feminist engagement – scholarly as well as activist – with the law, feminist goals are far from being realised. There is a daunting inertia and resistance against change in socio-legal settings, as well as the mind-boggling stickiness of conservative normative order that pulls backwards all attempts of legal reforms.[1] This serves as a reminder that dark times for feminism have far from ended. Moreover, feminism's engagement with the 'dark' – the darkness of individual and collective history, context and the dark side of the human – is far from complete.

For British psychoanalytic feminist Jacqueline Rose, feminism today needs a new language; a language different from the one based on the teleological grammar that seeks to end darkness with light, a language which is neither 'co-opted

1 The latest of these attempts is the replacement of existing criminal codes with 'new' laws deploying the rhetoric of decolonisation and progressive change. In December 2023 three new Criminal Laws: Bharatiya Nyaya Sanhita, 2023 ('BNS'), Bharatiya Nagarik Suraksha Sanhita, 2023 ('BNSS') and Bharatiya Sakshya Adhiniyam, 2023 ('BSA') (which replaced the Indian Penal Code, 1860 ('IPC'), Code of Criminal Procedure, 1973 ('CrPC') and the Indian Evidence Act, 1872 ('IEA') respectively) were enacted. The Bills received Presidential assent, and were published in the *Official Gazette* on December 25, 2023 and have come into force on July 1, 2024. It needs to be said that much of the 'old' is retained in these 'new' laws, making this endeavour a lost opportunity to re-imagine the space of criminal law (Tundawala & Choudhuri, 2023; Satish, Dash & Pandey, 2024; Uma, 2024). In this book, I will stay with the legal provisions of the IPC (as a large part of the IPC is verbatim reproduced in the BNS), and indicate the BNS provisions, wherever necessary.

DOI: 10.4324/9781003387411-1

by false pretension [n]or by the brute exertion of power for its own sake' (Rose, 2014, p. ix). It will not aspire to a 'sane, balanced, reasoned' world; rather it will dredge into the 'subterranean aspects of history and the human mind' to imagine feminist futures. She makes a plea for a 'bold and scandalous feminism' that does not sanitise itself but 'embraces without inhibition the most painful, outrageous aspects of the human heart, giving them their place at the very core of the world that feminism wants to create' (p. ix). 'Scandalous' thus is a plea for radical inwardness. Calling to reinvigorate the 'personal' in the old feminist slogan 'the personal is political', Rose asks: '[w]hat happens when we push that feminist insistence on the inner, private dimension of political struggle to the furthest limits of conscious and unconscious life' (p. x). This book is written as a response to this question in the domains of law and feminism in India.

Accepting Rose's invitation to move towards scandalous feminism, I explore the interface between law, feminism and emotions in this book. Emotions which are expelled from the dominant renditions of law and legal feminism, erupt into the scene precisely to scandalise the dominant imaginations of the law as well as feminist engagements with law. This enquiry into emotions looks beneath the dominant legal script of progressive reforms to examine how the rational legal edifice is constructed on popular sentiments. It explores how the personal and the intimate which inform the law materialise as 'the uncanny' – *unheimlich* (Freud, 1919/1955) – and are home to the darkest and the ugliest secrets of the individual and collective psyche. I intend to excavate and describe the unhomeliness that lurks in the home of legal imaginary.

While the relationship between law and feminism (in India and elsewhere) has resulted in a vast body of writings, designated as feminist jurisprudence (Kapur, 1996; Kapur & Cossman, 1996; West & Bowman, 2019; MacKinnon, 1983; MacKinnon, 1987; MacKinnon, 1989; Kannabiran, 2013; Agnes 1992; Agnes, 2004; Dhanda & Parashar, 1999), the 'emotion question' has not been foregrounded in the feminist legal scholarship in India. Emotions are seen as dangerous red flags for the rule of law, which ought to be contained (Bhattacharjee, 2017). In fact, feminists, located in different spacio-political contexts, have expressed concerns about 'rule by sentiments' to argue that reason and not emotion must form the foundational basis for all laws and legal reforms (Agnes, 2013; Kumari, 2015; Nussbaum, 2016). Theoretically, this argument leads to the re-reification of law and emotions as separate and distinct zones. Challenging this 'separation thesis' between the legal and the emotional is the entry point of this book.[2]

2 Herbert Hart's project is also founded on this separation thesis wherein he argues that law and morality are distinct spheres (Hart, 1994). Jeanne Lorraine Schroeder's Lacanian critique of Hart's positivism and separation thesis (Schroeder, 2008) provided a compelling background reading for me in thinking through the reason-emotion separation matrix. Schroeder is one of the few legal scholars who work on the intersection of Anglo-American jurisprudence, and speculative theory (including Lacanian psychoanalysis).

I will argue that our political demands which take the form of appeals to the law are tied to, and hence manifest, our innermost psychic states. The affective/the emotional/the psychic are intrinsically connected to the social/political/legal. This makes it pertinent for us, as feminists, to investigate the affective and psychic, alongside, with, and as internal to, the legal-socio-politico spaces. As Lacanian psychoanalytic theorist, Joan Copjec argued, contra Michel Foucault, 'some notion of transcendence is plainly needed if one is to avoid the reduction of social space to the relations that fill it' (1994, p. 7). The social space, if it only 'ground[s] being in appearance', can only offer a partial theory of power. Thus, Copjec urges the 'analysts of culture to become literate in desire, to learn how to read what is inarticulable in cultural statements' (p. 14). Extending Copjec's argument about the social to the terrain of the legal, this book contends that the legal is not only a discursive realm of significations or networks of power relations. The legal is also constituted by *desire*:[3] the desire of the legal subject as well as desire of the law, desire understood as 'unconscious desire' and as the 'other's desire' (Mitchell & Rose, 1985).

The opposition between reason and emotion is constitutive of the legal tradition. The law, it is claimed, is based upon reason and rational deliberation; and reason is superior to emotion. In this binary, emotion is understood to be an irrational drive that sweeps us and makes our cognitive faculties its slave. But law, we are well aware, has its own mythological world (Fitzpatrick, 2002). It is a world that selectively (de)recognises and (dis)acknowledges emotional experiences. The love and desperation of a mother who steals bread to feed her child is not recognised (she becomes a criminal deserving of punishment), while the jealousy and rage of a man who kills his partner's lover is sympathised with (and he is not a murderer, but only guilty of manslaughter/culpable homicide). It is reasonable in law to be blind to woman's despair but to recognise male jealousy. Such a selective and gendered approach to people's emotional responses constitutes the Reason of law.

The emotion-question seeks to expose these inconsistences and contradictions that are immanent in criminal law. For instance, when action arising from anger is accepted as a (partial) defence in criminal law, why does law not allow any defence to an individual who kills out of fear of her own life or the life of a loved one, owing to threats from another individual (as defence of duress) or difficult circumstances (as defence of necessity). How do we understand law's position of discounting fear, and privileging anger in principles of exculpation (Spain, 2011)? What are the gendered effects of law's capacity to account for only unidimensional emotions (like anger or fear), while sidelining 'multifaceted emotional situations in which people often find themselves, situations in which they feel competing and diverse emotions – fear and desire, love and hate – at the same time' (Baker, 2005, p. 447, fn. 1)?

3 I use the expression in the Lacanian sense. Desire is the remainder – 'something other' – that does not get fulfilled when a demand is met by the satisfaction of its needs.

Despite these stark inconsistencies, the law presents itself as rational, self-contained and objective. This image of law has been variously contested, with different aims and to different ends, in feminist jurisprudence (MacKinnon, 1983; MacKinnon, 1987; Williams, 1991; Smart, 1989, Kapur & Cossman, 1996; Gotell, 1995), the law and emotions scholarship (Abrams & Keren, 2010; Nussbaum, 2004; Bandes, 1999; Maroney, 2006; Sanger, 2001; Blumenthal, 2005) and also psychoanalytic jurisprudence (Goodrich & Carlson, 1998; Cornell, 1999; Douzinas, 2000; Aristodemou, 2014, Goodrich, 1997a; Schroeder, 2008). In this book, I will navigate through the crossroads of these three subfields. In what follows, I will begin with a broad overview of the law and emotions scholarship and outline my critique of this paradigm. I will then step into the domain of psychoanalysis, briefly explain the terms and concepts that I will be relying on in this book and devote the remaining part of this Introduction to show how a dialogue with psychoanalysis stretches the scope of our enquires by allowing us to ask those questions which are forbidden in the world of the law, and often even feminism.

The traditional view of emotions as enemies of reason – disorderly, irrational and outside of reason-driven conceptualisations of human nature and civic life – is no longer tenable. Significant advancements have been made in contemporary emotion research, making the study of emotion an exciting foray into trans-disciplinary thought.[4] However, there is no consensus in the field even about the fundamental assumptions about emotion, making it a 'wobbly compendium of thought' (Maroney, 2006, p. 136). There are two contradictory positions, running parallel in emotion research (Leys, 2017, Hutchinson, 2008). On one side are cognitivists who emphasise upon the intentionality of emotions, that is emotions are directed at objects, they are judgments, and have meaning (Lazarus, 1991; Solomon, 2003; Nussbaum, 2001; De Souza, 1990). On the other side, are non-cognitivists who highlight the significance of bodily changes and hold the view that emotions are triggered by subliminal stimuli, even in the absence of cognitive capacity (Sedgwick & Frank, 1995; Massumi, 2002; Damasio, 2005). Most legal scholars who inaugurated the law and emotions research aligned with the cognitivists, without paying much attention to the fundamental contradiction that lies at the heart of theorisation of emotion (Leys, 2017). It is not difficult to see why the contradiction did not bother them. If emotions were intentional and had meaning, then they could be easily brought, and accounted for, into the fold of law's reason.

In Anglo-American legal scholarship, the exploration of the emotion-question has led to a vast body of academic work on diverse emotions in different areas of law. While the intersection of law and emotion was never entirely ignored (Horder, 1992; Henderson, 1986–87; Pillsbury, 1989; Murphy & Hampton,

4 For developments in the field and cross-disciplinary dialogue, see *Emotion Review*, the first journal of the International Society for Research on Emotion, which was started in 2009.

1988), it was the conference on law and emotions at the University of Chicago Law School in May 1998 that foregrounded the relevance of studying emotions in law. Following this conference, *The Passions of Law* (1999), a collection of 13 essays, edited by Susan Bandes, was published in 1999. By now, 'the debate about whether emotion belongs in the law' was settled as it was widely accepted that emotions permeate the entire fabric of law and 'emotional content is inevitable' (Bandes, 1999, p. 7). The authors who contributed to this volume considered diverse emotions including disgust, shame, romantic love, remorse, revenge, anger, fear and cowardice to demonstrate that the law not only responds to emotions but the law also expresses as well as creates emotions.

Notwithstanding the "No-Emotion" claim of the law, the law and emotion scholarship has revealed that emotions are ubiquitous in law. Certain questions central to their enquiry are: which passions are willingly carved into legal theory and doctrine and which are left out as 'irrational' and thus, inappropriate to the legal process; when and how do emotions influence culpability; when is judicial reasoning guided by emotions; which approach to emotions guides the judges in decision-making; what social and ideological meanings are entrenched in and through judicial discourse by the recognition of emotions (Bandes, 2009a; Dubber, 2006; Finkel & Parrott, 2006)? These questions have pushed the limits of the hermeneutics of criminal law. Now it is clear that the official text might be speaking in rational-neutral terms but the sub-text of law-making is entrenched in emotions. Disgust, anger, repulsion determine what conduct should be criminalised and thus become instrumental in construction of the normative framework of the law (Nussbaum, 2004; Nussbaum, 2016; Nussbaum, 2010; Kahan, 1999); romantic love is powerfully structured, or even produced, by elaborate social scripts (Calhoun, 1999); 'global economies of fear' give shape to processes and institutions of law (Ahmed, 2004; Nussbaum, 2018); victims and their families bring raw emotions into the courtrooms to share their grief, sorrow, outrage and evoke compassion and sympathy from the justice system (Bandes, 2009b; Minow, 1993); vengeance, remorse, shame and considerations of mercy slide into sentencing (Nussbaum, 2004; Murphy, 2007); just as repentance, apology and forgiveness keep creeping into criminal justice (Murphy, 2006; Bibas & Bierschbach, 2004; Minow, 2001; Murphy & Hampton, 1988, Minow, 2015).

Significantly, many scholars in the field have taken a leap from description of law's relationship with emotion to prescriptive advocacy for law's purposeful cultivation of moral emotions (Minow, 2015; Nussbaum, 2013; cf: Sanger, 2001) without challenging the exclusionary logics of liberal legal order (Norrie, 2014). In such normative accounts, like Martha Minow's (2015) argument of cultivation of forgiveness via law, one finds an underlying faith in not just the authenticity of the emotion displayed but also transparency of the meaning attributed to it. This is the point where this book takes leave of this paradigm. The purpose of this book is to dent the enthusiasm of cognitivist law and emotions scholars premised as it is on affirmation of the liberal legal order. To this end, I will argue that the dominance of cognitivism in law and emotion scholarship has eroded the epistemo-ontological potential of emotions as a site of critique of law's rationality.

Rather than rupturing legal rationality and exposing its irrationalities, cracks and contradictions, the cognitivist conception of emotion strengthens the *status quoist* assumption of law as the domain of reason. In other words, the turn to emotions remains largely rooted in the possibility of reforming existing law to repair relationships. This reparative enterprise remains shallow and superficial in so far as it does not dare to confront the dark side of emotions. Instead, it prefers to efface and abdicate the deeper malaise in its preference of suturing the instituting wound of the legal institution. In this framework there is a prior agreement on what constitutes an egalitarian legal order based on equality and respect. An uncritical faith is retained in the liberal imagination of the law, as the overall argument is that the legal judgments and decisions based on certain (good) emotions will serve and advance the goals of liberal legal order better than those based on other (bad) emotions (Polletta, 2001). Emotion is tamed and subsumed within law's reason as legal prescriptivism takes over the 'social epistemologies that govern people's experiences, expressions, and interpretations of emotions' (Polletta, 2001, p. 490).

I will argue that the cognitivist strand of the law and emotion scholarship reifies the notion of abstract individualism. Even when emotions of the legal subject are discussed, the subject remains a rational, autonomous, choice-bearing actor. The frame of rationality remains paramount in describing, assessing and evaluating her emotions. Law itself is re-inscribed as a coherent, unitary system without any cracks or fissures bearing its own emotions. However, the moment one takes leave from the rigid constrictive frame of cognitivism, and takes the 'emotion question' to psychoanalysis, things fall apart. All assumptions about the law and the legal subject begin to crumble, and all certainties come to an end. This is where this book will begin, as we begin to see a less sure law, and a less safe feminism. A spilt law. A scandalous feminism.

It is important to understand what exactly is psychoanalysis. Psychoanalysis must be distinguished from psychologisation. The concept of psychologisation, in terms of conventional idioms of the discipline of psychology, reduces the experience of the subject to just one register – the psychological – and misses out on the complexity and mutual construction of the mind-body, psyche-social, mental-discursive in psychoanalysis.

In her Introduction to *Feminine Sexuality: Jacques Lacan and the école freudienne* (translation of selected works of French psychoanalyst, Jacques Lacan), Juliet Mitchell described psychoanalysis in one short sentence: 'psychoanalysis is about human sexuality and the unconscious' (Mitchell & Rose, 1985, p. 2). Mitchell clarified at the outset that psychoanalytically, sexuality cannot be equated with genitality or a biological drive: 'It is always psycho-sexuality, a system of conscious and unconscious human fantasies involving a range of excitations and activities that produce pleasure beyond the satisfaction of any basic physiological need' (p. 2). Sexuality and unconscious are 'causatively intertwined' (p. 2). Thus, sexuality is not reducible to sexual preference/ sexual identity and is not interchangeable with what we today understand as 'gender'.[5] As a system of unconscious fantasies, sexuality or sexual desire is not directly accessible because the unconscious is outside the logic of consciousness. At the same time, it is not a dark repository of emotions and thoughts; the unconscious is structured like language and 'governed by its own laws, its images do not follow each other as in the sequential logic of consciousness but by condensing onto each other and by being displaced onto something else' (Mitchell & Rose, 1985, pp. 2–3). Dreams, like parapraxia, slips of the tongue and pen, jokes and wit, are 'the royal road to the unconscious' (Mitchell, 2000, p. 102).

Jacques Lacan who is credited with the revolutionary 'return to Freud' (Grosz, 1990; Mitchell & Rose, 1985)[6] emphasised the significance of language in psychoanalysis.[7] He offered a theory of human subjectivity where the human subject, constituted through language (called the symbolic order), is created 'in the fissure of a radical split' (Mitchell & Rose, 1985, p. 5):

> The human animal is born into language and it is within the terms of language that the human subject is constructed. Language does not arise from within the individual, it is always out there in the world outside, lying in wait for the neonate. Language always 'belongs' to another person. The human subject is created from a general law that comes to it from outside itself and through the speech of other people, though this speech in its turn must relate to the general law.

5 Methodologically, feminists 'think of gender difference as both structuring and structured by the wide set of social relations' (Sangari & Vaid, 1989, p. 3). Gender is employed as an analytic category and 'the primary way of signifying relationships of power' (Scott, 1986, p. 1067). In the words of Judith Butler whose *Gender Trouble* is the definitive text for third wave feminism, gender should not be thought of 'merely as a cultural inscription of meaning on a pre-given sex (a juridical conception)'. Gender also refers to the 'very apparatus of production whereby the sexes themselves are established. As a result, gender is not to culture as sex is to nature; gender is also the discursive/cultural means by which 'sexed nature' or 'a natural sex' is produced and established as pre-discursive, prior to culture, a politically neutral surface on which culture acts' (Butler, 1999, p. 11).

6 After Freud, Freudian psychoanalysis went in different directions taking the form of American dominated ego-psychology, theories of Melanie Klein and of 'object-relations' (Grosz 1990, pp. 24–31).

7 Lacan interpreted Freud in the light of structural linguistics that foregrounded the divide between the signifier and the signified but more crucially, emphasised that signification (relationship between the signifier and the signified) was not the result of a direct relationship between the two, but an *arbitrary connection* that arises because of the differences between signifiers and differences between signs. But unlike structural linguistics that gave priority to the signified, Lacan prioritised the signifier: *how* I say something is more important than *what* I mean.

The unified identity of the subject is 'a mirage', as the subject's image of itself comes from outside; it is based on others' perception of the subject. This implies that all identity, including sexual identity, is a 'misrecognition' (Eagleton, 2009, p. 6). Thus, femininity and masculinity are not fixed, bounded and determined categories. As Rose explains: 'the unconscious undermines the subject from any position of certainty, from any relation of knowledge to his or her psychic processes and history, and *simultaneously* reveals the fictional nature of the sexual category to which every human subject is none the less assigned' (Rose, 1985, p. 29).

The symbolic order that we inhabit with others – the shared symbolic – creates both meaning as well as (a false sense of) identity, as it is with the order of the symbolic that social interaction and meaning-making becomes possible. The symbolic order is not only based on language; it also includes the written laws that govern our actions, along with the unwritten and unspoken rules (given to us by the Big Other, the invisible social authority) that inform our social interactions. The symbolic order – with the Big Other – binds us together as subjects. Both written and unwritten rules perform the unifying, and simultaneously the exclusionary, function. As Todd McGowan writes, '[t]he symbolic order unites subjects not through what it officially proclaims but through unwritten rules that provide a secret code for those who belong and always trip up those who don't' (2015, p. 33).

I take the above concepts of sexuality, unconscious, split subjectivity and the Symbolic to the registers to law and feminism, on the one hand, and to the concept of emotion, on the other. If the unconscious is at play and identity is created within a split, emotion can no longer be a transparent category whose meanings can be readily recovered. In Lacanian terms, 'emotion results from the way it gets caught up in a network of signifiers' (Glynosa & Stavrakakis, 2008, p. 267). Thus, the meaning of a particular emotion is not intrinsic to the emotion itself but determined by 'the subject's universe of meaning and the way that fantasy structures this' (p. 267). In other words, emotions do not necessarily emerge or are felt and acted upon based on reasons, beliefs, intentions. The psychoanalytic view of emotions neither classifies them with precision as positive-negative/good-bad nor endorses neuroscience techniques like brain-mapping, neuro-imaging to classify emotions as 'discrete, identifiable entities that can be found in the brain' (Hewitson, 2015).[8] The focus instead is on a person's experience (like feminism) which can be accessed not through body pulsations or brain images but testimony (like the law) of the psyche. Emotions are not always connected with conscious experience, 'given feelings can work to conceal other emotions and their associated thoughts (such as, to take one common example, affection/love masking aggression/hate and vice versa)' (Johnston,

8 Legal scholars like Ved Kumari (Kumari, 2014) and B. B. Pande (Pande, 2015) in their recent work on juvenile justice also rely on the technique of 'brain mapping' uncritically.

2009, p. 141). Without being more verbose about the matter, if one can be as straight-forward as Slovenian psychoanalytic philosopher, Slavoj Žižek, then 'emotions lie' (2006, p. 229)!

The work of psychoanalytic jurisprudence has been 'to introduce the question of emotion and the domain of subjectivity into the analysis of the institution and specifically of its law' (Goodrich, 1997a, p. 5). Legal scholars who work at the intersection of law and psychoanalysis have been able to transcend the foundational difficulties of bringing these two disparate disciplines to talk. This has been made possible by relying on psychoanalysis as a methodology of reading the law. Reading the law, as one would read the psyche. Psyche does not lend itself to easy reading and meaning-making. In a short piece titled 'A Note upon the 'Mystic Writing Pad', Sigmund Freud (1961) invoked the metaphor of the mystic writing pad to explain the writings on the psyche. Psychic writing is not easily legible, for it is two layered *simultaneously* (Dhar, 2008; Dhar, 2016), one layer is visible, the other is invisible, but both are intimately tied together. To read the psyche, both layers need to be acknowledged – one apparent, the other concealed.

As a critical methodology of reading the law, psychoanalysis acknowledges 'a relation between conscious and unconscious dimensions of human subjects and so also of the texts of law' (Goodrich, 1997a, p. 6). Peter Goodrich (1997a, 1997b), following Pierre Legendre, looks at the institution of law 'as if' it were a subject, driven to reproduce itself. If the legal institution acts as a subject and has a body (comprising of the whole corpus of texts that constitute the system of law), then this body has an unconscious, the 'legal unconscious'. Psychoanalysis here makes a hermeneutic intervention by providing 'an alternative technique for interpreting law' where legal texts are read 'in the symptomatic terms of their latent meanings' (Goodrich, 1997b, p. 1038) which manifest in repetitions, slips and accidental figures and clues smeared across the text. While the law makes claims to objectivity and rationality (it seeks to maintain its rationality at the performative level, in the rigour of legal textuality and also in the manner it constructs the legal subject), this book, with Goodrich (1997a), argues that the *legal unconscious* is at work (Bindal & Vashist, 2023). Two meanings of the legal unconscious operate simultaneously: the unconscious of the law and unconscious of the subject.[9]

9 Legal unconscious thus splits into two dimensions: one, the unconscious of law as subject, and two, the 'unconscious structured like law' and not just like language, given that the Law is an inalienable part of what constitutes the register of the symbolic order. Thus, the subject is constituted through Law/Symbolic; and law is like a subject. Here, it is important to distinguish between Law and law. Law (with capital 'L') refers to psychoanalytic laws, while 'law' refers to the legal system of rules, doctrines and principles enunciated in statutes and judicial decisions. The principle of sexual difference formed along the axis of masculine/feminine is based on two laws: prohibition on incest and prohibition on murder. In Lacanian terms, these universal laws constitute the Symbolic which in turn constitutes the subject. As David Caudill explains, 'the function of law is clearest in the so-called symbolic order (or plane, or register) of human experience and cognition, which is for Lacan the order of language – language not as a tool for communication between

The unconscious, it must again be emphasised, is not some hidden impulse which threatens or disrupts the stable surface order, or which is intrinsically subversive. Instead, the unconscious is constitutive of the contradictory desire to obey and flout the rules. This duality marks the nature of the unconscious. Thus, even as the hold of the law loosens on the subject externally – the expanding zone of external freedom displaces the subject's desire for prohibition into the unconscious – the internal prohibitions of the unconscious realm continue to work on her. The subject is, thus, not constituted by just the desire for freedom but by the desire for prohibition and obedience. This is why Goodrich (1997a) says that 'the legal order depends not simply upon fear of law's violence but much more generally upon a structure of political love' (1997a, p. 25). Law is an object 'of fascination and of love' (1997a, p. 10). The authority of law exists and continues only if the relationship between the legal subject and law is one of love. It excites as it kills. It secures *us* as it confines *them*.

With psychoanalytic reading of the law, the long-standing assumptions and concepts of legal theory start falling apart; the first being the distinction of 'public' and 'private'. The much-critiqued public-private divide of the liberal regime of law that conceives of the private realm of family, tradition and home as a law-free zone, becomes radically unsustainable. As Maria Aristodemou (2014) states 'the distinction between public and private is problematic because what is supposedly most intimate and hidden by and from the subject is taken from the outside, from the symbolic order of language and culture' (p. 4). In other words, the distinction between inside and outside is not clearly demarcated, as the inside (interiority, the unconscious) is constituted by language, culture, law (the symbolic order).

A psychoanalytically informed legal critique, thus, turns the legal order *inside out*. It is not about revealing the exclusions or antitheses of law; it instead takes the shape of uncovering the underside of law that sustains its outward logics. This underside is often the 'obscene underbelly' of ideologies, fantasies and unconscious desires that law hides and represses to maintain its legitimacy

relatively autonomous subjects but as a structure of governing signifiers, often unconscious in their operation and effects. At the most obvious level, legal processes and institutions function within the symbolic order, structuring our lives and stabilising our self-images and our relationships. On a deeper level, the logic and law of language is a feature of the symbolic order generally, so that specifically legal structures and other social codes and conventions share in the constitution of the subject by language, again including conscious and unconscious "discourse". At an even more foundational level, the Law is associated by Lacan with the Name-of-the-Father, a master signifier upon which the entire signifying network of culture and language relies – the fundamental Law of the Name-of-the-Father divides and differentiates, thereby supporting the unconscious representations and grammatical structures in thought and speech. The place (or locus or field) of the chain of determinative signifiers, as well as the Name-of-the-Father metaphor, is the Other – Lacan's ambiguous term for the paradoxically exterior field in which the subject appears and on which the subject is dependent for its very constitution' (Caudill, 1993, p. 422).

(Žižek, 1998). The subject is not always a rational, subject in-control who has the power to work on the social/legal register and introduce reforms to it. As the individual and the social are enfolded together in complex ways – there is a 'moebius strip' like continuity and indistinguishability of these realms – the capacity to re-form the social (including the legal realm) cannot be assumed. It has to be strived for and worked through by recognising our own unconscious resistance to change. The social is entrenched both in the Symbolic realm – which cannot be wished away – and our own unconscious – which is shaped by the Symbolic. Merely working to effect a change in the social/legal sphere will not produce feminist results, as our own unconscious is resistant to change. The unconscious comprises of our own fantasies which are much more difficult to let go. The fantasy of a common enemy, or a nation, or a common brotherhood, all work too well to sustain existing legal structures. No outside change can be successfully introduced to laws unless our unconscious fantasies and desires also undergo radical transformation. This is the radical inwardness that scandalous feminism demands.

The book can be divided into two parts. The structure of the book reflects the evolution of my thoughts and growing relationship with psychoanalysis. The first part, comprising of Chapters 1 to 3, seeks to mark a return of the repressed unconscious into prescriptive legal analysis of criminal law doctrines, the defence of loss of self-control and victim's retributive rage and desire for 'payback'. The second part, Chapters 4 to 6, of the book is on 'the sexual' where I attempt a theoretical move to complicate the accounts of gender and sexuality that inform feminism and law in India, offer a nuanced reading of sexual consent and raise the fraught question of child sexuality through age of consent law.

I start Chapter 1 with Martha Nussbaum's cognitivist view of emotion, what she calls the 'evaluative conception'. I will argue that the evaluative conception of emotions in criminal law, in as much as it presents the existing legal doctrines and principles as internally consistent and coherent, is a part of, what critical criminal law scholar Alan Norrie, calls the 'rationalising enterprise' of law. The evaluative view supports the orthodox criminal law scholarship in its claims that law is a rational system of clear and systematic doctrines and principles. In this framework, emotions (rather than being subversive forces) are allies which help in the reproduction of socially acceptable and morally appropriate norms. Law's evaluations chart out a hierarchy of appropriate and inappropriate emotions experienced by good and bad people in accordance with the prescribed codes of the social, cultural and sexual order. An artificial idea(l) of both the law and the subject is reinstituted by disproportionately focussing on what the law/subject ought to do, totally eclipsing what s/he actually ends up doing, despite the normative law, despite themselves. The assumptions of the liberal order stay in-tact as law comes to stand for equality and fairness and the legal subject is presumed to be the rational, autonomous, free-willed actor who has a direct and transparent access to her emotional motivations. Specifically, I offer a two-fold critique of Nussbaumian conception of law and emotions: the framing of the evaluative conception of emotion and her liberal imagination of the law.

In Chapter 2, I take this critique forward, focussing on the partial defence of loss of self-control which mitigates liability from murder to culpable homicide/manslaughter. Tracing the history of this defence, I will show how in the Indian context, it was always tied to the notion of male 'honour' which turned it into an instrument of murderous male rage. The study of provocation cases also reveals how evaluative conception of emotion barely touches the surface of emotions of the legal subject as well as emotions of the law. It is, as if, the legal discourse cannot make sense of the disproportionate emotional response of those who kill in anger (or out of fear). We see how the cognitivist frame erases experience, as pain and suffering enter the legal script. Rather, the cognitivist accounts of the law and emotion reinforce law's overarching dominance in our lives, of our subjectivities and affectivities. The translation of the suffering narrative into the legal narrative constitutes a loss – a loss of complexity, messiness, contradictions, intensity, indescribability of the experience of the victimised subjects. Focussing on the cases of women who kill their husbands out of anger, I will argue, that the Nussbaumian evaluative conception of emotion in criminal is, at best, an illustration of tyrannical legal prescriptivism. I call it 'tyranny of shoulds'.[10]

I then proceed to show how legal measures are emotive codes which are used to assuage grief and human-made suffering by translating these emotions into retributive rage. The death penalty demands as well as euphoric celebrations of stringent punishments are bound in this grief-rage knot, as are wars on terror backed by 'rule of law' regime (Rudy, 2020; Aladjem, 2008; Butler, 2004). Therefore, in our struggles for justice, we need to engage with difficult emotional states. If we believe that justice indeed is located outside the vicious cycles of violence and counter-violence, we cannot bypass the emotion question. As gender theorist Judith Butler (2004), writes, '[i]f we are interested in arresting cycles of violence to produce less violent outcomes, it is no doubt important to ask what, politically, might be made of grief besides a cry for war' (p. xii). And as '[o]ur affect is never merely our own: affect is, from the start communicated from elsewhere', I add that, the contours of feminist legal politics must expand to understand the collective *jouissance* (transgressive enjoyment)[11] in the enforcement of the masculine[12] order of the law.

10 I borrow this phrase from Grosz, 2014.

11 The French word, *jouissance*, in Lacan's corpus has been left untranslated in English. According to Lacan, there is *jouissance* beyond the pleasure principle (excessive enjoyment). *Jouissance* compels the subject to constantly attempt to transgress the prohibitions imposed on her enjoyment, to go beyond the pleasure principle. But the result of transgressing the pleasure principle is not more pleasure but pain, as the subject can bear only a certain amount of pleasure. Beyond this limit, pleasure becomes pain, and this is *jouissance*.

12 In Lacanian terms, masculine-feminine do not refer to persons either biologically (anatomy) or socially identified as male or female (gender). 'Rather', Jeanne Schroeder (2008, p. 1) points out, 'they refer to incompatible ways to confronting alienation and contradiction. The "masculine" attitude is denial. It attempts to resolve contradictions in order to create a complete and closed social universe. The

We cannot shut our eyes to the fact that popular sentiment moves the law in the direction of revenge and vengeance. The Supreme Court of India was quite candid about this, in its observations about the rationale of punishment: 'At times it is to satisfy the element of "emotion" in law and retribution/vengeance becomes the guiding factor'.[13] This compels me to re-turn to victim's grief-laden psychic states from where emerges the desire to annihilate the other, and ask: can we just stop our critique at calling the demands for retribution 'barbaric' or 'uncivilised'? Can we stop by merely urging the reason of law to take control of these unruly sentiments, yet again denying the unconscious (which seeks to 'satisfy the element of emotion') and reifying the law as a rational positivist institution? Is it not important to conceptualise the affective and the hegemonic along the axis of power as well as desire in order to understand the complexity of grief-rage-revenge connection?

This forms the backdrop of Chapter 3, where I reflect on the aftermath of the 2012 Delhi Gang Rape, which took the form of retributive reforms in criminal law in India. I first analyse feminist responses (or the lack of them) to the demand for death penalty for the rapists by the victim's parents, and second, feminist responses (or the surfeit of them) to Leslee Udwin's documentary *India's Daughter* which recounted the horror of the rape. My enquiry is directed at understanding the demands of justice which, often laden with retributive rage and feelings of vengeance, rise from abject grief. I will show how feminists confront this 'moebius strip' of grief and rage but tend to flatten its complexity by either erasing the retributive rage or pathologising it as irrational. I also reflect on the emotional roots of retributive theory of punishment, how the institution of punishment builds a 'hostile solidarity', creating a situation of release of otherwise banned emotions and giving a legitimate license to individuals to symbolically engage in acts of aggression mediated through the state. Thus, against these false notions of grief sans rage, and law sans hostility, I will argue that we need to build a more reflexive and robust legal feminism that engages with positions of difficulty, complicity and contradiction in theory as well as praxis.

I then move, in Chapter 4, towards a complete embrace of psychoanalysis, which inaugurates the labour of theorising the 'sexual' beyond the binary of 'sex as violence' (sex-negative feminism) versus 'sex as pleasure' (sex-positive feminism). Tracing the feminist debates around sexual imagery, I will show that the woman's movement in India was gravely influenced by dominance feminism's conceptualisation of the sexual as violence. To counter this position, the postcolonial feminist perspective sought to foreground the subject in pleasure in the larger project of rendering erotic supplement to the imagination of

feminine attitude is acceptance of contradiction's inevitability'. In Schroeder's analysis, the dominant theory of Law represented by positivist H.L.A. Hart is masculine in these terms, as Hart constantly outlaws morality in answering what is Law.

13 *Narinder Singh* v. *State of Punjab* (2014) 6 SCC 466.

justice. This binary formulation, however, gives us an incomplete picture of sexuality and desire. I will argue for a shift towards a psychoanalytic understanding of the sexual (desire) which transcends the dichotomy of violence/disgust and pleasure and draw out its implications for criminal law in India. Relying on the work of psychoanalytic feminists, I will argue that the sexual is tied to the unconscious where all certainties along with the fantasy of subject-in-control, on the path towards sexual freedom, end in grief. The sexual is a far more complex realm of *desire*: ridden with the desire for power, the desire to subjugate the one you love, very often, the desire to be subjugated, to be violated. This nuanced understanding of sexuality can introduce multilayered accounts into existing feminist narratives and produce a complex legal subject beyond the victim-agent binary.

In the final two chapters, I attempt to show, how a psychoanalytic account of the sexual offers a nuanced account of sexual consent, on the one hand and child sexuality, on the other. In Chapter 5, I attempt to work towards a psycho-sexual theory of consent. I push the limits of the juridical model of consent (which presumes a transparent access to the subject's desire), via the psychoanalytic idea of desire which by nature exceeds the limits of knowability. When one does not know one's own desire, how does one communicate what one wants? Engaging with diverse feminist critiques of sexual consent, I navigate through the domains of law and psychoanalysis, imagining where a disciplinary friendship, or even an intercourse between them, take us on the question of consent. The coming together of the two disciplines, I will argue, will offer us a theory of sexual consent which is based on a truer account of our sexual lives. The surrender, seduction and risk that accompany this intercourse will forge an empathic dyad of interdisciplinarity where juridical consent surrenders to 'limit consent'.

My final inquiry takes me to the child who appears in the law as an agencyless, asexual object to be protected, saved and represented. In Chapter 6, I take a step back from all the assumptions that frame the figure of the 'child' in law, specifically focussing on age of consent law, and ask: who is a child? Staying with Freudian insights on infantile sexuality, this chapter seeks to make a disruptive intervention in the existing legal discourse where the child is either appropriated or violently erased. I surface psychoanalytic accounts of listening which, I contend, will enable the transformation of the scene of law – from the liberal idea of consent and a simplistic libertarian understanding of desire as an act of choice – to a scene of listening which acknowledges the trauma of sexuality for the child.

In this book, I have worked with the hypothesis that an epistemic shift to 'emotion' in terms of both the law and the subject's *desire* will produce a more nuanced account of subjectivity and constitute a 'break' (Halley, 2006) which will free feminism of its dominant formulations of 'dominance', 'governance', 'cultural' and 'carceral' that have hijacked feminist imaginations. In recent years, especially with #metoo (Falkof, Phadke & Roy, 2022; Ahlawat, 2022; Page & Arcy, 2020), we have witnessed a debilitating feminist disillusionment with law, due process and even feminism (Cossman, 2021; Gangoli, 2023).[14] This disillusionment resulted from the stubborn persistence and stickiness of the dominant, conservative sexual and gender norms, what psychoanalyst and feminist, Mitchell has been calling, 'the undertow'. The undertow is a sort of 'statis' that 'makes progress regress on matters of 'gender' equality' (Mitchell, 2000, p. xviii). Mitchell recognises how 'feminism seems to be rowing against a current that is ultimately the stronger force' (2000, p. xviii), for there appear to be two levels of sociality- one induced by progressive gender reforms and the other is what performs the regressive and conservative function. While progressive social reforms are undertaken with a deliberate orientation, the regressive function is performed by 'a largely unconsciously acquired history' with 'a shared mental terrain' which impedes social change. Mitchell turned to psychoanalysis in early 1970s because for her 'Freud's account opens up ways in which we can think about why 'gender' conservatism persists in the face of change; why, indeed, the other side of progress seems always to be reaction' (2000, p. xxxi). Mitchell wants us to acknowledge the 'inherent pull backwards' that ordains our condition (Hollway, Mitchell & Walsh, 2015, p. 114):

> We want so much to go forward, to challenge and change the patriarchal world but there is something in the position of women, something in each of us as individuals and as a collectivity, that pulls us backwards all the time, and no matter how far we go forwards, there is an inherent pull backwards. That is not necessarily true, or so true, of other political movements, but it is deeply true of women. That is why I entitled the first essay I published, in 1966, Women: The Longest Revolution. [...] Is there anti-feminism lurking in the strongest feminist?

It is this statis that this book seeks to struggle with by invoking the emotion-question in law. In the context of law, one might ask why, despite the decades long work of the women's movement (despite feminists now walking the halls of power, Halley et al, 2018), gendered scripts have remained intact? Why men as well as women, despite the proliferation of feminist knowledge, remain emotionally invested in conservative institutions like marriage, family, nation, global capitalism, nationalism and neoliberalism? If these are only social, cultural and economic 'scripts', why has it been so difficult to undo them? If 'anti-feminist emotions' (retributive rage and revenge, for instance) are *merely* social and cultural constructs, why are we not able to unlearn them with progressive liberal education?

14 The #me too which arose from a feminist disillusionment with the law and legal processes led to many splits and fractures within the Indian women's movement. I have only signposted #metoo in this book; a fuller critical analysis deserves another study.

This book argues that socialisation and social constructionism are inadequate frames to explain the persistent existence of the 'undertow'. Therefore, our analysis of gender and sexuality,[15] law and desire must move away from social constructionism to the linguistically based symbolic order and the unconscious fantasy structure. Psychoanalysis – unconscious and sexuality – will open up novel ways of feminist engagement with the law which will save us from slipping into both liberal reformism and naïve radicalism. This is the hope with which this book is written. I invite the reader to share this hope with me.

References

Abrams, K. & Keren, H. (2010). Who's afraid of law and the emotions. *Minnesota Law Review*, 94, 1997.

Agnes, F. (1992). Protecting Women Against Violence – Review of a Decade of Legislation 1980–89. *Economic and Political Weekly*, 27(17).

Agnes, F. (2004). *Law and Gender Inequality: The Politics of Women's Rights in India.* Oxford University Press.

Agnes, F. (2013, September 18). The Rule of Sentiments. *The Asian Age.*

Ahlawat, I. (2022). The #MeToo Phenomenon on Indian Social Media: Moving Onward from the American #MeToo. *Asian Journal of Media and Communication*, 6(1), 19–38.

Ahmed, S. (2004). *The cultural politics of emotion.* Routledge.

Aladjem, T. K. (2008). *The culture of vengeance and the fate of American justice.* Cambridge University Press.

Aristodemou, M. (2014). *Law, Psychoanalysis and Society: Taking the Unconscious Seriously.* Routledge.

Baker, K. K. (2005). Gender and Emotion in Criminal Law. *Harvard Journal of Law & Gender*, 28, 447–466.

Bandes, S. A. (Ed.) (1999), *The Passions of Law.* New York University Press.

Bandes, S. A. (2009a). Repellent crimes and rational deliberation: Emotion and the death penalty. *Vermont Law Review*, 33(3), 489–512.

Bandes, S. A. (2009b). Victims, "Closure," and the Sociology of Emotion. *Law and Contemporary Problems*, 72(2), 1–26.

Bhattacharjee, M. F. (2017). The lynching of a nation. *The Wire.* https://thewire.in/communalism/the-lynching-of-a-nation.

Bibas, S. & Bierschbach, R. A. (2004). Integrating Remorse and Apology into Criminal Procedure. *The Yale Law Journal*, 114(1), 85–148.

15 The gender/sexual difference debate within feminism captures the fundamental split between Judith Butler and Juliet Mitchell. For Butler, Mitchell's position – how sexual difference is transmitted with immense power of Symbolic into the deepest recesses of our psyche – leaves us with a grim future. For her disagreements, see Butler, 2015. Mitchell, in response to Butler, holds that Butler's account of gender performativity does not take into account the psychological consequences of the prohibitions on desire and murder which every subject must face (the Law against murder and the Law against incest) which lead to sexual difference in men and women. See, Mitchell, 2000, pp. 111–129; Mitchell, 2015.

Bindal, A. & Vashist, L. (2023). The 'Legal Unconscious': Exploring the Intersection of Law and Psychoanalysis. *Asian Journal of Legal Education*, 10(2), 177–189.

Blumenthal, J. A. (2005). Law and the emotions: The problems of affective forecasting. *Indiana Law Journal*, 80(2), 155–192.

Butler, J. (1999) *Gender Trouble: Feminism and the Subversion of Identity*. Routledge.

Butler, J. (2004). *Precarious life: The powers of mourning and violence*. Seagull Books.

Butler, J. (2015). Ideologies of the Super-Ego: Psychoanalysis and Feminism, Revisited. In R. Duschinsky & S. Walker (Eds), *Juliet Mitchell and the Lateral Axis: Twenty-First-Century Psychoanalysis and Feminism*. Palgrave Macmillan.

Calhoun C. (1999). Making Up Emotional People: The Case of Romantic Love. In S. Bandes (Ed.), *The Passions of Law*. New York University Press.

Caudill, D. S. (1993). Name-of-the-Father and the Logic of Psychosis: Lacan's Law and Ours. *Legal Studies Forum*, 16(4), 421–438.

Copjec, J. (1994). *Read my Desire: Lacan Against Historicists*. London: MIT Press.

Cornell, D. (1999). *Beyond accommodation: Ethical feminism, deconstruction and the law*. Rowman & Littlefield Publishers.

Cossman, B. (2021). *The New Sex Wars: Sexual Harm in the #MeToo Era*. New York University Press.

Damacio, A. (2005). *Descartes' error: Emotion, reason and the human brain*. Penguin Publishing Group.

De Souza, R. (1990). *The Rationality of Emotion*. MIT Press.

Dhanda, A. & Parashar, A. (Eds). (1999). *Engendering Law: Essays in Honour of Lotika Sarkar*. Eastern Book Company.

Dhar, A. (2008). Return to Freud: Return to the Mystic Writing Pad. *Samiksha: Journal of the Indian Psychoanalytic Society*.

Dhar, A. (2016). What if, the hurt is "real": Psyche, neighbor and intimate? In R. Ramdev, S. D. Nambiar & D. Bhattacharya (Eds), *Sentiment, politics, censorship: The state of hurt*. Sage Publications.

Douzinas, C. (2000). *The end of human rights: Critical legal thought at the turn of the century*. Portland, OR: Hart Publishing.

Dubber, M. D. (2006). *The Sense of Justice: Empathy in Law and Punishment*. New York University Press.

Eagleton, T. (2009). *Trouble with Strangers: A Study of Ethics*. Wiley-Blackwell.

Falkof, N., Phadke, S. & Roy, S. (Eds). (2022). *Intimacy and Injury: In the Wake of #MeToo in India and South Africa*. Manchester University Press.

Finkel, N. J. & Parrott, W. G. (2006). *Emotions and Culpability: How the Law is at Odds with Psychology, Jurors, and Itself*. American Psychological Association.

Fitzpatrick, P. (2002). *The Mythology of Modern Law*. Routledge.

Freud, S. (1919/1955). The "Uncanny". In *The Standard Edition of the Complete Psychological Works of Sigmund Freud*, Vol. XVII (translated by J. Stratchey). Hogarth Press.

Freud, S. (1924/1961). A Note Upon the Mystic-Writing Pad. In *The Standard Edition of the Complete Psychological Works of Sigmund Freud*, Vol. XIX (translated by J. Stratchey). Hogarth Press.

Gangoli, G. (2023). The #metoo Movement in India: Emotions and (in)justice in feminist responses. *Feminist Legal Studies*, 32, 213–230.

Glynosa, J. & Stavrakakis, Y. (2008). Lacan and political subjectivity: Fantasy and enjoyment in psychoanalysis and political theory. *Subjectivity*, 24, 256–274.

Goodrich, P. (1997a). *Law and the Unconscious: A Legendre Reader*. Macmillan Press.

Goodrich, P. (1997b). Maladies of the Legal Soul: Psychoanalysis and Interpretation in Law. *Washington and Lee Law Review*, 54(3), 1038–1065.
Goodrich, P. & Carlson, D. G. (1998). *Law and the postmodern mind: Essays on psychoanalysis and jurisprudence.* University of Michigan Press.
Gotell, L. (1995). Litigating Feminist 'Truth': An Antifoundational Critique. *Social and Legal Studies*, 4(1), 99–119.
Grosz, E. (1990). *Jacques Lacan: A Feminist Introduction.* London: Routledge.
Grosz, S. (2014). *The examined life: How we lose and find ourselves.* Vintage.
Halley, J. (2006). *Split Decisions: How and Why to Take a Break from Feminism.* Princeton University Press.
Halley, J. (2018). Introducing governance feminism. In Halley, J., Kotiswaran, P., Rebouche, R. & Shamir H., *Governance feminism: An introduction.* University of Minnesota Press.
Halley, J., Kotiswaran, P., Rebouche, R. & Shamir H. (2018). *Governance feminism: An introduction.* University of Minnesota Press.
Hart, H. L. A. (1994). *The concept of law.* Oxford University Press.
Henderson, L. N. (1986–1987). Legality and Empathy. *Mich. L. Rev.*, 85, 1574.
Hewitson, O. (2015). Inside out and the 'science' of emotions. *Lacan Online.* www.laca nonline.com/index/2015/09/inside-out-and-the-science-of-emotions.
Hollway, W., Mitchell, J. & Walsh, J. (2015). Interview with Juliet Mitchell – Psychoanalysis and Feminism: Then and now. *Psychoanalysis, Culture & Society*, 20(2).
Horder, J. (1992). *Provocation and responsibility.* Clarendon Press.
Hutchinson, P. (2008). *Shame and Philosophy.* Basingstoke and New York.
Johnston, A. (2009). Affective Life between Signifiers and Jouis-sens: Lacan's Senti-ments and Affectuation. *Filozofski vestnik*, XXX(2), 113–141.
Kahan, D. (1999). The Progressive Appropriation of Disgust. In S. Bandes (Ed.), *The Passions of Law.* New York University Press.
Kannabiran, K. (Ed.). (2013). *Women and law: Critical feminist perspectives.* Sage Law.
Kapur, R. (1996). *Feminist Terrains in Legal Domains.* Kali for Women: New Delhi.
Kapur, R. (2013). Gender, Sovereignty and the Rise of a Sexual Security Regime in International Law and Postcolonial India. *Melbourne Journal of International Law*, 14(2), 317–345.
Kapur, R. & Cossman, B. (1996). *Subversive sites: Feminist engagements with law in India.* Sage Publications.
Kaul, N. (2023). *Consent: Fearful Asymmetry.* Zubaan: New Delhi.
Kotiswaran, P. (2017). A Bittersweet Moment: Indian Governance Feminism and the 2013 Rape Law Reforms. *Economic & Political Weekly*, 52(25–26), 78.
Kumari, V. (2014). Juvenile Justice Bill 2014: A Regressive Step. *Journal of Indian Law Institute*, 56(3), 303.
Kumari, V. (2015). Juvenile Justice in India. In F. E. Zimring, M. Langer & D. S. Tanenhaus (Eds), *Juvenile Justice in Global Perspective.* New York University Press.
Lazarus, R. S. (1991). *Emotion and Adaptation.* Oxford University Press.
Leys, R. (2017), *The Ascent of Affect: Genealogy and Critique.* University of Chicago Press.
MacKinnon, C. A. (1989). *Towards a Feminist Theory of the State.* Harvard University Press.
MacKinnon, C. A. (1983). Feminism, Marxism, Method, and the State: Toward a Feminist Jurisprudence. *Signs: Journal of Women, Culture, and Society*, 8, 635.
MacKinnon, C. A. (1987). *Feminism Unmodified: Discourses on Life and Law.* Harvard University Press.

Maroney, T. A. (2006). Law and emotion: A proposed taxonomy of an emerging field. *Law and Human Behavior*, 30(1), 119–142.

Massumi, B. (2002). *Parables for the Virtual: Movement, Affect, Sensation*. Duke University Press.

McGowan, T. (2015). *Psychoanalytic Film Theory and the Rules of the Game*. New York: Bloomsbury Academic.

Menon, N. (2019). Sexual Violence and the law in India. In R. West & C. G. Bowman (Eds), *Research Handbook on Feminist Jurisprudence*. Edward Elgar Publishing.

Minow, M. (1993). Surviving Victim Talk. *UCLA Law Review*, 40(6), 1411–1446.

Minow, M. (2001). *Between Vengeance and Forgiveness: Facing History after Genocide and Mass Violence*. Beacon Press.

Minow, M. (2015). Forgiveness, Law, and Justice. *California Law Review*, 103(6), 1615–1645.

Mitchell, J. (2000). *Psychoanalysis and feminism: A radical reassessment of Freudian psychoanalysis*. Basic Books.

Mitchell, J. (2015). Debating Sexual Difference, Politics, and the Unconscious: With Discussant Section by Jacqueline Rose. In R. Duschinsky & S. Walker (Eds), *Juliet Mitchell and the Lateral Axis: Twenty-First-Century Psychoanalysis and Feminism*. Palgrave Macmillan.

Mitchell, J. & Rose, J. (Eds). (1985). *Feminine sexuality: Jacques Lacan and the école freudienne*. Pantheon Books.

Murphy, J. G (2006). Well Excuse Me! – Remorse, Apology, and Criminal Sentencing. *Arizona State Law Journal*, 38(2).

Murphy, J. G. (2007). Remorse, Apology and Mercy. *Ohio State Journal of Criminal Law*, 4, 423–453.

Murphy, J. G. & Hampton, J. (1988). *Forgiveness and mercy*. Cambridge University Press.

Norrie, A. (2014). *Crime, reason and history: A critical introduction to criminal law*. Cambridge University Press.

Nussbaum, M. C. (2001). *Upheavals of thought: The intelligence of emotions*. Oxford University Press.

Nussbaum, M. C. (2004). *Hiding From Humanity: Disgust, Shame, and the Law*. Princeton University Press.

Nussbaum, M. C. (2010). *From Disgust to Humanity: Sexual Orientation and Constitutional Law*. Oxford University Press.

Nussbaum, M. C. (2013). *Political Emotions: Why Love Matters for Justice*. The Belknap Press of Harvard University Press.

Nussbaum, M. C. (2016). *Anger and forgiveness: Resentment, generosity, justice*. Oxford University Press.

Nussbaum, M. C. (2018). *The Monarchy of Fear: A Philosopher Looks at Our Political Crisis*. Simon & Schuster.

Otto, D. L. (2009), The Exile of Inclusion: Reflections on Gender Issues in International Law Over the Last Decade. *Melbourne Journal of International Law*, 10(1), 11–26.

Page, A. & Arcy, J. (2020). #MeToo and the politics of collective healing: Emotional connection as contestation. *Communication, Culture and Critique*, 13(3), 333–348.

Pande, B. B. (2015). 'Bad' Juveniles and the 'Worst' Juvenile Justice Law? The Second Challenge to Juvenile Justice Law in Darga Ram v. State of Rajasthan. *Journal of Indian Law Institute*, 57(1), 27–47.

Pillsbury, S. H. (1989). Moralizing the passions of criminal punishment. *Cornell Law Review*, 74, 655–677.
Polletta, F. (2001). The Laws of Passion. *Law and Society Review*, 35(2), 467.
Rose, J. (1985). Introduction – II. In J. Mitchell & J. Rose (Eds), *Feminine sexuality: Jacques Lacan and the école freudienne*. Pantheon Books.
Rose, J. (2014). *Women in Dark Times*. Bloomsbury.
Rottenberg, C. (2018). *The Rise of Neoliberal Feminism*. Oxford University Press.
Rudy, S. (2020), 'Human Rights', 'Rule of Law', and 'Violence'. In L. Vashist & J. Dogra (Eds), *Rethinking law and violence*. New Delhi: Oxford University Press.
Sangari, K. & Vaid, S. (1989). Introduction. In K. Sangari & S. Vaid (Eds), *Recasting Women: Essays in Colonial History*. Kali: Delhi.
Sanger, C. (2001). The role and reality of emotions in law. *William & Mary Journal of Women and the Law*, 8, 107–150.
Satish, M., Dash, P. P. & Pandey, A. (2024). Bharatiya Nyay Sanhita: Decolonising or Reinforcing Colonial Ideas? *The Wire*. https://thewire.in/law/bharatiya-nyay-sanhita-decolonising-or-reinforcing-colonial-ideas.
Schroeder, J. L. (2008). *The four Lacanian discourses: Or turning law inside out*. Taylor & Francis.
Scott, J. W. (1986). Gender: A Useful Category of Historical Analysis. *The American Historical Review*, 91(5), 1053.
Sedgwick, E. K. & Frank, A. (Eds). (1995). *Shame and Its Sisters: A Silvan Tomkins Reader*. Duke University Press.
Smart, C. (1989). *Feminism and the power of law*. London: Routledge.
Solomon, R. (2003). *Not passion's slave: Emotions and choice*. Oxford University Press.
Spain, E. (2011). *The role of emotions in criminal law defenses*. Cambridge University Press.
Tundawala, M. & Choudhuri, S. (2023). Does Today's India Need 'Decolonisation' Speak? *The Wire*. https://thewire.in/politics/does-todays-india-need-decolonisation-speak.
Uma, S. (2024). Why the Bharatiya Nyay Sanhita Is a Missed Opportunity for Gender Justice. *The Wire*. https://thewire.in/law/bharatiya-nyay-sanhita-women-gender-trans-queer-justice.
Vashist, L. & Bindal, A. (2023). Thinking Through Forgiveness: Towards Post Colonial Criminology. *Indian Journal of Criminology*, 51, 126–141.
West, R. & Bowman, C. G. (Eds) (2019). *Research Handbook on Feminist Jurisprudence*. Edward Elgar Publishing.
Williams, P. J. (1991). *The alchemy of race and rights*. Cambridge, MA: Harvard University Press.
Žižek, S. (1998). Why does the Law Need an Obscene Supplement. In P. Goodrich & D. G. Carlson (Eds), *Law and the Postmodern Mind: Essays on Psychoanalysis and Jurisprudence*. University of Michigan Press.
Žižek, S. (2006). *The parallax view*. MIT Press.

Chapter 1

The Limits of Nussbaum's Conception of Emotions

Cognitive appraisal theory is the dominant paradigm for understanding emotions in, what has come to be characterised as, the law and emotion scholarship. In this framework, promoted both by philosophers and psychologists, emotions are rational, informative and communicative. Legal scholars, Martha C. Nussbaum and Dan Kahan introduced cognitive appraisal theory as the evaluative view of emotions in criminal law. Criminal law (doctrines and principles), they argue, can only be explained through the evaluative view which holds that emotions are not 'unthinking energies' but judgments about the world which are amenable to moral evaluation.

In this chapter, I will argue that the evaluative conception of emotions in criminal law, in as much as it presents the existing legal doctrines and principles as internally consistent and coherent, is a part of the 'rationalising enterprise' of law. Alan Norrie (2014) explains 'rationalising enterprise' as an attempt of traditional criminal law scholarship to rationalise, and in so doing, sanitise the contradictions, fissures, chasms and antimonies which underlie the very formation and foundation of criminal law. For Norrie, "rationalising enterprise' is frequently rationalisation only in the pejorative sense of an apparent rationality papering over the cracks of deeper contradictions' (Norrie, 2014, p. 10). The evaluative view, I will contend, supports the orthodoxy of criminal law scholarship in its claims that law is a rational system of clear and systematic doctrines and principles. In this framework, emotions (rather than being subversive forces) are allies which help in the reproduction of socially acceptable and morally appropriate norms. Law's evaluations chart out and reinforce the hierarchy of appropriate(d) and inappropriate(d) emotions experienced by good and bad people in accordance with the prescribed codes of the social, cultural and sexual order.

While many criminal law scholars and legal philosophers endorse the evaluative view, Martha Nussbaum is my primary interlocutor. This is because of her comprehensive philosophical defence of the evaluative conception of emotions within criminal law. I will offer a two-fold critique of Nussbaumian conception of law and emotions: the very framing of the evaluative conception of emotions and her overarching liberal imagination of the law. My argument is

DOI: 10.4324/9781003387411-2

that even as she philosophises about emotions, she stays within the realm of rationality, tilting towards reason in Cartesian duality. But the body which bears the marks of trauma creates its own memories which stay in subterranean depths beneath the surface of thoughts and judgments behind emotions. It is the realm of the *unconscious* which belies the equality and temporality of measured responses which the law demands because the unconscious calculates and interrupts in uncanny ways, not in terms that can be 'evaluated' on the strict scales of the law. Further, Nussbaum's evaluative conception, guided as it is by rationality and moral appropriateness, is formulated on a simplistic understanding of how the human psyche works.[1] There is no shift in the conception of the subject of law even when her emotions are acknowledged; the reasonable person is never replaced by the *emotional person*, meaning thereby that the emotional excess that falls outside cognitive appraisals is never adequately captured by this framework of understanding the law.

I will close this chapter with a reading of an Indian case of homicide where the law confronts 'outlaw emotions'. In this case, the law is called upon to adjudicate and assess the emotional state of a soldier of the Indian army who killed his superior. I will read the verdict and its reasoning closely and argue for a theory of readability that enters the psycho-biographies of the subject.

A reductive view of psyche

All emotions, according to the cognitive evaluative theory, are a result of assessments and evaluations of a particular situation by an individual in the light of her needs, goals, moral beliefs and values as well as capabilities. Nussbaum distinguishes the cognitivist view from, what she calls, the mechanistic view of emotions. Nussbaum explains the two prevalent ways of thinking about emotions in law and otherwise: mechanistic and evaluative. Mechanistic conception sees emotions as free-floating energies which sweep the subject's rational capacity. Emotion, on this account, are 'energies that impel the person to action, without embodying ways of thinking about or perceiving objects or situations in the world [...] they follow laws of their own' (Kahan & Nussbaum, 1996, p. 278). As appetites and 'feelings relatively devoid of representational or cognitive content', emotions neither contain nor respond to 'thoughts'. The object of emotion is considered as an external cause or trigger which generates the emotion, and not something which is central to the emotion (Kahan & Nussbaum, 1996, p. 279). Differently phrased, it is an external trigger, or object, which constitutes the emotional flow without any internal, rational or examinable content. Within such a conception, people's emotional responses

1 Such framing disavows that emotions arise from complicated inter-subjective contexts, evolve over psychological time and not all their facets are accessible to the conscious and rational part of the mind.

cannot be morally assessed in a coherent manner and therefore, there can be no possibility of (re)shaping people's emotional lives.

On the contrary, according to the evaluative conception of emotion, emotions are thoughts that involve appraisals or evaluations: along with the appraisal of the object, emotions themselves can be subjected to evaluation. According to this definition, emotions are those feelings the experience of which brings about a change in a person's judgments about the world. This view holds that emotions as well as their appraisals can be morally evaluated. Individuals can and should, after a proper evaluation, shape their emotions through 'moral' education. The cognitive view advocates that emotions are rational as they respond to alterations in our knowledge, beliefs and thoughts: 'emotions change with our opinions, and so are "rational" in a very important sense' (Solomon, 2003, p. 5).

Nussbaum endorses the 'cognitive-evaluative' view of emotions.[2] She is categorical that 'the evaluative conception is true and the mechanistic conception false as accounts of what emotions are' (Kahan & Nussbaum, 1996, p. 350). Emotions are forms of evaluative judgment about an object's importance in one's own life. It is not possible to conceive of emotions without *an object*: emotions are always about something. The object is always *intentional.* This intentionality refers to how an object is viewed and interpreted by any singular individual. An object thus compels or occupies the central trigger for the emergence of emotions: in grief, the object is seen as lost, in love the object is seen to be important to one's own sense of being. Apart from intentionality, emotions embody and reflect (complex) *beliefs* about the object (e.g. only a real threat will give rise to fear). Beliefs and thoughts make the distinctions between emotion types. The intentionality and beliefs central to an emotion are concerned with *value,* i.e. the object is seen as valuable. In these terms, emotions are acknowledgments of one's own needs and neediness.

Nussbaum and Kahan club ancient Greek philosophers with Renaissance thinkers, as well as 20th-century psychoanalysts as they attribute the mechanistic view to Plato, Galen, René Descartes, David Hume, Immanuel Kant, Sigmund Freud, Melanie Klein and Richard Wollheim (Kahan & Nussbaum, 1996, footnotes at pp. 278–281).[3] In creating such a sweeping expanse of the mechanistic view, the binary

2 By cognitive, she simply means that which is concerned with receiving and processing information, and *not* the 'presence of elaborate calculation, of computation, or even of reflexive self-awareness'. Cognition, in Nussbaum's account, is not restricted to linguistically formulable propositions only and thus an account of animal emotions, infants' emotions and emotions of many adult human beings is a part of this framework. In her philosophical account, she finds resonance with cognitive psychology (where emotion is an 'appraisal' pertaining to a creature's flourishing), anthropology (emotion as evaluative social construction) and psychoanalysis (object relations and their evaluative dimensions). She makes a distinction between emotions and bodily appetites (hunger, thirst) and objectless moods (irritation and endogenous depression) (Nussbaum, 2001).

3 Mechanistic view, they argue, has been endorsed not only because of a certain branch of philosophical inclination towards it, but also because cognitive psychologists, under the influence of behaviourism, endorsed this view.

framework (mechanistic versus evaluative) presented by Kahan and Nussbaum (and endorsed by many law and emotion scholars, such as Abrams & Keren, 2010) is constructed on a reductionist understanding of not just emotions, but also the theories of our psychic lives. The understanding of both mechanistic and evaluative views is based on a superficial understanding of psychoanalysis, the discipline which has offered the most sophisticated accounts of the workings of our inner lives.

Sigmund Freud (along with Karl Marx and Fredrich Nietzsche) was at the centre of the intellectual revolution of 19th century that decentred the individual's pretension to sovereignty, self-knowledge and self-mastery. Freudian psychoanalytic perspective has disrupted the foundational assumptions about knowledge and subjectivity common to the social sciences and humanities (Grosz, 1990), but Nussbaum and Kahan relegated psychoanalysis (specifically, psychoanalytic account of emotion) to the mechanistic view – the *id* that holds sway over the subject in classical psychoanalysis/ego psychology (Grosz, 1990, pp. 24–31) – where emotions are objectless and purposeless stream of energy which sweep the subject away, or are oceanic currents which annihilate the agency of the subject. Even the evaluative view, where emotions are not thoughtless energies but are 'rational', does not engage with Freudian insights about the structure of the psyche, focussed as it is on cognitions and moral evaluations. There is no unconscious to human subjectivity in this view (Mitchell & Rose, 1985). As discussed in the Introduction, this book departs from both, such an understanding of emotions as well as the ego-psychology driven accounts of psychoanalysis.

Psychoanalytically, the binary of mechanistic and evaluative views would be untenable: they are neither uncontrolled energies, bodily pulsations and sensations (Sachdev & Vashist, 2021) nor easily accessible systems of meanings and beliefs directed towards specific objects. In fact, psychoanalysis tells us that emotions cannot exist in pure and transparent form. This makes the evaluative view specifically anti-psychoanalytic focussed as it is on cognitions, judgments and moral evaluations; as if, the unconscious does not exist. Moreover, the understanding of the object in the evaluative view is rather simplistic. Psychoanalysis would foreground the object in two senses: internal objects and external objects. It would then problematise internal and external by presenting the shadow of the internalised or introjected external object on to the ego and the projected out internal object onto the world. Further, *parts* of objects could offer an extraordinary kind of tractional pull on the psyche. Nussbaum misses out on the complexity of the object in psychoanalysis.

Emotions do not necessarily emerge and are felt and acted upon based on rational 'reasons, beliefs, intentions and meanings'. There is no direct connection between an emotion and the reason why it is felt. As already noted in the Introduction, it is for this reason, Lacanian philosopher, Slavoj Žižek (2006, p. 229) bluntly said that 'emotions lie'. Jason Glynosa and Yannis Stavrakakis explain the Lacanian rendition of emotion as follows (Glynosa & Stavrakakis, 2008):

> emotion results from the way it gets caught up in a network of signifiers (or "ideas" in Freudian terms). It is because of this, according to Lacan, that emotions such as depression or anger can deceive: their meaning and significance is a function not of their intrinsic properties, but rather of the subject's universe of meaning and the way that fantasy structures this. It is for this reason that Lacan cautions against the lures of emotions, paying special attention to the "letter" of what is said and the displacements of affect. This suggests that a key aspect of understanding the significance of emotions in the organization of social practices involves trying to map them in relation to the underlying fantasies that organize a subject's affective enjoyment.

The phrase 'subject's universe of meaning' in this passage might appear like Nussbaum's singularity of interpretation/evaluation of a situation by an individual. However, parsing this passage carefully one would note the importance of 'fantasy structure'. Eliding this important tenet makes Nussbaumian hypothesis simplistic. Žižek illuminates this dimension and gives another flip to the psychoanalytic meaning of emotions as he explains (2009, pp. 113–114):

> the emotions I perform through the mask (false persona) that I adopt can in a *strange way* be more authentic and truthful than what I really feel in myself. When I construct a false image of myself which stands for me in a virtual community in which I participate (in sexual games, for example, a shy man often assumes the screen persona of an attractive promiscuous woman), the emotions I feel and feign as part of my screen persona are not simply false: although (what I experience as) my true self does not feel them, they are nonetheless in a sense true. Say, what if, deep in myself, I am a sadist pervert who dreams of beating other men and raping women; in my real-life interaction with other people, I am not allowed to enact this true self, so I adopt a more humble and polite persona – is it not that, in this case, my true self is much closer to what I adopt as a fictional screen-persona, while the self of my real-life interactions is a mask concealing the violence of my true self?

This passage explains how an individual subject or 'self' is itself not a coherent, autonomous entity. The very subject formation, or in Lacanian terms, recognition of oneself as a subject is a misrecognition (Caudill, 1997). This complexity of 'self' only as a semblance of misrecognised self opens the complexity of emotions felt by the self in the first place. Simply put, unless we peel off the layers of the singularity of the subject's sense of self (which is taken for granted in Nussbaum), we would only be able to make superficial sense of our inner lives. Thus, emotions *per se* cannot give us clear accounts of our inner lives unless we consider repressions, resistance, distortions and displacements. There is no 'true' self with 'authentic' emotions (Johnston, 2009). The unconscious is always at work and therefore 'the link between what we feel and why we think we feel it can never be taken for granted' (Hewitson, 2015). Any straight-forward causal connection between any emotion felt, and reason(s) associated with it are nothing but reductionist psychological readings. Often the experience of an emotion hides the actual ideas associated with it; many times, 'what we think of as our emotions could actually belong to someone else'. A's anger against B could be an unconscious grievance against C. Repressed and unarticulable ideas (against C) manifest by making 'false connections' (here with B) based on some 'associative link' (between B and C). In other words, it is naïve to take emotions at their face value or evaluate them as readily available scripts, or ascribe to them easily accessible and obvious appraisals, meanings and intents. The psychoanalytic approach to emotion would thus labour to look beyond 'manifest emotions'[4] and compel us to look at the experience (Scott, 1992) behind expressed emotions which requires a critical and close attention to the psychic history of the legal subject.

Evaluative conception as a 'rationalising enterprise' of law

Which theory – mechanistic or evaluative – informs our understanding of emotions has significant implications for the paradigm of (criminal) law and emotions. Mechanistic and cognitivist/evaluative conceptions of emotion will offer distinct rationales for theories as well as doctrines of culpability or ascribing blame. If emotions make us lose self-control and detrimentally affect our capacities to think, then their irrationality should completely exonerate the offender (who acted under emotional influence) from criminal culpability. The offender will be given complete defence in criminal law if she acted under the influence of emotions, as emotions are taken as destroyers of rationality and hence, of responsibility (Pillsbury, 1989, p. 677). But if emotions are rational forces, then the offender continues to be the rational subject of law who is responsible for her actions, and therefore, can be held criminally culpable. In this latter view, as Eimear Spain contends, 'a conception of emotions as rational forces embodying reason and judgment may point towards an argument for a defence based on the rationality and acceptability of the emotions concerned' (Spain, 2011, p. 98). In the cognitive view, as emotions are rational, they help in the reasoning process and thus become an aid to law and legal interpretation. This explains the seductive appeal, for lawyer's reasoning, in favour of the evaluative conception. But if we wish to dream of 'doing justice', beyond any programmatic, mechanistic calculation, then such justice requires us to question simplistic assumptions and move toward a complex singularity of the subject.

4 This makes Eimear Spain (2011), as well as Jeremy Horder's (2005) classification of fear, anger etc. as separate realms, too simplistic. My position is that such reform proposals based on inclusion of woman's emotions in law are reductionist as well as essentialist (i.e. contrary to psychoanalysis as well as feminism).

Nevertheless, before pursuing another effort for 'justice', we must venture into a nuanced understanding of the evaluative conception.

At the outset, it must be stated that Kahan and Nussbaum offer a sophisticated argument in favour of the evaluative understanding of emotions in criminal law. According to them, 'an account of the law informed by the evaluative conception is [descriptively] superior to any informed solely by the mechanistic view' (Kahan & Nussbaum, 1996, p. 301). The rationale and logic of criminal law's doctrines and principles can be explained fully and coherently in evaluative terms. Within the frame of this overall contention, they challenge both the 'voluntarist' approach (Hart, 1968, pp. 46–49) (where an individual is held criminally accountable for 'willed' violations of law) and the 'consequentialist' approach (Bentham, 2014; Posner, 1985) (which is premised on justification for punishment when an individual frustrates preferred states of affairs). They argue that these approaches are rooted in the mechanistic conception of emotions. For voluntarists, emotions impair the accused's capacity for self-control and therefore, diminish her culpability. Emotions in such formulation, for Kahan and Nussbaum, remain conceptually within the mechanistic conception, featuring as 'forces' or 'impulses' that sweep over an individual's capacity to act rationally. In this account, there is no assessment of the valuations internal to emotions while determination of criminal liability. In the consequentialist view, on the other hand, what really matters is whether an emotion inclines or disinclines an individual to produce the desired state of affairs: emotions which will frustrate desired states of affairs will furnish grounds for increased culpability and vice versa. Kahan and Nussbaum in their criticism of these approaches contend that substantive criminal law and the criminal law doctrines cannot be wholly explained through these approaches, as criminal law doctrines are structures to assess 'the moral quality of the values that a person's emotions express' (Kahan & Nussbaum, 1996, p. 304). And therefore, criminal law's theory of culpability can only make sense if it is consistent with the evaluative conception of emotion.[5]

Nevertheless, the evaluative conception, rooted in rationality, leaves untouched the kernel of law and keeps its internal logics (of rationality) intact. If emotions are rational, they can be easily brought within the rational fold of law, and subjected to legal reasoning, assessment and evaluations. The rationality of emotions – the internal assessments and judgments of emotions – will be made to stand the test of legal rationality even when the 'emotion question' is posed to the rule of law.

5 The authors clarify that '[t]he evaluative position, as we develop it, is much less ambitious than is either the voluntarist or the consequentialist accounts. The evaluative view does not assert that appraising the quality of offenders' emotions is the only object of criminal law or that individuals must invariably be punished or condemned whenever they experience morally inappropriate emotions. It asserts only that the quality of the offenders' emotion is *one* consideration that matters in substantive criminal law' (Kahan & Nussbaum, 1996, pp. 304–305).

Criminal law and 'normative acceptability of emotions'

The unquestioned and unexplored assumption in the dominant frame of modern criminal law is 'that the law is mainly rational' (Williams, 1983). Nussbaum's evaluative conception of emotions in criminal law appears to be a part of this 'rational reconstruction' in as much as she takes the principles of law as *a priori* and given. She only seeks to explain and describe the rationale behind those principles. Her rejection of mechanistic view and endorsement of evaluative view *vis-à-vis* criminal law is premised on the idea that evaluative view enables us to understand why criminal law acts in the way it does, why it mitigates some killings and not others.

While the principles and doctrines of criminal law are presented as 'free-standing foundations for a rational criminal law', in reality, Norrie rightly contends, 'the central principles of the law are the site of struggle and contradiction' (Norrie, 2014, p. 10). Norrie shows how 'general principles' of criminal law function as ideological forces which obscure the real workings of the power of criminal law machinery. He demonstrates that these general principles are a product of particular historical context and are neither trans-historical nor transcendental. Through a historical analysis, Norrie unmasks the particular and political contexts of English criminal law, despite the posture and pretence of universal/general principles of criminal law. Such an analysis also helps us to appreciate how through such a construction, the social, cultural and political are ostensibly and artificially separated from the legal, and the latter is accorded a distinct, separate and elevated status.

Commenting on the artificial separation of 'intention' (a voluntary action) and 'motive' (the ulterior objective of an action) in determining criminal culpability, he writes: 'universality was proclaimed in opposition to the interests of the poor, for whom poverty was 'the common excuse' in the eighteenth century' (Norrie, 2014, pp. 44–45). Furthermore:

> The ruling classes sought a universal definition of right and wrong that could legitimate extremely dubious processes of property expropriation of the poor by the rich [...] The rule of private property became the 'rule of law', so that attacks on the former could be condemned as attacks on a universal social good.
>
> (Norrie, 2014, p. 45)

This critical history of criminal law tells us that the legal commonsense, (that eventually comes to be known as the 'rule of law') conceals the property related interests of the ruling classes. That is to say, historically it was easier to erase the claims of the propertyless as irrelevant by relegating 'motive' into the zone of irrelevance in criminal law. A principle which seems universal and general only till we historically deconstruct the politics behind the principle. This historicity enables us to critically scrutinise the existing conceptual framework that determines the imputation of criminal liability *viz.* the focus on intention as opposed to motive, substantive justification of conduct, legal duty to act, etc.

Motives, intentions, emotions

Criminal law makes a crucial distinction between motive and intention: unlike the latter, the former is not considered relevant in the determination of criminal culpability or guilt. If a person puts poison in his uncle's tea to cause his uncle's death in order to inherit his property (Ormerod, 2011, p. 117), the desire to inherit money (greed/jealousy) is no part of crime. Law will only see that the intention was to kill which was acted out by poisoning the tea. By excluding motives, law also excludes the social and political contexts that give rise to this criminal act. In doing so, a mercy killer is equated with a serial killer in so far as the determination of guilt in criminal law is concerned. The conceptual understanding of human emotions in this framework is governed by utilitarian psychology where every individual is an independent, isolated monad harbouring her own personal motivations and emotions. Law's 'psychological individualism' has created an ideal image of 'man': an abstract, rational, juridical individual. This 'isolated psychological figure' is a responsible actor who is present in the real world but is not affected or constrained by the social and moral contexts of the real world.

It is noteworthy that in advocating for the evaluative conception, Nussbaum acknowledges the relevance of motives and emotions in making moral and legal assessments of culpability. The evaluative view, she contends, ruptures the dominant understanding of culpability in criminal law, as motives and emotions are central to the evaluative enquiry. The evaluative view in criminal law substantiates a theory of moral assessment that pertains to not only *what* act an individual has done, but also *why* she has done the same. Thus, motive becomes central to the enquiry of moral assessment and in turn to the determination of criminal liability. The evaluative view says 'that act has greatest moral worth when it is the product of motives (including emotions) that themselves express an appropriate evaluation of the actor's circumstances. Similarly, an undesirable act can be carried out for a variety of reasons and is more or less worthy of condemnation depending on what the actor's motives for doing that act express' (Kahan & Nussbaum, 1996, p. 315). An angry mother becomes entitled to mitigating consequences because her anger (towards her daughter's abuser) is considered appropriate in her situation. Her 'emotional motivations' (i.e. what made her angry and whether in that background her emotional reaction can be adjudged appropriate) distinguish her from the homophobic killer, whose emotional motivations are fully inappropriate (Kahan & Nussbaum, 1996, p. 361).

While this account appears compelling, and disruptive of the orthodox view in which motive is excluded or made irrelevant to guilt determination, it does little to contest the psychological individualism located at the heart of law. In assessing and comparing a mother's emotional motivations with that of the homophobic killer, certain value judgments are necessarily made about a mother's love for her daughter, the value of other's life, disgust towards the homosexual. In making these assessments, some values are accepted and others rejected. Nussbaum believes that it is important for law to make these evaluations, as:

> Under the evaluative view [...] we are continually (except in a small number of cases of extreme mental disorder) treating our fellow citizens as reasonable, and promoting in society at large a view that human beings are or should be reasonable and rational. This is both more appropriate as a view of one's fellow citizens under liberal constitutionalism and more effective in promoting the stability of such a regime.
>
> (Kahan & Nussbaum, 1996, p. 361)

Consider another illustration taken by Nussbaum: theft and not competition is wrongful (even though both may equally harm a merchant) because 'theft expresses – in a way that competition (ordinarily) does not – a false assessment of the merchant's worth [...] the thief's behaviour communicates to the merchant and to others that she views the merchant's interests as unworthy of her respect' (Kahan & Nussbaum, 1996, p. 352; Murphy & Hampton, 1988). The emotional motivation of a thief is wrongful because merchant's interests are disrespected by her. Individual emotional motivations – in this case, motive behind stealing (deprivation, unequal distribution of resources, monopolistic control over property) – are often products of a long history of social and political conditions but in an evaluative assessment these linkages are often lost. Nussbaum's inclusion of motive or the 'why-question' remains limited to the individual assessment with complete erasure of the structural violence that contributed to that emotional motivation. Consistent with the utilitarian psychology (the consequentialist approach), in this view, no serious thought is given to the social, cultural and political contexts within which emotions are stimulated and nurtured. The moral assessments leave little scope of raising questions around already entrenched ideas within criminal law, which are products of historical forces and social conflict. In evaluative assessments, it is not clear to what extent the link between socio-political causes and individual motives can be explored. This view of emotions in law reinforces the insular logic of law where legal theory not only becomes alien to structural and social violence, but it also shuts itself to the voices and traces of violent histories of the subjects before the law.

How are these moral assessments made? Would the evaluative conception contest the gendered assumptions and prejudices internal to the rule of law? Is there is way to view theft other than as a communication that the thief views the merchant's interests (i.e. her right to private property) as unworthy? Under the evaluative view, can theft *ever* communicate acute deprivation and need? In what follows, I will show how the evaluative conception does not disrupt or complicate the presumption of 'reasonable man' – a rational being who exercises rational control over his passions – rather reifies and solidifies it: the reasonable person becomes the one who feels the reasonable emotion and acts in consonance with it.

The criteria of reasonableness under the evaluative view

Following Nussbaum's argument closely, the evaluative conception in criminal law entails enquiring whether the experienced emotion is rational and reasonable (not whether emotions are experienced for a reason). The rationality of emotions is tested on the touchstone of their social appropriateness and moral evaluation. Rationality is equated with reasonableness and emotions are tested on moral grounds. The enquiry is one of 'normative acceptability of the emotion' (Spain, 2011, pp. 98, 103). The assessment of the emotion (as rational and therefore acceptable) 'take(s) place against the background of a shared judgment that emotions are sometimes reasonable, in the normative sense. In other words, these emotions are justified by what has happened, against the background of reasonable views about what matters' (Nussbaum, 2004, p. 12). Therefore, Nussbaum argues that reasonableness of emotions is to be adjudged against the backdrop of the (moral) values and (social) norms.

However, the criteria of reasonableness that pervades the enquiry into emotional states also brings with it judgments rooted in the dominant sexual, social and cultural norms as well as perceptions of reasonable behaviour. Consequently, emotions sanctioned by social and cultural norms are scripted into law, leaving little space for expression of what feminist thinker Alison Jaggar termed 'outlaw emotions' (we will return to this in a while). But this does not daunt Nussbaum's enthusiasm about the evaluative conception for, she believes, law 'is itself normative, playing a dynamic educational role' (Nussbaum, 2004, p. 12). For Nussbaum, the normative aspect of law is its strength. For she believes that law itself is rational and moral, that law will progressively change over time, that the 'reasonable man' will ensure that law's evaluations will take us towards feminist futures. It may be briefly stated here that Nussbaum's framework fits into, what Jeanne Schroeder describes as, feminist 'policy-based scholarship'[6] where justice is an achievable and teleological possibility, following a linear trajectory of moral and rational progress, where one norm is displaced with the other better norm. The conservative norm is seen as outside, even though connected with, the law and which can be shed off easily through moral education. The question that is never asked is: how can any evaluation be done when law, or socio-symbolic order itself internalises the conservative

6 Schroeder (2001) writes: 'policy scholarship reflects a fundamental fear of freedom. Policy oriented scholars to [sic] use the law as a tool to subject others to their control in order to achieve what they see as society's objective purposes'.

norm? In this scenario, as law and norm collapse into a singular entity, there would be no scope of assessing the moral appropriateness of the emotion from the reasonable person's standpoint. The reasonable person of the Nazi regime and law, for instance, was the one who had internalised the values of Aryan supremacy and whose emotional motivations and responses were in conformity with those values. These laws were valid and good laws (except when seen from the external viewpoint of Lon Fuller, 1958), even though the emotions codified within these laws were racist and anti-semitic.

One finds a similar uncritical approach towards the reasonableness criteria in the work of Eimear Spain who takes Nussbaum's framework seriously. She builds an argument towards a reformulated defence of 'duress' based on fear. In the reformulated defence of duress, where fear would be a recognised emotion, a person would be granted this defence if 'his or her actions represent a prudent and *reasonable* response to the *rational* fear engendered by the predicament' (Spain, 2011, p. 272, emphasis mine). To grant the defence, the experience of fear is to be evaluated on the touchstone of the standard of behaviour expected from the 'reasonable man' of law. Put differently, the fear experienced by the defendant should be morally appropriate. Spain categorically affirms that emotions that result from a "bad' belief system' (say, when fear is unwarranted because the perceived threat is mistaken or when fear results from a value system which is morally reprehensible) cannot be acceptable in law. Only those emotions can form the basis of criminal law defences which are based on beliefs and values acceptable to democratic societies.

In consonance with the cognitive view, Spain maintains that '[emotional] urges are spurs to action, but an individual retains control over his or her reactions and is not compelled to act upon them' (Spain, 2011, p. 266). Thus, even when fearful, an individual continues to act voluntarily. Far from displacing the subject of law, this framework, even while inaugurating emotions within legal discourse, reifies abstract legal individualism where the emotions of a person are her private concern, with no social history or responsibility. Society will share no accountability for the emotions that a person feels. It is an individual's responsibility to modulate her emotions to conform to social norms and abide by legal rules; neither the law nor the society will share the moral or criminal responsibility for the 'inappropriate' emotions (Spain, 2011, p. 266):[7]

> Each person has a duty to educate him or herself and alter his or her underlying values if they represent socially unacceptable views. So, a person who grew up in a dysfunctional household where physical aggression was

7 In Macaulay's Draft Penal Code, we find a similar emphasis on changing underlying values in accordance with what is socially acceptable. Giving explanation for punishing homicide committed in heat of passion, Macaulay writes, that it deserves to be punished (though not as severely as murder) 'to teach men to entertain a peculiar respect for human life [...] to give men a motive for accustoming themselves to govern their passions' (Macaulay et al, 2002, p. 107).

> the norm cannot claim an excuse for losing his or her temper unreasonably and assaulting another. Society has a right to expect that individuals will alter their underlying perceptions to overcome such a tendency and this may be enforced by law. Inherent in this view is a respect for the person, as to excuse those who had a bad upbringing on the basis of that upbringing alone would be to exhibit disrespect for their power and individuality as people.

The dominance of moral considerations in evaluative conception makes it an enquiry less about people's emotional states and more about social/legal appropriateness. The evaluative view stresses the objective assessment of the moral quality of an individual's emotions as well as her responses. Legal doctrines are operationalised on the basis of those emotions that are capable of rational explanations[8] and are formulated on morally and socially acceptable beliefs.[9] Law thus aligns with the social to sit in judgment over people's inner motivations. Further, it will be wrong to presume that evaluations will always be based on progressive ideals. In fact, often it is the regressive norms of the social that inform the value structure for adjudging and evaluating emotions.[10]

The rationality of emotions is defined in normative terms. Irrationality, according to Nussbaum, may be understood (Nussbaum, 2004, p. 11):

> in terms of thought that is bad thought in some normative sense. Thus, the person who says that two plus two is five, even after repeated teaching, is irrational, because he thinks badly. So, too, in a different way, we typically hold that racism is irrational, based on beliefs that are false and ungrounded.

Such rationalisation of emotions, even though Antonio Damasio acknowledges 'that emotions and feelings can cause havoc in the processes of reasoning under certain circumstances' (Damasio, 2005, p. xii), is a reductive exercise that erases the complexity of psychic processes and excesses as well as the long history of lived experience – including childhood experiences – that produces a particular emotion.

In contrast, a grounded understanding of emotions in law requires a complex theory of the 'subject of law' as well as 'law as subject' which is beyond the cognitive and evaluative frames. A preliminary account of such a conception is provided by psychoanalytic reading of the law which provides a nuanced

8 Spain argues that emotions may be irrational, when the individual overestimates 'the personal relevance of the situation [...] make[s] a mistake of fact when appraising the situation [...] [or assessment is] based on a flawed value system' (2011, p. 105).

9 As Berger states '[t]he evaluation taking place is not just of the state of the accused's will, but of the emotions that informed her action and whether these emotions are emotions that are legitimate in the eyes of the community' (2006, p. 109).

10 Though Spain categorically states that cultural pluralism should not become the excuse to accommodate misogynist and racist emotional responses (e.g. honour-based killings).

understanding of the unconscious. As Peter Goodrich and David Gray Carlson note: "the intentional subject and the 'reasonable man' are disassembled in psychoanalysis to reveal a chaotic and irrational libidinal subject, a sexual being, a body and its drives. Behind the mask of reason, the unconscious plays the role of law and emotion determines both judicial judgment and the subject's deeds' (Goodrich & Carlson, 1998, p. 3). It is precisely this chaotic and disaggregated notion of subjectivity that is absent in the evaluative account of emotions.

Evaluative anger and the defence of provocation

Kahan and Nussbaum argue that neither voluntarist nor consequentialist account of criminal law can explain the requirements of a successful 'plea of provocation' in criminal law (Kahan & Nussbaum, 1996). The 'plea of provocation', if successfully pleaded, leads to mitigation of guilt, in common law jurisdictions, from murder to manslaughter even in a case of intentional killing. If provocation is granted because accused's choice capabilities have been partially undermined, owing to anger (voluntarism) or because investing heavily in the punishment of individuals who kill in the heat of passion is wasteful (consequentialism), then the essential ingredients of this defence in its common law formulation cannot be explained. The defence of provocation[11] in common law was not granted to an angry defendant who killed without 'adequate' provocation or if the victim was someone besides her provoker. These salient requirements of the defence, according to Kahan and Nussbaum, can only be explained through evaluative approach to emotions in law. Law does not accept mere impairment of volition as the ground for mitigation of liability, as anger is considered appropriate only in response to serious and not any slights; again, mitigation is offered only if anger is directed at the provoker because it is the latter's conduct that formed the object of the defendant's anger.

Nussbaum explains the cooling down requirement (if the accused had enough cooling down time, she is not entitled to the defence) in evaluative terms as follows (Kahan & Nussbaum, 1996, pp. 317–318):

> It is much easier to make sense of "cooling time" in evaluative terms. We assess the appropriateness of emotions against a complex of social norms. Some of these, as we've explained, specify which goods are valued by a reasonable person, and how much a reasonable person should value such goods in relation to each other. Still other norms, however, specify how long a person should persist in a state of strong or intense anger when someone has interfered with some good essential to his well-being.

11 For a fuller discussion of the defence, cast as deprivation of loss of power of self-control, see Chapter 2.

> [T]he duration of a person's anger is particularly relevant to the assessment of his relative valuations. When an offense is fresh, we tolerate – indeed, expect – strong anger; it is precisely because a person *ought* to value fidelity intensely that the law is prepared to mitigate the punishment of the cuckold if he kills shortly after learning of the adultery. But if the cuckold continues to be obsessively angry for days, weeks, months, or even years, then we will regard his view of what's important in life as skewed. Unshakable rage reveals that he values something – honor, control – too much. It also reveals that he values other things that matter – like the life of the victim and the lawful resolution of disputes – too little. If a person has good character, he won't stop valuing fidelity as time passes, but he will take the steps necessary – perhaps divorcing his wife, or possibly notifying authorities of the transgression of the offending man – to restore "tranquillity of ... judgment" in a way that reflects an appropriate valuation of all the goods and interests at stake.

The authors, however, concede that the evaluative account of 'cooling time' requirement for the defence of provocation is not perfect as there can be cases where a defendant's brooding anger appears morally appropriate and understandable, but legally one can establish 'cooling time'. The authors attribute 'this lingering imprecision [...] to the inherent impossibility of devising legal rules that perfectly capture the relevant moral judgments' (Kahan & Nussbaum, 1996, p. 318). Despite this imprecision, the authors assert that '[t]he flexible conception of "cooling time" reflected in case law works adequately well for evaluative purposes and otherwise marks a reasonable accommodation between the evaluative view and other legitimate concerns in criminal law, including deterrence' (Kahan & Nussbaum, 1996, p. 318). However, the acceptance of imprecision as a 'reasonable accommodation' between evaluative and deterrence goals is an uneasy resolution. Law's 'cooling period' in its evaluation of defendant's rage seldom considers the perspective of the *activated-afterness-of-events (Nachtraglichkeit)*: a delayed and deep reaction which appears to have no semblance of a justification (Lacan, 2006, p. 711).

Further, under the evaluative approach, 'the quality of a person's character, not simply the quality of her volition, is the touchstone of moral assessment' and as a moral author of her acts 'she remains accountable for experiencing good rather than bad emotions' (Kahan & Nussbaum, 1996, p. 307). The evaluative conception can thus successfully explain why common law treated an enraged man who killed his girlfriend's lover differently from an enraged man who killed his wife's lover. They were punished differently not because they experienced different emotional intensities. But because the emotional valuations of their honour and dignity were adjudged differently by law. A boyfriend did not have the control that a husband possessed over the woman. The evaluations, Nussbaum points out, change with shifting community standards: the enraged husbands are no longer granted the defence in many jurisdictions,[12] while a battered woman who kills is covered within the defence (though in India this change is yet to come).

The evaluative approach also explains the distinctions in criminal law between situations where culpability is mitigated and where there is complete exculpation.[13] This is based on relative evaluations that are integral to the evaluative conception (Kahan & Nussbaum, 1996, p. 313):

> The evaluative view does not assume that any particular act expresses only one emotional evaluation, which is either "appropriate" or "inappropriate". Acts may be attended by multiple evaluations varying in their moral quality. Thus, for the law to be evaluative in nature, it is enough for it to condemn acts that reflect at least some appropriate emotional motivations less severely than acts that reflect only inappropriate emotional motivations.

This is explained by ascertaining the position in law of a woman who kills the abuser of her daughter. The moral assessment of the anger of this woman who kills a man after discovering that he sexually abused her daughter is not a straightforward enquiry. Her emotion embodies different appraisals not all of which will be endorsed by law: 'She has appraised her circumstances in a way *correctly*, as her anger reflects her appropriate valuation of her daughter's well-being; but in a way she has also appraised them *wrongly*, as she should not have thought that this good was all-important, taking precedence over all other considerations, including the value of the man's life and the importance of lawful resolution of disputes' (Kahan & Nussbaum, 1996, p. 313). Because of these varied appraisals, not all of which are correct in the eyes of law, the woman's guilt will be mitigated and not exculpated in law.

In contrast, a man who killed out of homophobic hatred should not get the defence. This is because *all* appraisals embodied in this emotion are inappropriate and hence undeserving of mitigation. In other words, the evaluative

12 See *R* v. *Tran* [2010] SCC 58 (Supreme Court of Canada). In the UK, the loss of control defence is illustrated in ss. 54–55 of the Coroners and Justice Act, 2009. S. 55(6)(c) provides that 'the fact that a thing done or said constituted sexual infidelity is to be disregarded' in determining whether loss of self-control had a triggering quality. However, in *R* v. *Clinton* [2012] 1 Cr App R 26, the court interpreted the new offence as allowing for sexual infidelity – if there are other circumstances (in light of ss. 54(1)(c) and 54(3)) where sexual infidelity is integral to the facts as a whole, and then is one of the many factors which caused the loss of self-control.

13 In the voluntarist account, the distinction between exculpation and mitigation can also be explained in the following terms: provocation defence only mitigates culpability because the individual continues to be seen as a 'reasonable person' who ends up losing self-control. The passion impairs 'choice capabilities' partially, not fully. For exculpation from guilt, there should be complete impairment of choice-capabilities. Consequentialists would say that provocation calls for mitigation because provoked killers should be punished less than the unprovoked killers.

conception is premised on prior moral judgment of the emotional responses which varies according to the moral standards of a society. In this view, law's assessment of the appraisals embodied in the emotions will change over time. Only the evaluative view, for the authors, can explain the changing legal assessments of emotional responses according to changing social norms (for instance, the rage of the cuckold is no longer accepted as a defence, while the battered women who kill are not judged severely under law). Clearly, the changing legal assessments are not because the intensity of cuckold's rage is doubted *but because moral quality of this rage is suspect.*

In her book *Anger and Forgiveness*, Nussbaum while offering a normative argument against anger,[14] contends that the doctrine of provocation is completely in line with her normative thesis on anger. She observes that people will feel anger towards their perpetrators, but:

> victims should turn the business of dealing with the perpetrator over to the law, rather than taking matters into their own hands [...] It's very understandable that the individual face and body of the perpetrator may dominate a victim's thoughts and dreams for a while. If the fixation on the perpetrator becomes an ongoing obsession, however, we would be correct in blaming the person (and urging her to seek treatment for the problem). What would be acceptable would be anger for a brief period, followed by movement towards a Transition, in which the victim's focus now becomes social welfare, and how the legal system can promote it.
>
> (Nussbaum, 2016, pp. 165–166)

According to Nussbaum (2016), in the 'middle realm' ('people with whom we are not involved in relations of intimacy and deep trust', p. 138), the relationship between the offender and the victim is different than the one in the 'intimate realm'. While in the 'intimate realm' people are bound in a reciprocal relationship of trust, in the 'middle realm', people generally share a very thin relationship with little or no expectations. Therefore, in the 'middle realm', she believes, often the victim does not become a perpetrator and instead hands over the matters to law. Law then takes into account the anger felt as a result of injury in the 'middle realm': 'Why should that conduct have the power to make me turn into a dog? Whether the offender should be made to suffer becomes a purely forward-looking question, which institutions will handle in their way' (Nussbaum, 2016, p. 166). What victims need to do is 'to mourn and to deal with the losses they have experienced'. This 'need not entail ongoing payback fantasies about the perpetrator. By turning things over to the law, they transform the injury, making it not just about them, but about what makes society go better [...] Letting impartial justice take its course is not a pusillanimous response' (Nussbaum, 2016, p. 166).

14 For a critique of Nussbaum's normative account of anger, see Vashist (2021).

These heightened *ought* propositions – *tyranny of shoulds* – and wishful prescriptions to mourn, and deal with losses might shock anyone familiar with elementary understanding of the complexity of human psyche (Leader, 2008). In such description, what Nussbaum misses out is the traumatic dimension of such emotional responses, triggered both by political structures and personal histories. Evaluative view obscures any enquiry into the gendered experience that has triggered the emotions under law's scanner. Would law investigate the fact that the mother who killed in the above example had known the perils of patriarchy and lived in the discriminatory institution seamlessly pervading her life, which in fact compelled and entrenched her response? There is no reflection on the post-event trauma that haunts the perpetrators (or the fact that the perpetrator was also an institutionalised victim of patriarchy). To the law, she is a criminal. Terming the mother's appraisals as *wrong* from the external standard of moral/legal appropriateness, is a cold and objective denial of the institutional violence normalised by law. Further, 'punishing' her for the neglect of the *lawful resolution* presumes that the lawful resolution is always and automatically just.[15] The trauma of being a victim of institutional violence (of patriarchy, family, marriage, state) as well as the trauma of being a perpetrator of violence, this liminal position always escapes the law. The logic of the evaluative conception forecloses any understanding of and attention to the traumatic kernel in the subjectivity of those who are pushed to commit crimes.

Any lawful resolution that fails to engage with the traumatic subjects (victims-agents-perpetrators) of sexist, heteronormative cultures is bound to erase that mother's trauma which carries the burden of being both the victim and perpetrator of violence. The subject remains, or is expected to remain, in control in the 'blindfolded' eyes of the evaluative law. Referring to Toni Morrison's *Beloved* in which Sethe, the central character, kills her own daughter, Gabriele Schwab argues that it is 'Sethe's personal history as a slave that triggers the killing of her baby daughter [...] Sethe's mother [who was never allowed to keep her own children] passed down to her the sense that it is better to be dead than to be a slave' (Schwab, 2010, p. 79) and better as a slave to avoid attaching oneself to the children. A previous slave who was orphaned by the death of her slave parents, Sethe had a brutal experience of slavery. Such violence of the institution of slavery and its gendered nature requires acknowledgment, if not healing, for taking the affectivity of the subject and the possibility of justice seriously. The evaluative conception seems to be 'silencing the traumatic histories' in the garb of the rational legal culture. In the eyes of law, these mothers who ended up killing their children in their attempt to escape domestic violence are criminals who took neither life nor morality seriously. Law in such cases is doomed to neither understand the loss of children nor the loss of self in the homicidal emotional outburst that led to the loss of the loved one. Evaluative law merely consolidates the *inability to mourn* the loss

15 For a distinction between a lawful and a just act, see Derrida (1992).

and re-institutes the impossibility to confront or understand the traumatic histories that trigger emotional responses in the subject.

How a past wound would incite a particular reaction is not accessible through the available legal categories of tangible evidence, as it is not 'available in terms of what gets written on the "transparent surface sheet" of the Mystic Writing Pad'. It rather needs to be 'retroactively recuperated with difficulty–patience–care from the somewhat illegible script, from the Other language inscribed–encrypted on the wax slab underneath' (Dhar, 2016, p. 23). To read the stories beneath the surface of the *mystic writing pad*, which I have discussed in the Introduction, one needs to find the traces borne elsewhere – illegible and unintelligible – not on the surface. The limits of judicial interpretation and understanding the injuries through the calculus of cause and effect would invariably read the action as 'cruel', exaggerated, violent rage. Perhaps this calls for an alternate 'theory of readability' such that 'interpretation is possible even in the face of obvious obstruction' (Dhar, 2016, p. 23). It is not a plea for excusing but *understanding* the victim[16] who 'chose' to kill.[17]

Postscript: 'Outlaw emotions' of an Indian army *jawan*

B. D. Khunte was a *jawan* (foot-soldier) in the Indian army.[18] He was convicted and sentenced for the murder of his superior, Subedar Randhir Singh by the orders of Armed Forces Tribunal, New Delhi. This order was upheld by the Delhi High Court. Khunte preferred an appeal before the Supreme Court, challenging conviction for murder and seeking the plea of provocation which is present as an exception to the offence of murder under section 300 of the Indian Penal Code (IPC) [now section 101 of BNS]. Exception 1 requires that the provocation must be 'grave', it must be 'sudden' (i.e. there must be no 'cooling down' period), it must cause the loss of power of self-control. It may be noted that the law on provocation in India also includes the concept of cumulative or

16 Contrary to the linguistic shift from victim to survivor, I retain the word 'victim' but I do not use it in the sense of an identity as the victim is not totally deprived of agency for all times. As Hydén (1999) argues that even in victims, there is a 'hidden transcript' of resistance in the fear of the victims. And therefore, it is no use to work with the binary of victim and survivor: 'the identity as a 'battered woman' [...] offer[s] a too-limited base on which to build a self-understanding'.

17 The law assigns blame which is mitigated by absence of volition or freewill. But if the subject has the capacity to choose her actions, she is legally responsible. Feminists have often confronted this conundrum of legal ethics where escape from punishment is at the cost of the loss of legal capacity. The ethic of psychoanalysis, in contrast, would ask the subject 'to take responsibility for [her] own symptom, simply because their [sic] is no one else who can take responsibility for it. To take responsibility for one's own symptom is to have some say in one's destiny. It is to refuse victimhood, a paranoid form of being wherein one is only ever the object of the actions of larger and powerful forces' (Seymour, 2017).

18 *B.D. Khunte* v. *Union of India* (2015) 1 SCC 286.

successive provocation whereby even after the cooling down the exception can be claimed if the subsequent conduct of deceased ignites the initial provocation. Khunte gave the following account of the incidents that led to the killing of his superior (paras 4–6):

> On 28-6-2006 [I was] resting in [my] bunk after lunch when the deceased Subedar Randhir Singh came to [my] cot in an inebriated state, slapped [me] mildly twice and asked [me] to follow him. Thinking that [I] was being called for some kind of duty, I followed the [Subedar] to the storeroom where [he] bolted the door from inside and asked [me] to remove [my] pant suggesting thereby that [he] intended to sodomise [me]. When [I] declined, [Subedar] punched [me] and kicked [me] repeatedly and asked [me] to put up [my] hand and hold the side beams of the top berth of the double bunk in the storeroom [...] the [Subedar] thereafter made unwelcome and improper advances like kissing [my] body, cheeks and stomach. While this was going on, two other personnel viz. Hadgal Vilas and Anil Gadge knocked at the door of the store room. The [Subedar] opened the store room door and asked them to go away and shut the door again only to continue the [my] torture for half an hour. [I] somehow managed to free [my]self and return to barrack, shaken and crying inconsolably. [I] shared [my] grief and sorrow about the whole episode with [my] colleagues and immediate superior officers. No formal report was, however, lodged by [me] before the superior officers, although [...] the superior officers pacified and advised [me] to remain calm and keep [my] cool.
>
> [I] and [my] colleagues planned to gather near the water heating point in the evening and beat up the [Subedar]. With that resolve [I] performed [my] administrative tasks during the day till it was time for [me] to go for night picket guard duty commencing at 2000 hrs. along with Hadgal Villas carrying [my]service weapon duly loaded as the place where [I] was posted was an operational area [...] [A]fter taking early dinner [I] reached [my] place of night guard duty. While on duty [I] saw someone approaching [me]. As per the prevailing drill and procedure [I] challenged the approaching person, but the person paid no heed to the warning and continued to approach till [I] could recognise him to be Sub Randhir Singh. Seeing the [Subedar] and still seething with anger [I] opened fire upon him from [my] service weapon. Sub Randhir Singh was hit and dropped dead on the spot. [I] was immediately taken into custody handcuffed and tied to the cot in the barrack.
>
> [T]he daytime incident in the storeroom had so deeply shaken [me] that [I] was gravely and suddenly provoked when [I] saw the [Subedar] approaching the picket in the evening.

In the light of the above, Khunte's counsel argued that even though there was a gap of several hours between the attempted sodomy and the killing, Khunte had not 'cooled down' and 'had been all the while seething with anger'. On the other hand, the Union of India (who represented the deceased as well the army) contended that a long interval had lapsed ('cooling off') between the alleged provocation by the deceased and the murderous assault by the appellant.

The Supreme Court conceded that 'an incident' did take place in the store-room, as the appellant was seen crying by many of his colleagues, and he had reported to them: '*sahib ney mere ko bahut mara aur pant kholney ko bataya aur mere mana karne par mujhe phir pita* (Sahab beat me up and asked me to remove my pant and on my refusal to do so beat me again)' (para 9). However, drawing a distinction between the *attempt* at sodomy and the *fact* of sodomy, the court observed that there is no evidence that the 'deceased had actually sodomised him', but then goes to record that '[w]hether or not the deceased had sodomised the appellant is not material' (para 10). The extent to which the court believed the appellant was that he was 'beaten and humiliated' (para 19).

The court rejected the plea that Khunte was provoked [again] when the Subedar refused to stop despite appellant's call of halt. According to the court, 'the deceased had [not] come close to him or tried to act fresh with him so as to give to the appellant another provocation that could possibly justify his losing self-control and using his weapon' (para 19). Moreover, '[t]he deceased, at any rate, could not be accused of having given any provocation to the appellant by moving towards the place where the appellant was on guard duty for the deceased was well within the sphere of his duty to keep an eye on those who were performing the guard duty' (para 19). It is interesting to see how the court continues to operate within the sacrosanct framework of duty. The Subedar was 'within the sphere of duty' in approaching Khunte despite the physical/sexual assault and humiliation to which that he had subjected the appellant. Even after attempting sodomy in the afternoon, the Subedar continues to claim the right 'to keep an eye on those who were performing the guard duty' (para 19). Even though it was the Subedar who had exhibited callous disregard for the protocol of identifying himself on call, it was Khunte who violated the norms through his retaliation.

The State read Khunte's response as retaliatory and thus not deserving of mitigation of culpability. He should have kept his faith in law and let law take its own course. As he did not behave like the reasonable person who would not obsess about anger, he failed to live up to the normative expectations of law. However, such a construction of Khunte's response – unreasonable, criminal rage – is possible only by effacing the institutional apathy towards his complaint. He was asked to 'remain calm and keep cool' when he complained about the incident. In this context, can we see Khunte's anger as an 'outlaw emotion' in the deeply hierarchised and closed institution of the army? Isn't Khunte's violent outrage an expression that subverts the dominant institutional norms marked by an uncritical obedience to a superior's orders and a silence (and secrecy) around the internal workings of the armed forces? Outlaw emotions, according to Alison Jaggar:

> provide the first indications that something is wrong with the way alleged facts have been constructed, with accepted understandings of how things are. Conventionally unexpected or inappropriate emotions may precede our conscious recognition that accepted descriptions and justifications often conceal as much as reveal the prevailing state of affairs. Only when we reflect on our initially puzzling irritability, revulsion, anger, or fear may we bring to consciousness our "gut-level" awareness that we are in a situation of coercion, cruelty, injustice, or danger.
>
> (Jaggar, 1989, p. 167)

Khunte's anger was a rejection of the culture of silence. A culture that expected him to remain calm and maintain his cool. In his defence, Khunte's lawyer argued that an 'incident of this nature [attempted sodomy] taking place in the Army is usually underplayed by the authorities by either denying the same totally or presenting a different picture which is neither true nor realistic' (para 5). Not surprisingly, no part of the judgment responds to this assertion.[19] In the way the court proceeds in its legal reasoning, there is not only a denial of the truth of Khunte's testimony but a complete suppression of such violence internal to (the logic of) armed forces (across the world). Euphemistic descriptions of the violation as 'misdemeanour' and 'humiliation' are the linguistic strategies which maintain the 'unknown known' (an active not knowing, Žižek, 2016) quality of the obscene underbelly of the armed forces. The myth of honour must stay in-tact and that is why there is such a refusal to see the unconscious even when it spills out.

While the armed forces often come under the critical scanner for the excesses externally committed by them (on civilians, prisoners of war, women), the excesses that produce the disciplined soldier through years of tormenting physical, mental and emotional training go unaddressed and unattended. The logic of the severity of the training and the ethos on which it is premised are never questioned. The making of a soldier is a psychological exercise of ridding him of the wrong emotions and breeding the right ones. The right emotional character forms the ethos of the army. Humiliation is the way through which camaraderie is built. The apparent appearance of camaraderie conceals the 'ontological wounding' that goes to the heart of one's being (Geetha, 2009, p. 95; Rao, 1964; Pandit, 2017).[20] The psychic abuse inherent in the training regime aims to induce a psychological regression that infantilises the subject and causes a 'loss of autonomy' to re-make his character through suggestions to

19 This needs to be contrasted with *Ravi* v. *State of Karnataka*, ILR 2001 Kar 71, where the court recognised that homosexual assault on a person against his will 'would trigger off a violent physical reaction of wanting to hit back at the person who is making such advances'.

20 That the caste position of B. D. Khunte (he belonged to the backward caste) is totally suppressed is not only pertinent to understand the violence of the liberal individualism that sustains the law but also the illusion of secular harmony in armed forces.

which he will be more receptive now. It is first through infantilising that the army constructs the masculinity ready to kill (Grossman, 2009).

The impunity given to the violence of the armed forces is not difficult to explain. The violations are committed not by the enemy *other* whom it is fairly easy to despise but by the institution that constructs its self-image through collective national pride. The truth is buried through denial and even when violence is acknowledged, it is often seen as an exception or an aberration so that the founding faith and allegiance to the institution and the values it stands for, remain intact. The erasure of sexual violence marked by the Indian Supreme Court in this case is symptomatic of the fact that the judiciary works with the state to keep the 'official secret' of the (sexual) violence that lies at the foundation of the nations and nationalisms. The complicity of the judiciary, the ultimate guarantor and protector of human rights, with this official secret is in the service of rule of law that binds all state institutions, especially the state forces that claim to protect 'us' from the enemy.

It is important to reiterate that the exception of provocation would not take into account *all* cases of real momentary anger but only where anger is an 'institutional emotion', i.e. when anger falls in line with the logic of social, cultural and political institutions or it is in tune with power-based interests. Nussbaum might not want the law to endorse honour or status related ideas (and therefore she argues that anger at diminished honour/status should not be given the defence of adequate provocation) but this naïve desire emerges from a liberal view of law and emotions where both law and emotions exist outside and independent of the social/cultural/political and are independent of one another. However, *Khunte* shows that emotions acquire meanings and legitimacy within larger institutional settings. The validity and desirability of emotions are tied to the institutions within which they circulate. Perhaps this explains why male anger at 'loss of honour' (discussed in Chapter 2) is readily appreciated by the courts. The institutional logic of family, marriage, community and state construct zones of permissible emotional expression. Khunte's expression of anger was unacceptable because it went out of bounds, in its exposé of the internal violence of the armed forces. It will always be difficult to secure a place for such 'outlaw emotions' within law, owing to law's own identification with social and political hegemony. This is the tragedy of Nussbaum's normative stance on emotions: it will outlaw subversive emotional outbursts but will never manage to disrupt institutionally sanctioned and privileged emotional scripts.

References

Abrams, K. & Keren, H. (2010). Who's afraid of law and the emotions. *Minnesota Law Review*, 94, 1997.

Bentham, J. (2014). *An introduction to the principles of morals and legislation*. Universal Law Publishing.

Berger, B. L. (2006). Emotions and the veil of voluntarism: The loss of judgment in Canadian criminal defenses. *McGill Law Journal*, 51(1), 99–109.

Caudill, D. S. (1997). *Lacan and the subject of law: Toward a psychoanalytic critical legal theory*. Humanities Press.

Damasio, A. (2005). *Descartes' error: Emotion, reason and the human brain*. Penguin Publishing Group.

Dhar, A. (2016). What if, the hurt is "real": Psyche, neighbor and intimate? In R. Ramdev, S. D. Nambiar & D. Bhattacharya (Eds), *Sentiment, politics, censorship: The state of hurt*. Sage Publications.

Finkel, N. J. & Parrott, W. G. (2006). *Emotions and Culpability: How the Law is at Odds with Psychology, Jurors, and Itself*. American Psychological Association.

Fuller, L. (1958). Positivism and fidelity to law — A reply to Professor Hart. *Harvard Law Review*, 71(4), 630–672.

Geetha, V. (2009). Bereft of being: The humiliations of untouchability. In G. Guru (Ed.), *Humiliation: Claims and context*. Oxford University Press.

Glynosa, J. & Stavrakakis, Y. (2008). Lacan and political subjectivity: Fantasy and enjoyment in psychoanalysis and political theory. *Subjectivity*, 24, 256–274.

Goodrich, P. & Carlson, D. G. (1998). *Law and the postmodern mind: Essays on psychoanalysis and jurisprudence*. University of Michigan Press.

Grossman, D. (2009). *On killing: The psychological cost of learning to kill in war and society*. Back Bay Books.

Grosz, E. (1990). *Jacques Lacan: A Feminist Introduction*. London: Routledge.

Hart, H. L. A. (1968). *Punishment and responsibility*. Oxford University Press.

Hewitson, O. (2015). Inside out and the 'science' of emotions. *Lacan Online*. www.lacanonline.com/index/2015/09/inside-out-and-the-science-of-emotions.

Horder, J. (2005). Reshaping the subjective element in the provocation defense. *Oxford Journal of Legal Studies*, 25(1), 123–140.

Hydén, M. (1999). The world of the fearful: Battered women's narratives of leaving abusive husbands. *Feminism & Psychology*, 9(4), 449–467.

Jaggar, A. M. (1989). Love and knowledge: Emotion in feminist epistemology. *Inquiry*, 32(2), 151–167.

Johnston, A. (2009). Affective Life between Signifiers and Jouis-sens: Lacan's Senti-ments and Affectuation. *Filozofski vestnik*, XXX(2), 113–141.

Kahan, D. M. & Nussbaum, M. C. (1996). Two conceptions of emotion in criminal law. *Columbia Law Review*, 96(2), 269–278.

Lacan, J. (2006). *Écrits*, B. Fink (transl.). New York: W.W. Norton & Company.

Leader, D. (2008). *The new black: Mourning, melancholia and depression*. Penguin UK.

Macaulay, B., Macleod, J. M., Anderson, G. W. & Millett, F. (2002). *A penal code prepared by the Indian law commissioners*. The Lawbook Exchange.

Mitchell, J. & Rose, J. (Eds). (1985). *Feminine sexuality: Jacques Lacan and the école freudienne*. Pantheon Books.

Murphy, J. G. & Hampton, J. (1988). *Forgiveness and mercy*. Cambridge University Press.

Norrie, A. (2014). *Crime, reason and history: A critical introduction to criminal law*. Cambridge University Press.

Nussbaum, M. C. (2001). *Upheavals of thought: The intelligence of emotions*. Oxford University Press.

Nussbaum, M. C. (2004). *Hiding From Humanity: Disgust, Shame and the Law*. Princeton University Press.

Nussbaum, M. C. (2016). *Anger and forgiveness: Resentment, generosity, justice*. Oxford University Press.

Ormerod, D. (2011). *Smith and Hogan's criminal law*. Oxford University Press.

Pandit, R. (2017). Army rejects calls to raise new units based on caste or religion. *The Times of India*. https://timesofindia.indiatimes.com/india/Army-rejects-calls-to-raise-new-units-based-on-caste-or-religion/articleshow/18248941.cms.

Pillsbury, S. H. (1989). Moralizing the passions of criminal punishment. *Cornell Law Review*, 74, 655–677.

Posner, R. A. (1985). An economic theory of the criminal law. *Columbia Law Review*, 85, 1193–1231.

Rao, M. S. A. (1964). Caste and the Indian army. *The Economic Weekly*.

Sachdev, D. & Vashist, L. (2021). Introduction. *Journal of Practical Philosophy*, 2(1). http://practicalphilosophy.co.in/wp-content/uploads/2021/01/1.-Introduction_Deepti-Sachdev-Latika-Vashist.pdf.

Schroeder, J. L. (2001). *Fear of freedom: A polemic against policy scholarship*. Working Paper Series No. 35, Jacob Burns Institute for Advanced Legal Studies, Cardozo Law School. https://ssrn.com/abstract=262349.

Schwab, G. (2010). *Haunting Legacies: Violent Histories and Transgenerational Trauma*. Columbia University Press.

Scott, J. (1992). Experience. In J. Butler & J. W. Scott (Eds), *Feminists theorize the political*. Routledge.

Seymour, R. (2017). *The murder of Hélène Rytman*. www.versobooks.com/blogs/3324-the-murder-of-helene-rytman.

Solomon, R. (2003). *Not passion's slave: Emotions and choice*. Oxford University Press.

Spain, E. (2011). *The role of emotions in criminal law defenses*. Cambridge University Press.

Vashist, L. (2021). Total control: Nussbaum's normative account of anger. *Journal of Practical Philosophy*, 2(1). http://practicalphilosophy.co.in/wp-content/uploads/2020/12/5.-Total-Control_Latika-Vashist.pdf.

Williams, G. L. (1983). *Textbook on criminal law*. Stevens.

Žižek, S. (2006). *The parallax view*. MIT Press.

Žižek, S. (2009). Discipline between Two Freedoms – Madness and Habit in German Idealism. In M. Gabriel & S. Žižek, *Mythology, Madness, And Laughter: Subjectivity in German Idealism*. London: Continuum International Publishing Group.

Žižek, S. (2016). Rumsfeld, UNKNOWN KNOWNS, and Psychoanalysis [Video file]. www.youtube.com/watch?v=4SQpczc8mGg.

Chapter 2

Gendered Emotions in the Provocation Defence

> Situations of marital discord do give rise to very strong feelings, and psychiatrists and social scientists alike who have done deep research in this field have now clearly laid down that particularly in situations of extra marital lessons very strong emotional reactions are quite natural particularly from the aggrieved spouse [...] Psychiatrists have very clearly expounded the theory that sexual jealously which is the root cause of hostility in such a situation is sufficient to disturb the aggrieved human being to the extent of even creating a situation of temporary loss of control. It is precisely this emotion or this state of mind that the law takes into account while considering exemption (1) to Section 300 of the Indian Penal Code (IPC) [now section 101 of Bharatiya Nyaya Sanhita, 2023, BNS].
>
> –*K.M. Balakrishna v. State of Karnataka*, 1996[1]

> My name is Manju Lakra. The incident took place last Sunday night. My husband was in the habit of coming home in a drunken state at night and beat me up. On the night of the incident also he came home drunk and beat me up [...] Failing to bear it anyone [sic], I beat my husband with that lathi. I hit him in the legs, head and back of the neck. He had been in a drunken state and could not get up again. Later, he died [...] Since husband used to always commit atrocity on me, I killed him out of anger. I have spoken exactly what happened, or else God shall not forgive me.
>
> –*Smt. Manju Lakra* v. *The State of Assam*, 2013[2]

Indian law partially diminishes criminal liability if the offender was 'deprived of the power of self-control' and acted under 'grave and sudden provocation', mitigating culpability from murder to culpable homicide not amounting to murder ('manslaughter' under common law). Even though the law does not name or specify any emotional state as an impetus for losing 'the power of self-control', the exception has privileged the emotion of anger, particularly male

1 1996 SCC Online Kar 682, para 14.
2 MANU/GH/0272/2013 (Hereafter, '*Manju Lakra*'), para 19.

DOI: 10.4324/9781003387411-3

anger (tied to sexual infidelity and notion of 'honour') in offering this limited concession to human frailty. Murderous rage arising from sexual jealousy, as the first epigraph from a High Court judgment reveals, has been naturalised in a way that, for the defence of provocation, it has acquired the status of legal commonsense. Even as emotions pervade the text, sub-text and the cultural life of law, there is no other site of law where the emotion question has emerged in such profound gendered complexity as in the defence of provocation.

The exception of provocation, Exception 1 of section 300 of the 1860 IPC (section 101 of the BNS) reads as follows:

> Exception 1.: When culpable homicide is not murder. Culpable homicide is not murder if the offender, whilst deprived of the power of self-control by grave and sudden provocation, causes the death of the person who gave the provocation or causes the death of any other person by mistake or accident.

In context of the IPC, it has been long recognised that 'sudden' refers to the *unexpected* provocative conduct of the victim – which took the accused by surprise – and not when the accused lost self-control (Yeo, Morgan & Cheong, 2012, pp. 804, 815). Thus, there can be an interval between the provocative incident and the homicidal act, as long as the accused does not regain self-control. However, the interval should not be long enough to allow premeditation and impulse of revenge to take over. In this legal provision we find a glimpse of the emotional, raging subject-out-of-control, repressed *other* of the autonomous, free-willed, always-in-control liberal subject, who can lose itself when provoked. Here, emotionality is not *othered* as monstrosity or primitiveness of the criminal but recognised as an aspect of universally shared human frailty.

Historically, the defence of provocation, characterised as loss of self-control, has been one of the most contested and controversial provisions. Criminal law scholarship is inundated with literature on analysis and critique of provocation. The range of critical scholarship spans from philosophical enquiries into its rationale (whether provocation should be categorised as an excuse or a justification; see Berman & Farrell, 2011) to psychological basis of mitigation of liability, discussing, *inter alia*, the intentionality of emotional defendants (Hollander-Blumoff, 2012; Weisberg, 2009). The gender critique, has been the strongest where, across jurisdictions, criminal law scholars (not necessarily 'feminist') have shown how in its historical evolution as well as modern re (formulations) it has not just disproportionately protected violent men who killed in rage, but also privileged a masculine worldview in its gender-neutral stance (Horder, 1992; Forell, 2006; Nourse, 1997; Ramsey, 2010; Horder & Fitz-Gibbon, 2015; Dressler, 2002; Pillsbury, 2009; Lacey, 2002). In tune with such pervasive criticisms, calls for structural reforms have ranged from re-conceptualisation to proposals for complete abolition of the defence (Gruber, 2015; Wells, 2000; Medarametla, 2017).

The story of provocation defence in India has not been different. However, unlike other common law (UK, Australia) as well as IPC jurisdictions (Pakistan), in India the defence of provocation has been largely ignored. The criminal law reform efforts spearheaded by Indian women's movement have disproportionately focussed on offences against women and sexual offences at the risk of bypassing how gendered violence is normalised through gender-neutral homicide provisions in the penal code. The provision has stood uninterrogated even in the face of long-standing criticism by IPC scholars (Leader-Elliott, 2011; Yeo, 1998; Kumari, 1999). While the BJP-led central government introduced the criminal law changes, employing the rhetoric of decolonisation, to free Indians of Thomas B. Macaulay's colonial legacy, many critical criminal law scholars have insisted that a serious criminal law reform exercise requires us not to disown and disavow, but a *return to* Macaulay (Chan et al., 2011). I will touch upon all these aspects in this chapter, but my primary aim is to show how the defence of provocation, historically premised on a gendered account of anger, emerges as a contentious site where law's encounter with its other, an emotional subject-out-of-control betrays its own internal inconsistencies and contradictions.

Haunting spectres of Macaulay

The provocation provision in Macaulay's original penal code of 1837 appeared as section 297: 'Voluntary culpable homicide is 'manslaughter' when it is committed on grave and sudden provocation, by causing the death of the person who gave that provocation'. The Explanation to this section stated that provocation would be 'designated as 'grave' when it is such as would be likely to move a person of ordinary temper to violent passion'. Provocation, thus, from its inception is a legal defence that recognises and encodes emotions in law; provocation mitigates culpability when it 'moves' a person to violence. This word used in the explanation of Macaulay's draft has a useful etymological link with the English word 'emotion'. 'Emotion' has Latin roots, and its English language usage is foundationally derived from the Latin 'emovere': '*e*' (out) and 'movere' (to move), which means to stir, to move, to agitate. However, legal recognition for mitigation was not accorded to any or all emotions, but only those that 'move a person of ordinary temper to violent passion'.

'It would be a fortunate thing for mankind' contended Macaulay, 'if every person felt an outrage which left a stain upon his honour more acutely than an outrage which had fractured one of his limbs' (Macaulay et al., 2002, p. 108). In so conceptualising the defence of provocation, he brought gross insults by words at par with the passions aroused by physical injuries, as 'all wise legislators desire to encourage' the value and importance of 'honour' in the population. Here, 'honour' was invariably masculine 'honour' which led to justifiable male rage. The circumstances which wounded such 'honour' were spelt out in detail: wounded 'honour' of a husband who finds his wife in adultery;[3] 'an affectionate and high spirited brother' who killed 'in a paroxysm of rage the seducer of his sister'; one who took 'indecent liberties with a modest female in the presence of her father, her brother, her husband, or her lover' would also invoke 'intemperance of anger [which] ought to be treated with greater lenity' (Macaulay et al., 2002, p. 108).

Provocation was understood 'as a harm to 'honour', which may be affronted, slighted, stained, traduced, diminished or lost as a consequence of the conduct or words of another' (Leader-Elliott, 2011, p. 293). Macaulay, thus, implicitly endorsed the 'evaluative conception of emotion', which I have elaborately discussed in Chapter 1, as for him the tenets of culpability depended upon 'a blameable excess of an *appropriate* feeling' (Leader-Elliott, 2011 p. 294). '[W]hy should we treat an offence produced by the blameable excess of a feeling which all wise legislators desire to encourage, more severely than we treat the blameable excess of feelings certainly not more respectable?', Macaulay had asked (Macaulay et al., 2002, p. 108). As Leader-Elliot points out, the 'idea of a wrong done within a community of feeling is the argumentative spine of Macaulay's explanation of provocation as a partial defence that extenuates a resort to violence' (Leader-Elliott, 2011, p. 294). Because the ideas of honour, and attached shame, 'bind people together in a community of feeling' (Williams, 1993), they perform the explanatory function of why law compassionately responds to violent anger provoked by an onslaught on honour.

In Macaulay's criminal code, male 'honour' came to be the privileged emotion that deserved not just law's acknowledgement but also support.[4] Colonial law came to fully empathise with husbands, fathers and brothers who lost self-control and killed infidel wives, non-conforming daughters and sisters. 'Honour' was not singularly tied to male rage but was coalesced with other 'good' emotions of the familial order: affection and love. The violent rage directed at erring, transgressive women in the family, was after all, a product of love and affection. Familial love and affection extracted the price of conformity with social mores, cultural practices and sexual norms, as women's sexuality was considered the repository of familial male honour. This is how 'the realm of emotion provided the basis here for a legal crystallisation of masculine authority, rather than a point of resistance to colonial penetration' (Singha, 1998, p. 167). Radhika Singha remarks, '[i]nstitutionally, patriarchal power over women was provided with an anchorage in judicial narratives about emotional states which justified or mitigated the infliction of injury or death by men upon their female relatives' (Singha, 1998, pp. 166–167).

3 Adultery, however, was not termed 'adequate provocation' as a matter of universal rule. Because it could so happen that the husband in such a case had acted not from a feeling of 'wounded honour or affection'; instead he acted 'from mere brutality of nature, or from disappointed cupidity' (One is aware of the limits of this rationale, as the distinction between 'wounded honour or affection' and 'disappointed cupidity' itself may be falsely created).

4 Macaulay's broad conception of the right of private defence was also to 'encourage a manly spirit' (Ling, 2011, p. 189).

It is difficult to suggest if the positing of patriarchal mores into the legal script was a British colonial imposition, or whether it was merely consolidation of existing community mores into the script of codified law. The passage from Macaulay's notes which I will cite below will only complicate any categorical assurance that the patriarchal honour coding was imposed by an alien colonial authority.

One is tempted to ask, what is it about the nature of some emotions that allows law to mobilise them to its own ends to draw the limits of lawful and unlawful violence? Why is that a violent outrage incited by an attack on honour 'would be a fortunate thing for mankind' but not a lashing out in despair? If sentiments of honour and shame bring people together (which explains law's partial exculpation in the defence of provocation), why is collective sympathy for those who are pushed into violence as a result of social and structural burdens, say starvation, homelessness, impoverishment, not accounted for in the 'loss of self-control'? We are tapping, then, on a political economy of emotions, an account where a certain collective is discounted against others which are counted and credited. More questions on this economic logic can be posed, *viz.*, why does the legal presumption of 'rational subject-in-control' remain in-tact when a mother kills her children one after the other to save them from wretched pangs of hunger?[5]

Macaulay's draft did not contain any reference to 'loss of self-control'. What mitigated the guilt of the accused was not loss of self-control but the gravity of the transgression which provoked the accused's reaction (Yeo, Morgan & Cheong, 2012, p. 796). In accounting for the weight of the transgression, in an extremely illuminating passage from notes appended to Macaulay's draft code, we learn that the colonial legislators and the law sought to respond to and encode the feelings of the native subject:

> A person who should offer a gross insult to the Mahomedan religion in the presence of a zealous professor of that religion, who should deprive some high-born Rajpoot of his caste, who should rudely thrust his head into the covered palanquin of a woman of rank, would probably move those whom he insulted to more violent anger than if he had caused them some severe bodily hurt. That on these subjects our notions and usages differ from theirs is nothing to the purpose. *We are legislating for them, and though we may wish that their opinions and feelings may undergo a considerable change, it is our duty, while their opinions and feelings remain unchanged, to pay as much respect to those opinions and feelings as if we partook of them.* We are legislating for a country where many men, and those by no means the worst men, prefer death to the loss of caste, where many women, and those by no means the worst women, would consider themselves dishonoured by exposure to the gaze of strangers; and to legislate for

5 *In Re: Sreerangayee* v. *Unknown* (1973) 1 MLJ 231.

> a such a country as if the loss of caste, or the exposure of a female face were not provocations of the highest order, would, in our opinion, be unjust and unreasonable
>
> (Macaulay et al., 2002, p. 108, emphasis mine)

The 1860 Code had substantially deviated from Macaulay's draft but the colonial presumptions about the native subjects, we will see in cases discussed below, remained etched in the law. Now the offenders are required to establish that they committed the act while they were 'deprived of the power of self-control' (a vocabulary which slipped into the 1860 legislation). Loss of self-control is a subjective condition, a liminal state between the autonomous 'subject-in-control' and its contrary, i.e 'total deprivation' of self-control which would be tantamount to automatism and attract complete exoneration. The emotional state of the offender here, thus, is an 'intermediate stage between icy detachment and going berserk'.[6] This emotional state of in-betweenness has irked many commentators who, subscribing to the evaluative conception of emotion, have argued that the terminology of 'loss of self-control' ought to be deleted. I will return to this critique in a while, but for now it is sufficient to note that provocation 'must have destroyed the capacity for reasoning' *and* inspired the intention to kill in the offender (Yeo, Morgan & Cheong, 2012, p. 814). Simply, it should be established that 'the accused's intention came from his or her highly charged emotional condition' (Yeo, Morgan & Cheong, 2012, p. 814).

A close look at the cases emerging from colonial archive establishes that provocation in Indian criminal law took the rigid shape of 'defence of male honour'.[7] The judicial discourse, notwithstanding some important yet marginal deviations, aligned itself with caste, class and gender hierarchies of the 'honour' codes which made some lives less worthy in the eyes of law. Fatal violence which could be traced to the slightest disruption of established normative framework was partially excused as it could be characterised as *appropriate* 'blameable excess of feelings'. While Macaulay was careful in not casting all adultery cases as 'adequate provocation' and insisted on a distinction between cases of 'brutality of nature or disappointed cupidity' and 'wounded honour or affection', the colonial courts were less nuanced in their interpretations. Rather, 'brutality' was seen as a natural consequence of 'wounded honour'.

Lahore High Court's 1929 decision in *Jan Muhammad* v. *Emperor*[8] is illustrative of how the emotional core of provocation defence sought to both excuse and justify male violence within intimate spaces. Jan Muhammad was convicted

6 *Phillips* v. *R* [1969] 2 AC 130.

7 I use the term with awareness that in naming this form of violence as 'honour' based violence/murder (as honour killing), we end up accepting and perpetuating the ideology which masks the violence. I am taking this risk because, I believe, that *mere* linguistic reformulation would not do the work that needs to be done to pull the carpet from under patriarchy's sticky feet.

8 AIR 1929 Lah 861.

in the trial court for murdering his 21-year-old wife, Mussammat Bhago. Against this verdict, he filed an appeal in the Lahore High Court. The woman, it was recorded in the High Court judgment, had 'an evil reputation' and was 'leading an immoral life' (para 2). Sympathising with the husband who must have felt 'extreme mental agony, shame and humiliation' on account of 'the previous conduct of the woman' and her 'evil ways [which] were the common scandal of the village' (para 7), the court granted him the defence of provocation. Commenting on the brutality of the blows inflicted on the wife's body, including her private parts, the court said: '[s]ome blows undoubtedly were struck upon the private parts of the unfortunate woman and their significance is apparent' (para 7). For the court, the wife was justifiably, though unfortunately, punished for her sexual excesses. And this is how the court explained husband's 'savage protest' against wife's 'continued and notorious immorality' (para 7): the 'unfortunate affair' (para 7) in which the woman lost her life was not an 'isolated incident' but against 'the whole chapter of the deceased's wicked conduct' which caused the husband 'prolonged agony' (para 7).

In *Kadir Bakhsh* v. *The Crown*,[9] Lahore High Court allowed the defence to the appellant-accused who had confessed to his crime saying '[m]y honour has been spoiled and ruined' and so 'I killed my wife, *Mussammat* Nurai, and Muhammad, son of Lal' (para 4). In a 1923 case,[10] the Court of Judicial Commissioner, Oudh granted the defence to the appellant who had killed his wife because she had developed intimacy with a neighbour. In the court's reasoning, her 'determination to leave him and to disgrace him must have come upon him with a sudden force' (para 1).

While it was well-established in the law that if a husband discovered his wife in the act of adultery and thereupon killed her, he was guilty of only manslaughter and not murder,[11] a successful plea of provocation did not require proof of the sexual act between the wife and her lover; any inappropriate or even innocuous conduct that evoked the suspicion of the man was considered sufficient in order to exercise householder's sovereign power to punish and claim the defence. Mere presence of wife's lover in her company was considered enough for the husband (and his relatives) to lose self-control and kill the intruder.[12] Loss of 'honour' was not contingent on actual proof and verifiable facts; the network of rumours, gossip and suspicion was sufficient to dishonour and disrepute. One is tempted to say, the legal system recognised this precarity of 'honour' and purity and the psychic burdens that cultures of honour impose on men, and (partially) condoned the violence it led to.

9 1920 SCC OnLine Lah 95: AIR 1920 Lah 501.
10 *Gurdin* v. *Emperor*, 1923 SCC OnLine Oudh 196: AIR 1925 Oudh 288.
11 *Emperor* v. *Dinbandhu Ooriya*, AIR 1930 Cal 199.
12 *Raham Shah* v. *The Crown*, 1923 SCC OnLine Lah 450: (1924) 6 Lah LJ 437.

It is not just adulterous wives whose murders by their husbands have been mitigated in law. Wives' killings in general were also condoned because they were not good enough wives. Being subservient is the being of a wife as *Mahadeo* v. *Emperor* makes amply clear.[13] Mahadev hit his wife thrice with a *gandasa* (chopper). The reason for his loss of self-control was her refusal to accompany him back to his home. She had instead, it was alleged, abused him. The woman's conduct was considered a grave provocation in view of the assigned normative roles 'of an Indian household where the wife is expected to obey and respect her husband' (para 3). Even though the court found this act 'cruel and merciless' (para 3) – the woman was in advanced stage of pregnancy – it believed that 'the accused had a chopper in his hand at the time accidentally and not with an intent to hit' (para 3). The sentence was reduced to rigorous imprisonment for eight years having regard to his youth.[14]

Remaining true to Macaulay's legislative intent, colonial courts re-instituted provocation as the male 'honour' defence. But here loss of the power of self-control cannot only be read as exertion of male power; in fact, it is quite the opposite, i.e. it is the loss of (masculine) power of control over the other. It is masculinity crumbling under its own weight, the loss of phallic power within the affective registers of the familial. Familial violence against women, in the words of Jacqueline Rose, 'is a form of radical self- deceit [...] that punishes the world, punishes women we can say, for the limitations of human power' (Rose, 2016, p. 7). Women are not just victims of male rage [and law's violent injustice], that comes from the privilege of male/law's power, but they are also 'the scapegoats for man's [law's] unconscious knowledge of his [its] own human, which means shared – that is, shared with women – frailty' (Rose, 2016, p. 10). Violence, as Rose says, 'is man's response to the fraudulence of his power and the limits of his knowledge' (Rose, 2016, p. 10). Law's sympathetic response to the violence triggered by an anxious masculinity is not just an expose of, what feminists for the longest time have termed, law's complicity in the patriarchal order. In (partially) condoning the violence, provocation defence also becomes the site where the law unconsciously admits that 'impotence breeds violence' (Arendt, 1970, p. 54). Law admits its own impotence. Unfortunately, courts of 'decolonised' India have continued with this legacy of 'impotence of bigness' (Arendt, 1972, p. 34).

13 922 SCC OnLine Oudh 107: AIR 1923 Oudh 112.

14 But not all cases of wife killing were granted the defence. In *Bhopal* v. *King Emperor* (1931 Cri LJ 1244 (1)), the court maintained that if an accused killed his wife under provocation which was grave but not sudden, Exception 1 won't be applicable. In *Kakar Singh* v. *Emperor* (AIR 1924 Lah 733), the Lahore High Court dismissed the appeal of Kakar Singh who was sentenced to transportation for life for a conviction under section 302 of the Indian Penal Code, of having murdered his wife *Musammat* Karmon. Karmon had eloped with one Gorkhi and after staying with him for a month had been induced to return to her husband's house.

Reasonable person: jealous, insecure, angry victim

In post-independence India, legal assessment of emotional reactions of persons who, 'deprived of self-control', are impelled into homicidal acts is based on a dual test: whether they were subjectively provoked, and whether objectively – as per a 'reasonable man' – losing self-control was justified.[15] However, there is a colonial continuity in court's normative reasoning both with respect to the interpretation and application of legal provisions as well as cultural, social and psychic formations of the 'reasonable man' of free India. For the 'reasonable man' of free India, his 'honour' continues to be the most prized possession, a guarantee of his secured masculinity (Ramanathan, 1999). Any actual or perceived threat to his 'honour' is met with extreme violence against the woman (and the seducer/intruder man) who has endangered the secured masculinity of the 'reasonable man'. This violence – a symptom of 'masculinity in panic' (Rose, 2021, p. 48) – is mitigated by law (seen both as a 'justification' and an 'excuse') and the honour codes of the patriarchal social order are reinforced.

The figure of the 'reasonable man' was introduced in Indian law of provocation[16] in the 1962 decision of the Supreme Court, *K.M. Nanavati* v. *State of Maharashtra* (1962).[17] Though the facts of *Nanavati* did not typify a rare occurrence – in the court's own words, the case presented a 'common place problem' (para 1) – it became determinative of the legal interpretation of the provocation provision in the penal code. Nanavati's was the story of a betrayed husband, an officer in the Indian Navy who killed his wife, Sylvia's lover. The prosecution case was that when Sylvia confessed about her intimacy with Ahuja, Nanavati got enraged, went to his ship, took a revolver on a false pretext, went to Ahuja's flat and shot him dead. The defence, however, presented a completely different story. That after his wife confessed, 'he [had] decided to settle the matter with him' (para 5). Nanavati first dropped her and the children to a cinema, went to the ship, picked up the revolver on some false pretext, 'though [Nanavati said that] the real purpose was to shoot himself' (para 5). The defence argued that Nanavati had gone to meet Ahuja to ask him if the latter would marry his wife and look after his children. When Ahuja retorted with 'Am I to marry every woman I sleep with?' (para 5), he became enraged and in a struggle between them, accidentally Ahuja was shot.

15 Contrast, the decision of the Supreme Court of Canada in *R* v. *Tran*, 2010 SCC 58, where the court observed: 'the ordinary person standard must be informed by contemporary norms of behaviour, including fundamental values such as the commitment to equality provided for in the Canadian Charter of Rights and Freedoms' (para 34).

16 This case introduced the 'reasonable man's standard' from the then English common law to the Indian law on provocation. For a critique see, Yeo, Morgan & Cheong (2012, pp. 817, 818).

17 AIR 1962 SC 605.

The court ruled out defence's version and held that it was a premeditated, intentional killing. It laid down that the objective test of provocation in the following terms (para 152):

> No abstract standard of reasonableness can be laid down. What a reasonable man will do in certain circumstances depends upon the customs, manners, way of life, traditional values etc.; in short, the cultural, social and emotional background of the society to which an accused belongs. In our vast country there are social groups ranging from the lowest to the highest state of civilization. It is neither possible nor desirable to lay down any standard with precision: it is for the court to decide in each case, having regard to the relevant circumstances.

Despite laying down this test, in this case, the court did not 'ascertain whether a reasonable man placed in the position of the accused would have lost his self-control momentarily or even temporarily when his wife confessed to him of her illicit intimacy with another' (para 152). Nevertheless, it constructed an account of reasonability which was far more complicated than an 'evaluative appraisal' of his emotional reaction. For the court, Nanavati would have, in fact (subjectively) lost self-control but he had regained the same and 'killed Ahuja deliberately' (para 152). The rejection of defence version was because it '[did] not appear to be natural' to the court. Rather, '[i]t was *natural* that the accused was enraged at the conduct of the deceased and had, therefore, sufficient motive to do away with the deceased' (para 126). The court wonders:

> Is it likely that a person, situated as Nanavati was, would have reacted in the manner stated by him? It is true that different persons react, under similar circumstance, differently. A husband to whom his wife confessed of infidelity may kill his wife, another may kill his wife as well as her paramour, the third, who is more sentimental, may commit suicide, and the more sophisticated one may give divorce to her and marry another. *But it is most improbable, even impossible, that a husband who has been deceived by his wife would voluntarily go to the house of his wife's paramour to ascertain his intentions, and, what is more, to ask him to take charge of his children.*
>
> (para 70, emphasis mine)

Furthermore:

> We cannot visualize Nanavati as a romantic lover determined to immolate himself to give opportunity to his unfaithful wife to start a new life of happiness and love with her paramour after convincing him that the only honourable course open to him was to marry her and take over his children. Nanavati was not ignorant of the ways of life or so gullible as to

> expect any chivalry or honour in a man like Ahuja. *He is an experienced Naval Officer and not a sentimental hero of a novel.* The reason therefore for Nanavati going to Ahuja's flat must be *something other than* asking him for an explanation and to ascertain his intention about marrying his wife and looking after the children.
>
> (para 72, emphasis mine)

The other, and only reason, for the court, would be to shoot the lover which would be 'the conduct of an enraged man who had gone to wreak vengeance on a person who did him a grievous wrong' (para 74). The court could not accept Nanavati, 'an experienced Naval Officer' (para 72) to be such a sentimental lover which the defence made him out to be. The only expected reasonable conduct of an experienced Naval officer would have been to avenge his honour. It was the manly thing to do.

The court had already laid down by tracing precedents that homicidal rage (towards the wife or her paramour) on account of 'loss of self-control' was a justified emotion of a husband whose wife was unfaithful to him. Not just justified but it was an expected emotion too, therefore, when Nanavati had pleaded that he was not taken over by rage, rather was reflecting on the future of his wife and children, the court could not believe his story. In court's re-construction of the story, he had indeed lost control, but sufficient time had passed for him to cool down during the day, and therefore, he was denied the defence.

In fact, had the defence taken a different line of argument – that he had initially lost self-control, then despite cooling down, he flipped with Ahuja's abusive words – they could have pleaded successive provocation.[18] The court traced a series of cases where husbands of adulterous wives were granted the defence of successive provocation when they had killed the wives[19] or the paramours.[20] Specifically, the court had concluded that (i) the adultery of the wife is accepted as 'grave' provocation for the husband and (ii) the gravity of adultery is such that it can impact the accused for a long time such that the 'mental state created by an earlier act may be taken into consideration in ascertaining whether a subsequent act was sufficient to make the assailant to lose his self- control' (para 147). In other words, the impact of the confession of adultery at a given time period can impact how the provoked man received another act of the victim at a later time period.

Nanavati, tracing the law from colonial times, established male rage as a reasonable emotion. This is despite denying the defence of provocation to Nanavati on the technical ground that his anger had cooled off. The terms of

18 I would like to thank B. B. Pande (former Professor, University of Delhi) for all his classes where these alternate arguments and readings emerged.

19 In re Murugian, AIR 1957 MAD 541; In re C. Narayan, 1958 CRILJ 476.

20 *Boya Munigadu* v. *The Queen*, ILR 3 MAD 33; *Babu Lal* v. *State*, AIR 1960 ALL 223; *Emperor* v. *Balku*, AIR 1938 ALL 532.

reasonability in post-independence provocation cases where male 'honour' was threatened were such that the reasonable man of law identified and empathised with the offender. Affective solidarity with the offender turns the offender-victim categorisation upside-down: the offender is the real victim and the deceased the real culprit. In legitimising man's anger, law nevertheless betrays the crisis of masculinity: male rage, a symptom of panic-struck masculinity, is a desperate attempt to reclaim manhood.

Post-*Nanavati*, it is established in various court judgments that 'no man could have possibly resisted the impulse of punishing a faithless woman',[21] that '[a]ny ordinary man with normal senses or even sangfroid would be outraged at such a scene',[22] that '[p]robably finding the situation to be intolerable the man was probably goaded to turn into a demonical killer'[23]. While allowing the defence to men, courts have not resisted from performing the pedagogic function, teaching duties of domesticity of married life to the dead woman: 'all the time the accused was considerate to her with the fond hope that she will mend her ways and live as a dutiful wife for the husband. However, she was not found to be of that type, but was found to enjoy her lust with the company of so many males'.[24]

It is not merely sexual infidelity which allows a man to get justifiably provoked, in the eyes of law, to the extent of fatally wounding his wife. It is not just adulterous wives whose murders by their husbands have been mitigated in law. As I said earlier, those Indian women who did not perform their wifely duties – chief among them obedience to the husband – met the same fate at the hands of their provoked husbands. Here, 'honour' is no longer a category marked by sexual governance (Baxi, 2009) but a much broader idea which seeps into nitty-gritty of ordinary, everyday existence of women. A delay in preparation of meals by the wife, even after she has contributed her share of wage-labour to earn for the family, is sufficient provocation to enrage a married Indian man.[25] Besides husbands, in a series of precedents, fathers and brothers who lost their self-control on the pretext of being dishonoured by the sexually transgressive women of the families, have killed them and their lovers have also been granted the defence of provocation.[26]

21 *Madaiah* v. *State*, 1991 SCC Online Kar 572, para 21.
22 *State of U.P.* v. *Lakhmi*, MANU/SC/0126/1998, para 23.
23 *Madaiah* v. *State*, 1991 SCC Online Kar 572, para 21.
24 *Perumal* v. *State*, MANU/TN/0018/2001, para 4.
25 *Laughanbai Devjibhai Vasava* v. *The State of Gujarat*, 2018(3) SCALE 309.
26 *State of Rajasthan* v. *Ramesh* 2015(2) SCALE 550. Amid the shrill rhetoric of arresting 'honour crimes', in India there is a total silence on the judicial indulgence of honour-based killings through the evocation of defence of provocation. In the last two decades, 'honour crimes' in India have received considerable attention and at the behest of women's organisations and human rights bodies, it has been recognised that 'honour' based crimes violate constitutional rights of women as citizens. The Supreme Court of India, in 2018, responding to a writ petition filed the organisation, Shakti Vahini (*Shakti Vahini* v. *Union of India*, 2018(5) SCALE

Unreasonable and unjustified: Reading the excess

In identifying with male-rage, the defence of provocation has been called out by critical criminal law commentators, not just feminists, as a gendered defence that atones male violence. It has been argued that women who kill are labelled as 'mad, bad or sad' (Weare, 2017) and '[s]ymbiotic to this labelling of women who kill is the denial of their agency by society, the law and the criminal justice system' (Weare, 2013, pp. 337–338). They are either penalised (by being denied the defence) or erased (by viewing them as depressed, unsound, victims who acted more out of fear than anger) (Young, 1992). One crucial aspect of these reform proposals and critiques has been the erasure of women's violent passion in provocation cases. In Australia, Canada and England, this has led to the acknowledgement of women's 'slow burn' anger, by allowing the expert evidence of battered woman's syndrome, which does not meet the common law requirement of 'suddenness' of loss of self-control. Specifically, the argument has been that women react very differently in the face of provocation; their homicidal acts are explained either by slow burn or fear. However, the debate around gendered nature of emotional dimension of provocation has not assumed the form that it has in most other common law jurisdictions. In India, slow burn has not been a matter of discussion (Medarametla, 2017) – perhaps because provocation has always included sustained provocation – and thus violence of women, on account of 'loss of self-control' is invariably rendered 'excessive' and incomprehensible within the register of law (even otherwise, the approach of the Indian courts has not been consistent on the applicability of sustained provocation. As we saw in *Khunte's* case discussed in Chapter 1, slow burn is not conceptualised within the frame of sustained provocation).

In 1997, a woman named Girja Devi appealed against her conviction before the Himachal Pradesh High Court. Girija Devi was convicted for the murder of her husband and was sentenced to life imprisonment. In her appeal,[27] she pleaded the right to private defence and, alternately, the exception of provocation. She testified that her husband, under the influence of alcohol, would beat her and other family members. On the fatal night, he was drunk and had again assaulted her. She described the turn of events in her statement to the police: 'He had the [sic] sex in natural course with me then he gave beating to me.

51), directed the Central and State Governments to take preventive steps to combat 'honour' crimes. Here, it may be useful to draw a comparison with Pakistan where the history of provocation defence has been similarly tied to 'honour-based' considerations. In 1990, the exception of grave and sudden provocation was removed from the Pakistan Penal Code by the Qisas and Diyat Ordinance. This Ordinance allowed for private settlement of these offenses which continued to allow lenient treatment of 'honour killings', as offenders were forgiven by the legal heirs of the victim who were often complicit in the crime. The law was again amended by the Criminal Law (Amendment) (Offences in the Name or on pretext of Honour), 2016 to ensure that killers get a mandatory life sentence (Cheema, 2008).

27 *Girja Devi alias Gita Devi* v. *State of Himachal Pradesh*, 2000 CriLJ 1528 (HP).

Thereafter, he directed me to put his organ into mouth. I refused. Again, he insisted upon to do, lest I would be killed along with my son Chaman Lal. He tried to put his organ forcibly in my mouth and took 'Darat' [a sharp grass-cutting agricultural weapon] in his hands and threatened to kill. I was able to get hold of sickle as I was too much afraid of and then I hit his private part with the sickle. He fell down and thereafter, I hit him whatever came in my hands and went on hitting with that' (para 12).

The testimony of this woman was set against the versions of a few other witnesses: her son, her husband's aunt and a villager. The son, nine years old, told the court that his father had not consumed liquor on that occasion, and he was sleeping at the time of murder. He also stated that there was no quarrel between his parents that night. The other witnesses denied that the deceased used to drink alcohol or beat up his wife, children or parents. The High Court thus refused to grant the right of private defence and considered it an afterthought on the part of the defence strategy. According to the court, if she were really beaten up by her husband 'there certainly would have been some tell-tale signs of the same on her body', and so she should have got herself medically examined, 'so as to establish her bona fides' (para 28).

This judicial demand of making the body testify so that the woman's speech became credible is discursively situated within the gendered nature of the production of evidence in cases of violence against women (Baxi, 2005; Kolsky, 2010). The history of domestic abuse in the marriage was completely erased as she was established as a lying woman whose plea of self-defence was a 'false plea'. Though not private defence, the court did accept the ground of sudden and grave provocation. Significantly, it was the testimony of the investigating officer (IO) that established that there were exculpatory grounds of losing her self-control. The IO had recorded that 'deceased used to keep the appellant naked and [she] was made to stand throughout the night in that position' (para 22). That her husband used 'to do unnatural offence on her and also enjoyed oral sex' and the night 'prior to his death', her husband had unnatural sex with her and 'had insisted upon her to suck his organ for which she refused' (para 23). The court noted that the 'deceased Pal Chand was somewhat of a pervert in his sexual habit and [...] wanted to satisfy his perverted lust on his helpless wife' (para 30). Therefore, his wife killed him under grave and sudden provocation. Significantly, it was not the history of domestic abuse – the everyday beatings and humiliation to which the appellant was subjected but husband's sexual habit which militated against the sexual code of conduct between husband and wife (for it was criminal 'carnal intercourse against the order of nature')[28] and granted partial relief to the wife.

28 IPC, section 377 criminalised carnal intercourse against the order of nature. Here, it may be noted that s. 377 criminalised 'unnatural sexual intercourse' between heterosexuals as well as homosexuals. On the one hand, it was used to delegitimise homosexual relationships (to this extent the provision was read down in *Navtej*

The evaluations in the judicial acceptance of her anger (to grant provocation) puts the Nussbaumian evaluative thesis of emotions in crisis. The pent-up rage that flared out of her wounded history, evidenced in the nature of injuries on her husband's body was accommodated within the socio-legal code of (hetero)sexual morality. One wonders if, within the liberal imagination of the subject of law, there is any opening to see how psychic wounds are 'felt, held, and savoured in the very gut of our existence, in the core of our being'. (Geetha, 2009, p. 255). Even as the law seeks to reduce her rage into moral terms, her testimony and actions refute such domestication. Girja Devi's was not a 'moral anger' of a woman suffering at the hands of a pervert; hers was a defiant 'outlaw anger' – woman's unfeminine expression of anger – made 'unintelligible by discourses of power'. Can law accommodate such an 'outlaw emotion' which protests against the formal equality in distribution and experience of affects and 'unequivocally highlights that the anger of the marginalized is different than the anger of the privileged' (Applebaum, 2014, p. 134)? Even as her rage is rendered unintelligible, the limits of intelligibility of the legal discourse itself emerge in the judgment. Especially important are the contradictions in the judgement with regard to her son's testimony, a simultaneous acceptance and disavowal. The child had said that his father was asleep when he was attacked and there was no quarrel on the day of the incident. The court had accepted this, as 'having already lost his father in the occurrence, he would have no reason to depose against his own mother, rather natural mother, he having been borne from the womb of the appellant, in order to falsely implicate her and thus lose both his parents in the bargain' (para 25). But, in granting her provocation – which should never be couched as desire for retaliation and revenge – there is a disavowal of exactly what the court had believed! If the father was asleep, then how does one read Girija Devi's violent act, except as one inspired by the desire to retaliate and seek revenge? To account for slow burn, the immediacy requirement will have to be dispensed with but always at the risk of allowing the prohibited affectivity of retaliation and revenge. Law hits the ends of its own rationality when confronted with woman's outlaw emotions. Girja Devi's 'slow burn' – effectively erased – coincides, as if, with the uncontainable excess that marks her actions: 'I hit him [with] *whatever* came in my hands and *went on hitting* with that'.[29] It is this excess that puts law's rationality under erasure.

Johar v. *Union of India*, AIR 2018 SC 4321), on the other hand, in the backdrop of marital rape exemption, it was invoked in cases when wives were sodomised by their husbands. Legally, while marital rape was not a crime, s. 377 could be invoked to 'protect' this wife. However, after the 2013 amendments to criminal law, husbands have marital immunity for sexual intercourse as well as sexual acts (IPC, s. 375, exception 2). BNS does not have a corresponding section to section 377 of the IPC; significantly, section 377 is removed in its entirety without creating a separate provision criminalising sodomy.

29 This needs to be contrasted with how the nature of injuries inflicted by angry husbands are read as proof of their 'rage'. Also see, 'honour killing' cases in this context. *Mohd Hanif* v. *State*, 2016 SCC Online Del 2475; *Jaspal Singh* v. *State*, 1986 SCC Online Del 46.

Kuvariben is another example where the 'excess' was rendered unreadable within the script of law. Kuvariben killed her husband, Mahendrasinh while he was asleep.[30] She inflicted multiple blows on him using an axe and locked the room. She then went to the police station, reported the incident and took the police inspector to her house, where her husband was found dead in a pool of blood. She had sent her son, Bachu, to her mother's place with the blood-stained maxi after the incident. The maxi was collected as evidence, along with other incriminatory articles. In the morning of the day of the incident, the husband in an inebriated state, had abused Kuvariben and beaten their son. During this quarrel between husband and wife, a police constable had gone to their house to pacify them.

Kuvariben was charged with murder. The sessions judge acquitted her of the charges, disbelieving the evidence furnished by the prosecution and accepting the plea of *alibi* she had put refuting the prosecution version. In the appeal preferred in the Gujarat High Court, it was argued that the trial court had failed to appreciate the evidence on record, it solely relied on the testimony of accused's mother and son (who were hostile witnesses) and overlooked the significant fact of 26 injuries on the person of the deceased which, according to the prosecution, dispelled the contention of provocation. The high court sentenced Kuvariben for murder in the light of the 'undisputed' facts which provided the circumstantial evidence against her.

It was established that there was a quarrel between the husband and the wife on the day of the incident. However, the court did not accept it as a ground for provocation, as she 'had sufficient time for subsiding her passion/anger, and there were [sic] sufficient interval between the last quarrel and the time of murder of the deceased' (para 9.15). The court also accepted that Kuvariben faced severe domestic violence at the hands of her husband. But this fact was taken, not as slow burn, but as the motive behind the crime for which there was only circumstantial evidence. One is compelled to ask, why the long history of domestic violence was acknowledged to establish the motive for the crime, but not viewed as a provocation that led her to lose her self-control? Is it because it is not natural for women to exhibit such excessive loss of control? Is it because the outlaw emotions are uncontainable within evaluative judgments of law?

The court noted that 'she had taken undue advantage of her husband who was fast asleep and acted in a very cruel manner by using a deadly weapon' which resulted in the fatal injuries. Kuvariben acted 'cruelly' by using a 'deadly weapon against unarmed husband who was under the influence of alcohol and fast asleep' (para 9.14).[31] There was 'no justification at all' in her act as 'she did not stop with first blow, but inflicted as many as 6 to 7 blows' (para 9.14). Is

30 *State of Gujarat* v. *Kuvariben w/o Mahendrasinh Nanaksingh*, 2009 SCC Online Guj 1186.

31 Technically, this is not an essential ingredient of the 'defence of provocation' but of 'sudden fight'.

there any other way to read Kuvariben's excess – wounds inflicted without justification – without reducing it to cruelty and retribution? Is excess *ever* justifiable? In imputing criminal liability on her, law's concern was not that she acted too late – and so there was premeditation for revenge – the concern is that she acted *too much* – and that *too-muchness* made her reaction cruel and vindictive. It is uncontainable within both anger and fear as triggering emotions that led to the loss of self-control. The loss of self-control was, as if, the loss of the self itself. Cruelty, perhaps an expression of desire to inflict the same suffering on one's tormentor, takes it outside both justified anger and legitimate fear. Abused women who kill out of fear often attack their abusers while they are asleep, but this fear does not always fit the normative script of helplessness and vulnerability. To read the loss of (the) self (in) control, existing legal frame of evaluative judgments of emotions would not do. We need an alternative theory of readability to render scrutable this incomprehensible and reprehensible violence.

On January 22, 2006, 'god-fearing' Manju Lakra killed her husband. The second epigraph at the beginning of this chapter is a part of Manju Lakra's judicial confession which she had later retracted. It sums up the history of her marriage with Bhadra Lakra and acknowledges what this marriage had done to her: turned her into a killer. 'Since husband used to commit atrocity on me, I killed him out of anger' (para 20), she confessed, not without heavy weight of guilt, her desire for retaliation, if not directly 'payback' (Nussbaum, 2016). The compulsion to confess – to report the matter herself and say 'exactly what happened' – tied to the desire to be punished by the law, as if, it would atone her sin, and god will forgive her. The trial court nevertheless convicted her for murder, sentencing her to life imprisonment. The Guwahati High Court granted her the defence of provocation, making this the first case in India where provocation defence has been granted invoking the 'battered woman's syndrome'.

The high court begins the judgment with some literary, more accurately theologico-literary flourish, citing a popular quote by playwright, Wilson Mizner: 'All anger is not sinful because some degree of it, and on some occasions, is inevitable. But it becomes sinful and contradicts the rule of Scripture, when it is conceived upon slight and inadequate provocation, and when it continues long'. To ascertain the nature of her anger and determine degree of her guilt, judges Indira Shah and I. A. Ansari asked, 'whether her act was *sinful* or was she just a *victim* of the circumstance?' (para 1, emphasis mine). Sin and victimhood thus became pegs through which the court proceeded to adjudge the criminality of her angry conduct. Her anger would not be sinful if it aligned with 'the rule of the Scripture' *and* she was a victim of the circumstances. There are no scriptures invoked in the judgment, except of course the meta scripture of criminal law in India, the IPC [now BNS], and the unwritten scriptural rules of marriage for dutiful, forbearing wives. Manju Lakra, the court had concluded, did not violate these rules and *therefore,* mitigated the liability from murder to culpable homicide.

According to the court, this was one of those cases in which 'the victim seemingly is the husband, and the aggressor is the wife; but *in reality*, it is the wife, who is the victim' (para 98). Offering an exceptional reading to establish culpability of the deceased husband, the court noted 'that if not *cruelty* within the meaning of Section 498A [section 85 of BNS], the circumstances, prevailing in the family of accused, were nothing short of *domestic violence* as conceived under the Protection of Women from Domestic Violence Act, 2005' (para 66). And hence, 'the deceased *had facilitated his own death by inviting fatal response* from the accused' (para 66, emphasis mine).

In an adjacent move, the court sought to prove that Manju Lakra was indeed the victim in this case and should be seen and adjudged as such. The court invoked the UK's Court of Appeal decision in *Kiranjit Ahluwalia,*[32] which had exposed the cracks of provocation defence in the UK and led to the re-formulation of the law. In *Ahluwalia*, the defence was not granted but her appeal was allowed on the ground of diminished responsibility.[33] Uncritically endorsing *Ahluwalia's* reliance on battered wife's syndrome (Young, 1992), the Gauhati High Court noted that 'a battered woman had special knowledge of the imminence of an attack and as to why retreat was not a reasonable alternative' (para 101). The 'victim's'[34] behaviour is 'indicative of "learned helplessness"' (para 102).

In an unprecedented way, the court went on to examine section 304B (dowry death) [section 80 of the BNS] in the light of the battered woman's syndrome: 'If circumstances create a level of provocation so much so that the *person feels that nothing but an end to his/her life would be a solution*, then, the offense may, depending upon the circumstances, be one under Section 304B or Section 306 IPC' (para 107, emphasis mine). This detour to sections 304B and 306 of the IPC [sections 80 and 108 of the BNS respectively] is significant to understand the court's reasoning. While section 304B [section 80 of the BNS] criminalises the husband or husband's relatives if dowry-based harassment compels a woman to commit suicide, section 306 [section 108 of the BNS] punishes abetment to suicide. Drawing an analogy with these sections, the court asked: 'If, instead of committing suicide, the victim takes the life of her aggressor, whether the case can be brought within Exception 1 to Section 300' (para 107). And concluded (para 108):

32 *R* v. *Ahluwalia* (1993) 96 Cr App R 133.

33 Indian law does not grant the defence of diminished responsibility. Diminished responsibility is a defence where criminal responsibility is reduced on account of mental disorder. However, this defence is only limited to the offence of murder and mitigates criminal liability instead of complete exculpation. (Yeo, Morgan and Cheong, 2012, pp. 757–783).

34 As I said before, in the feminist discourse, there is a marked shift from the category of 'victim' to 'survivor' to contest the victimisation thesis. My argument, however, is to hold on to the category of 'victim', not as an identity category, but to acknowledge the trauma and psychic complexities that are immanent with victimhood. The quick (and often only linguistic) jump to 'survivor' has the danger of smoothening the contradictory and conflicting emotions experienced by the victims.

> if circumstances, potential enough to provoke a person to commit suicide, has [sic] been recognised, it should be equally recognized, going by the victim's level of trauma, that the same set of circumstances are potential enough to turn her into an aggressor so much so that she kills her husband or kills any of her provocateur.

Instead of ending the husband's life, had she committed suicide,[35] the husband would have been convicted under section 306 of the IPC. In other words, the husband was the culprit. If the wife would not have killed him, the law would have punished him! This is a strange and certainly unintentional sanctification of private vengeance – the victimised wife, by virtue of being a victim has come to replace the law. No doubt the court sought to establish absence of intentionality: 'more than the intention to kill her husband, the *intention of the accused was to put an end to the continuing violent acts of her husband* and as a consequence whereof, she felt that nothing short of putting an end to the life of her husband would be a solution' (para 113, emphasis mine). In other words, she did not want to kill her husband but merely wanted to stop his violence, 'without really intending to put an end to his life' (para 116).[36] Here the crack in the reasoning – how slow burn rage slips into revenge diluting the legal insistence on the absence of premeditation – exposes the ever-present difficulty in crafting provocation as a compassionate excuse.

While in *Kuvariben*, motive was relied upon to establish intention, in this case the motive (of ending the violence) negated the very intention to kill. This affective gendering of *mens rea* (Vashist, 2016), I argue, is on account of court's differential reading of Kuvariben's violent rage and the god-fearing Manju Lakra's pent-up resentment and anger which burst out finally. Manju Lakra's 'slow burn rage' and 'strong resentment and rage' which 'had been building up inside her [...] waiting to erupt at any further violent conduct of her husband' (para 116) – a volcano waiting to explode any time, is collapsed with the emotion of fear (para 113, emphasis mine):

> The continuous turmoil [...] created by the violent conduct of the deceased husband, was potential enough to create a fear in the mind of the accused-

35 The reliance on *Suyambukani* v. *State of Tamil Nadu*, 1989 LW (Cri) 86, is again to make a similar analogical move. In *Suyambukani*, the Madras High Court had conceived of 'Nallathangal syndrome' based on Nallathangal ballad which narrates the tribulations of a woman who succumbed her poverty and committed suicide with her children. Here, the court's conception is that the victimised woman might turn on her aggressor, instead of committing suicide.

36 The court convicted her under s. 304 (Part II) because looking at the nature of injuries and the weapon, it could not be said that she had intention to cause death. Though she could have the knowledge that her act was likely to cause death. Here, it may be noted that though the court is saying that her intention was to end the violence, they do not go on to say that she acted in self-defence.

> appellant. The fear was not only *real*, because even before the date of occurrence, accused was beaten up by the deceased [...] but also *perceived* in the sense of imminent threat to life and safety [...] Such perceived fear is possible only when continuous ill-treatment is shown to exist.

There is no doubt that anger would have co-existed with fear (of not just the husband, but the wider kinship structures that demand conformity even in the wake of extreme violence) but in the absence of any evidence or argument to buttress the case for 'fear', the emotion of fear here served the legal hermeneutics for a linear construction of a 'battered wife', as if, legal justice could be scripted only within the rhetoric of victimisation.

Even as Manju Lakra was granted the defence, this case shows the ever-present analytic risk of falling into the gendered script of reading women's rage as 'fear'. As stated before, this is not to suggest that anger and fear cannot be co-present – in most situations of long-term abuse, the two emotions cannot be separated. But the label of 'victim', while acknowledging the history of domestic abuse, not only eternalises the victim status (Fattah, 2010, p. 59) but by confining the victim condition singularly to narratives of pain, suffering and victimisation suppresses the complex reality of victim's experiences. Enmeshed with pent-up resentment, fear offers account of 'an unarticulated knowledge of what she wants and what she does not want' (Hydén, 1999, p. 462; Sen, 2010). Here, loss of self-control emerges neither as a pathological symptom of irrational subjectivity which the law should guard against, nor as a readily available emotional trope couched in a sense of entitlement or power. It is also not merely an expression of socially and culturally inherited emotional scripts. It is an expression of resistance through which she rejected what she was being subjected to.

In the cases analysed above, we saw how the law does not respond to anger in a similar fashion all the time. Instead, the normative gender roles determine law's reading of the emotional states. When law rejects 'payback-anger' and when it tolerates it is itself constructed by law's own complicity in the masculine social order which is sustained through gendered emotional scripts.

Reforming the law? From emotion to reason?

Despite the apparent gender bias in the application of the provocation defence, Indian feminists have not recommended that this exception be abolished or radically altered.[37] Even the 'decolonised' BNS reproduces Exception 1 of

37 Even as the 'Verma Committee' (2003) acknowledged the urgent need to arrest 'honour' based crimes, it maintained total silence on judicial acquiescence of 'honour' based killings when the defence of provocation is granted to men who kill their wives, daughters and sisters. For an argument of reconstruction of the provocation defence in the IPC, see Leader-Elliott (2011). Leader calls for replacing the 'reasonable man's test' with an 'ordinary law-abiding citizen standard' (who has internalized the values of liberal democratic society and is not guided by the

section 300 of the 1860 IPC verbatim [as Exception 1 of section 101 of BNS]. In contrast, many jurisdictions, in recognition of the fact that the provocation doctrine disproportionately benefitted men[38] and has entrenched sexist stereotypes into the law, have introduced feminist homicide law reforms.[39] In this concluding section, I will stay with the reforms that have taken place in the British law. To exclude defendants who killed for reasons of sexual infidelity and to include situations of 'slow burn', the UK abolished provocation and replaced it with the new 'partial defence to murder: loss of self-control'.

Section 54 of the (UK) Coroners and Justice Act 2009 states that a person (defendant) who kills may be convicted of manslaughter, and not murder, if:

a there is a loss of self-control;
b the loss of self-control had *a qualifying trigger*; and
c a person of D's sex and age, with a normal degree of tolerance and self-restraint and in the circumstances of D, might have reacted in the same or in a similar way to D.

Section 55 explains 'a qualifying trigger': the loss of self-control may be attributed to D's 'fear of serious violence' or to 'circumstances of an extremely grave character' which 'caused D to have a justifiable sense of being seriously wronged'. Sexual infidelity is explicitly cast off as a legitimate trigger for loss of self-control.

It is noteworthy that the requirement of 'suddenness' was abolished in the UK. This move aims to account for the gendered ways in which men and women kill: while men claimed to kill when feelings of anger caused them to 'snap', women did not snap but killed in response to being subjected to years of

strength of feelings within a community). He further asserts that the victim's conduct should qualify as a serious wrong resulting in 'extreme emotional disturbance of temporary duration' in the 'law-abiding citizen of ordinary temperament'. And finally, he clarified that 'anything done in the exercise of one or more of the fundamental rights included in the Universal Declaration of Human Rights' should not amount to provocation.

38 This is not to suggest that the law is more severe with women. In fact, in *In Re: Sreerangayee* v. *Unknown* (1973) 1 MLJ 231 and *Emperor* v. *Mt. Dhirajia*, AIR 1940 All 486, reduced sentences were recommended and given. The point however is that provocation does not seem to recognize the situations in which women kill. In none of the following cases – *Sreerangayee, Dhirajia, Gyarsibai w/o Jagannath* v. *The State*, 1953 CriLJ 588, *Supadi* v. *Emperor*, 87 IndCas 840 a, Baijanti Bai v. State of M.P., 2000 CriLJ 3253 – was the provocation plea even made.

39 Three Australian states of Tasmania, Victoria and Western Australia abolished the provocation doctrine as a partial defence to murder. See, (Tasmania) Criminal Code Amendment (Abolition of Defense of Provocation) Act, 2003; (Victoria) Crimes (Homicide) Act, 2005, s. 6; (Western Australia) Criminal Law Amendment (Homicide) Act, 2008, s. 12. In the U.S., the Model Penal Code (MPC), (1962), s. 210.3(1)(b) which mitigates murder to manslaughter refers to 'extreme mental or emotional disturbance'.

violence and abuse, and often out of fear. These legislative changes sought to recognise that the 'loss of self-control' may occur not only because of anger but also in response to emotions like fear. And that self-control can be eroded over a long period of time, not just in the heat of the moment.

Nevertheless, these new provisions retain the vocabulary of 'loss of self-control'. Commentators as well as law reform bodies (Horder & Fitz-Gibbon, 2015; Law Commission, 2006),[40] fear that it will bring back the traditional common law understanding of acceptable/unacceptable emotional states, and that loss of self-control is not 'doing any real work' (Baron, 2011, p. 15). It only creates 'a convenient but perhaps illusionary impression [...] that *something happens* to the agent who kills in the heat of passion that is similar to, but not as extreme as, what happens to someone who really does act involuntarily and that, therefore, warrants mitigation' (Baron, 2011, p. 15). Moreover, 'loss of self-control' is inconsistently applied in the law, as not all situations of 'loss of self-control' (for instance, addiction) are mitigated.

Emotion theorists, relying on the cognitivist/evaluative conception of emotion, have added to the critique of 'loss of self-control'.[41] Sarah Sorial, for instance, has argued that 'even when agents 'lose it', they are still able to make rational assessments of a situation, including assessments about their chances of success in committing acts of violence and whether there will be adverse consequences for them' (Sorial, 2019, p. 261). For Sorial, loss of self-control as a defence is problematic because it does not consider the fact that emotions are learned and hence can be unlearnt: 'while we may be socialised to express emotions in certain ways, we can develop a critical distance from this socialisation and train our emotional responses in socially and ethically appropriate ways' (Sorial, 2019, p. 264). Furthermore, 'while it is true that our self-control is sometimes vulnerable to emotional forces or can be vulnerable in the face of prolonged stress or excessive fatigue, there are many less extreme ways this loss of self-control can be expressed' (Sorial, 2019, p. 264). In other words, there is always a choice when it comes to expressing one's emotions.

40 As the UK Law Commission noted, 'a positive requirement of loss of self-control is unnecessary and undesirable'. This requirement privileges 'men's typical reactions to provocation over women's typical reactions [...] women's reactions to provocation are less likely to involve a 'loss of self-control', as such, and more likely to be comprised of a combination of anger, fear, frustration and a sense of desperation' (Law Commission, 2006, para 5.18).

41 Unfortunately, mainstream legal literature, even when it attends to the emotion question, simplifies self-control by subsuming it within the evaluative frame. Those working on the intersection of law and psychology recognise the mismatch between psychological research and the legal position on this issue. While the advances in psychological research on loss of self-control reflect empirical reality of the subjects – a reality far from rational and control- law insists upon normative judgments about individual behaviour. Hollander-Blumoff's thought-provoking paper challenges criminal law scholars who, at their own peril, have neglected the developments in psychological studies on self-control. Hollander-Blumoff (2012).

For these critics of loss of self-control, 'claims about loss of self-control are not really cases of loss of self-control' because we all have some control on expression of our emotional responses. In fact, Sorial goes on to say that cases of 'loss of self-control' are cases where people acted 'because they felt a sense of entitlement, or simply because they thought they would get away with it' (Sorial, 2019, p. 266). Getting herself caught in the gendered script of emotions (which she herself is critical of) she posits that 'a person might kill because she sees no other way out of a situation or to protect herself and/or her children from further violence' (Sorial, 2019, p. 266). Men kill because of entitlement; women kill out of helplessness. Evaluative account of emotions structures this distinction: while the former expression of emotion is unjustifiable and inexcusable, latter may be found justifiable.

Sorial thus argues for replacing 'loss of self-control' with a *reason-based approach* grounded in *normative moral rights-based theory*. Meaning thereby, a 'justifiable sense of being seriously wronged' ought to be restricted to only those cases where defendant's rights and autonomy (or rights/autonomy of someone close to the defendant) were violated. Under this reason-based approach the defence will be granted to those cases 'in which the provocation was a clear and a serious *wrong*, rather than simply an upsetting situation' (Sorial, 2019, p. 267, emphasis mine) and a 'wrong' is what undermines the rights/autonomy of others in a serious way.

This interesting spin towards *reason* in and through the evaluative conception of emotions is not surprising (see Chapter 1 on Nussbaum's evaluative conception). But this neat policy proposal does not take us closer to just outcomes. Sorial's subject, like Nussbaum's, is a liberal autonomous subject who can choose how to express emotions and who ought not lose her self-control. Losing self-control is a sign of deviation from rationality which deserves legal censure. But by abandoning loss of self-control as a ground of mitigation, law does not necessarily make moral progress. This is what Alan Norrie has usefully shown in his analysis of the new provocation law in the UK. Norrie, whose project – one of revealing 'cracks and contradictions' in criminal law – I read as psychoanalytic (even before his explicit turn toward psychoanalysis), continually reminds us of the quicksand of policy recommendations and legal reforms premised on the myth of liberal individualism.

Norrie has demonstrated that the changes in British law, inspired by the recommendations of the Law Commission of England and Wales (2004), recast the provocation defence in terms of 'imperfect justification' rather than its earlier formulation of a 'compassionate excuse' (Norrie, 2010). For the Law Commission, anger *per se* is not morally inappropriate; it 'can be an ethically appropriate emotion and that [...] it may be a sign of moral weakness or human coldness not to feel strong anger' (Law Commission, 2004, para 3.38). However, anger cannot justify all violent responses: 'a killing in anger produced by serious wrongdoing is ethically less wicked, and therefore deserving of a lesser punishment, than, say, killing out of greed, lust, jealousy or for political reasons' (Law Commission, 2004, para 3.38). The same was true for 'fear' which was included as an acceptable emotional state to claim the defence: fear ought to be appropriate and justified too.

It is significant to note that the Law Commission had recommended dropping the requirement of loss of self-control. This recommendation must be understood in the light of Commission's focus on accepting 'appropriate' emotions as mitigating factors deserving the defense of provocation. With this perspective, dropping 'self-control' made sense, as 'to be out of control might take the moral edge off what has been done in righteous, but sanctionable, anger' (Norrie, 2010, p. 278). But as we have seen, the new law continues to retain the requirement, while subjecting it to qualifying triggers of 'fear of serious violence' or 'a justifiable sense of being seriously wronged'. Norrie terms it 'imperfect justification' because the action of the defendant is evaluated for '*both* its particular rightfulness *and* its overall wrongness' (Norrie, 2010, p. 278) – rightfulness of justifiable action and wrongness of losing self-control.

The old law of provocation in the UK (now repealed section 3 of the Homicide Act, 1957[42]), Norrie writes, was based on an understanding of provocation as a 'compassionate excuse'. The fact that the defendant lost self-control was seen as morally inappropriate from the beginning, as '[i]t can never be right at any level to lose one's control, for this entails a defect in one's rationality, the sine qua non of moral action' (Norrie, 2010, p. 279). However, in certain circumstances the moral quality of the act, despite the loss of self-control, evoked sympathy. As some cases of loss of self-control could be sympathised with, law partially condoned or excused them. The rationale of the law was that it condemned *both* the loss of self-control (for law never expects the legal subject to lose control) and the wrong done by the defendant, *but still* approached the actor with compassion. Thus, provocation was understood as 'a concession to human frailty, for the loss of self-control and its consequence is condemned, but the weakness it represents is viewed with sympathy' (Norrie, 2010, p. 279).

'Under the new ethical approach', writes Norrie, 'this sympathy for human frailty is rejected in favour of a recognition of imperfectly justified anger' (Norrie, 2010, p. 284). The assumption is that the law is making normative moral progress, very much like Sorial's rational for reason-based approach grounded in moral rights theory. Norrie shows us that this teleological argument – from unruly to justifiable emotion and from emotional to rational subject – is not necessarily a sign of moral progress. On the contrary, it exhibits law's perverse side in its insistent search for justifiable reasons which overlook tragic

42 S. 3 of the Homicide Act, 1957 read: 'Where on a charge of murder there is evidence on which the jury can find that the person charged was provoked (whether by things done or by things said or by both together) to lose his self-control, the question whether the provocation was enough to make a reasonable man do as he did shall be left to be determined by the jury; and in determining that question the jury shall take into account everything both done and said according to the effect which, in their opinion, it would have on a reasonable man'.

circumstances which may turn ordinary persons into killers. Unlike Sorial, for Norrie, the pressing question is: how would the new law account for those cases where the defendant may not have acted by a 'justified sense of being wronged' but nevertheless acted in a context of 'sympathetic or tragic plight'? Should law not have 'compassion for the weakness of one who in sad or tragic circumstances did what was wrong without justifiable sense of being seriously wronged' (Norrie, 2010, p. 284)?

One wonders how Sorial's self-contained, self-assured critique of loss of self-control would respond to Norrie's well-founded objections. Relying on evaluative conception of emotion, Sorial pushes for a harder 'imperfect justification' which solidifies law's mythical assumption of abstract liberal individualism – where the legal actor may be affected by emotions but ought to remain in control such that the reasons for the emotional response can be evaluated before it takes the form of appropriate expression.

In lieu of conclusion

I did not intend to arrive at a (feminist) reform proposal with respect to the defence of provocation. Or, to argue for/against the category of loss of self-control. My quest was to find out: what conceptual understanding can emerge with a closer and comparative study of the category of 'loss of self-control'? How does loss of self-control, if at all, offer a glimpse into the mythically constructed 'in-control' subjecthood of law? How does it challenge the rigid formulations of legal subjectivity? How it encodes within itself the unwritten rules of gendered institutions? How do we read law's condonation of masculinity-in-panic that gets manifested as violence against women? How do we make sense of outlaw, emotional excesses that defy the evaluative terms of law? To work with it as a conceptual category, we need to disentangle loss of self-control from the evaluative judgments that get attached to it. The question which is always asked is, whether the subject's loss of self-control was justified or not. Instead, we should ask a more preliminary question: who is the subject?

In showing – what was already known – that provocation is a male 'honour' defence and that it discounts and erases emotional subjectivities of women, I was not building an argument to suggest how to re-form it. Instead, my aim was to peel the layers of judicial reasoning to reveal the meanings and possibilities that remain buried under law's evaluative judgments of emotions of the legal subject. Posing the emotion question while keeping the frames of legal evaluation in-tact would do little to destabilise both law's self-presentation as rational as well as the dominant view of the subject as one in-control. Evaluative view's seductive appeal lies in the mythic illusion of a complete reason-based law. An imaginary law that can read and assess the emotions of a presumably transparent legal subject. But, by betraying the emotion question – turning it into a question of reason – it re-institutes reason-emotion hierarchy within the law. More problematically, it refuses to take up the challenge of 'loss of self-control' as a conceptual category to (re)think the law.

Undoubtedly there is an inherent limitation in the idea of loss of self-control – it will always have a tendency to condone violence caused by those who are taught/can afford to lose self-control – which makes it a threat to those reform projects that seek to regulate gendered expression of emotions. Nevertheless, loss of self-control allows, permits and opens up a space for compassion. It serves as an opening for those unfortunate offenders who truly find themselves at the limits of rationality. Especially in those tragic cases, which are far too many, where extreme acts of violence are individuated, exonerating social and cultural structures, and state apparatuses which create conditions for violence. Norrie (2010) reminds us of the case of a sleep-deprived and fatigued father who killed his 17-day-old infant because he could not bear the baby's incessant cries.[43] Who would say that cries of a baby constitute justified reasons to lose self-control? In such cases, law's evaluative conception of emotions is bound to fail because actions of offenders would not easily fit within the realm of im/morality. Yet there is something not right about the law that refuses to see the broken subject that stands before it.

References

Applebaum, B. (2014). Learning from Anger as an Outlaw Emotion: Moving Beyond the Limits of What One Can Hear. *Philosophy of Education*, 70, 132–140.

Arendt, H. (1970). *On violence*. Harcourt Brace Jovanovich.

Arendt, H. (1972). Lying in politics: Reflections on the Pentagon Papers. In H. Arendt (Ed.), *Crises of the republic*. Harcourt Brace Jovanovich.

Baron, M, (2011). Gender Issues in the Criminal Law. In J. Deigh & D. Dolinko (Eds), *The Oxford Handbook of Philosophy of Criminal Law*. Oxford: Oxford University Press.

Baxi, P. (2005). The medicalisation of consent and falsity: The figure of the habitué in Indian rape law. In K. Kannabiran (Ed.), *The violence of normal times: Essays on women's lived realities*. Women Unlimited in Association with Kali for Women.

Baxi, P. (2009). Habeas Corpus juridical narratives of sexual governance. Working Paper Series, Centre for the Study of Law and Governance, Jawaharlal Nehru University, New Delhi. www.jnu.ac.in/sites/default/files/u63/09-Habeus%20%28Pratiksha%20Baxi%29.pdf.

Berman, M. N. & Farrell, I. P. (2011). Provocation manslaughter as partial justification and partial excuse. *William & Mary Law Review*, 52, 1027.

Chan, W. C., Wright, B. & Yeo, S. (Eds) (2011). *Codification, Macaulay and the Indian Penal Code: The legacies and modern challenges of criminal law reform*. Ashgate Publishing Company.

Cheema, M. H. (2008). Judicial patronage of 'honor killings' in Pakistan: The Supreme Court's persistent adherence to the doctrine of grave and sudden provocation. *Buffalo Human Rights Law Review*, 14(1), 51–99.

Dressler, J. (2002). Why keep the provocation defense: Some reflections on a difficult subject. *Minnesota Law Review*, 1712.

43 *R* v. *Doughty* (1986) 83 Cr App R 319.

Fattah, E. A. (2010). The Evolution of a Young, Promising Discipline: Sixty Years of Victimology, a Retrospective and Prospective Look. In S. G. Shoham, P. Knepper & M. Kett (Eds), *International Handbook of Victimology*. CRC Press, Taylor & Francis Group.

Forell, C. (2006). Gender equality, social values and provocation law in the United States, Canada and Australia. *Journal of Gender, Social Policy & the Law*, 14(1), 27–71.

Geetha, V. (2009). Bereft of being: The humiliations of untouchability. In G. Guru (Ed.), *Humiliation: Claims and context*. Oxford University Press.

Gruber, A. (2015). A provocative defense. *California Law Review*, 103(2), 273–332.

Hollander-Blumoff, R. (2012). Crime, punishment, and the psychology of self-control. *Emory Law Journal*, 61(3), 501–533.

Horder, J. (1992). *Provocation and responsibility*. Clarendon Press.

Horder, J. & Fitz-Gibbon, K. (2015). When sexual infidelity triggers murder: Examining the impact of homicide law reform on judicial attitudes in sentencing. *The Cambridge Law Journal*, 74(2), 307–328.

Hydén, M. (1999). The world of the fearful: Battered women's narratives of leaving abusive husbands. *Feminism & Psychology*, 9(4), 449–467.

Kolsky, E. (2010). The body evidencing the crime: Rape on trial in colonial India, 1860–1947. *Gender & History*, 22(1), 109–130.

Kumari, V. (1999). Gender Analysis of Indian Penal Code. In A. Dhanda & A. Parashar (Eds), *Engendering Law: Essays in Honour of Lotika Sakar*. Lucknow: Eastern Book Company.

Lacey, N. (2002). Why keep the provocation defense: Some reflections on a difficult subject. *Minnesota Law Review*, 86(5), 1712–1735.

Law Commission (2004). *Partial Defences to Murder*. Law Com. No. 290.

Law Commission (2006). *Murder, manslaughter and infanticide*. Law Com. No. 304.

Leader-Elliott, I. (2011). Provocation. In W. C. Chan, B. Wright & S. Yeo (Eds), *Codification, Macaulay and the Indian Penal Code: The legacies and modern challenges of criminal law reform*. Ashgate Publishing Company.

Ling, C. W. (2011). Private Defence. In W. C. Chan, B. Wright & S. Yeo (Eds), *Codification, Macaulay and the Indian Penal Code: The legacies and modern challenges of criminal law reform*. Ashgate Publishing Company.

Macaulay, B., Macleod, J. M., Anderson, G. W. & Millett, F. (2002). *A penal code prepared by the Indian law commissioners*. The Lawbook Exchange.

Medarametla, K. (2017). Battered women: The gendered notion of defences available. *Socio-Legal Review*, 13(2), 108–129.

Norrie, A. (2010). The Coroners and Justice Act 2009 – partial defences to murder (1) Loss of control. *Criminal Law Review*, 275.

Nourse, V. (1997). Passion's progress: Modern law reform and the provocation defense. *The Yale Law Journal*, 106(5), 1331–1448.

Nussbaum, M. C. (2016). *Anger and forgiveness: Resentment, generosity, justice*. Oxford University Press.

Pillsbury, S. H. (2009). Misunderstanding provocation. *University of Michigan Journal of Law Reform*, 43, 143.

Ramanathan, U. (1999). Images (1920–1950): Reasonable man, reasonable woman and reasonable expectations. In A. Dhanda & A. Parashar (Eds), *Engendering law: Essays in honour of Lotika Sarkar*. Eastern Book Company.

Ramsey, C. B. (2010). Provoking change: Comparative insights on feminist homicide law reform. *Journal of Criminal Law & Criminology*, 100, 33.

Rose, J. (2016). Feminism and the abomination of violence. *Cultural Critique*, 94, 7–36.

Rose, J. (2021). *On Violence and On Violence Against Women*. Faber and Faber.

Sen, R. (2010). Women's subjectivities of suffering and legal rhetoric on domestic violence: Fissures in the two discourses. *Indian Journal of Gender Studies*, 17(3), 375–401.

Singha, R. (1998). *A despotism of law: Crime and justice in early colonial India*. Oxford University Press.

Sorial, S. (2019). Anger, provocation and loss of self-control: What does 'losing it' really mean? *Criminal Law and Philosophy*, 13(2), 247–269.

Vashist, L. (2016). Feminist methodology and legal education: Some reflections. In M. K. Sinha & D. Kharb (Eds), *Legal research methodology*. Lexis Nexis.

Weare, S. (2013). "The mad", "the bad", "the victim": Gendered constructions of women who kill within the criminal justice system. *Laws*, 2(3), 337–358.

Weare, S. (2017). Bad, mad or sad? Legal language, narratives, and identity constructions of women who kill their children in England and Wales. *International Journal for the Semiotics of Law – Revue internationale de Sémiotique juridique*, 30(2), 201–222.

Weisberg, R. (2009). The values of interdisciplinarity in homicide law reform. *University of Michigan Journal of Law Reform*, 43(1), 53–82.

Wells, C. (2000). Provocation: The case for abolition. In A. Ashworth & B. Mitchell (Eds), *Rethinking English homicide law*. Oxford University Press.

Williams, B. (1993). *Shame and necessity*. University of California Press.

Yeo, S. (1998). *Unrestrained killings and the law: A comparative analysis of the law of provocation and excessive self-defence in India, England and Australia*. Oxford University Press.

Yeo, S., Morgan, N. & Wing Cheong, C. (2012). *Criminal law in Malaysia and Singapore*. LexisNexis.

Young, A. (1992). *Imagining crime*. Sage Publications.

Chapter 3

Glimpses of our Darker Selves

In 2016, a Research Scholars' Workshop titled "Engendering Social Change: Practices of Resistance" was organised by the Centre for Women and Development Studies, New Delhi (CWDS). The focus of the conference was on understanding and foregrounding the practices of resistance which push for social change. Theorising resistance, the concept note read as follows:[1]

> Resistance is conscious, it is oppositional, it contests existing ways of being and thinking, including structures of power and injustice – based on gender, class, caste, dominant religious or regional identities, or a state system that maintains an order that rests on these hierarchies. Resistance may take the form of everyday acts, subaltern dissent, or organised collective campaigns and protests. The scope of intentionality, the elements of conscious mapping and directionality of the acts of resistance, the layers of collectivity and the depth of critique of the existing gender structures, relations and practices are and may be extremely diverse.

In this feminist formulation, resistance is understood as resistance to forms of oppression and control from above and outside, something that challenges power and injustice, and leads to social and political change. However, resistance is not always conscious and not necessarily oppositional. Psychoanalytically, resistance is internal to the self, often not progressive and in fact inhibiting progress or change.[2] One may describe it as a conservative internal

1 A part of this chapter was presented at the workshop titled "Engendering Social Change: Practices of Resistance" organised by the Centre for Women and Development Studies, at IIC, New Delhi, on January 30–31, 2016, organised as part of CWDS-VMMF (Vina Mazumdar Memorial Fund) activities.

2 Law's resistance against change has recurrently surfaced in the area of sexual consent. The Delhi sessions court in the case of *State* v. *Mahmood Farooqui* (Sessions Case No.118/15 (New SC No.1590/2016) concretised the definition of consent which was introduced in the 2013 criminal law amendments. In convicting Farooqui of rape, the judgment noted that '[t]he essence of rape is the absence of consent. Consent means an intelligent, positive concurrence of a woman.' The Delhi High Court (*Mahmood Farooqui* v. *State [Govt. of NCT of Delhi*], 2017 SCC OnLine Del 6378), in a regressive move, reversed this decision, and observed: 'Instances of

DOI: 10.4324/9781003387411-4

mechanism which spurs resistance against the instinct which resists. Thus, far from being a tool *for* transformation, resistance operates *against* the possibilities of transformation. As in the struggle for 'change', the 'social' has emerged as a far more rigid and powerful zone than we would have expected, I will argue in this chapter, we need to make continuous revisions in feminist practices of resistance by continually attending to this resistance within.

In *The Last Resistance*, Jacqueline Rose writes: 'Resistance is blindness.' (Rose, 2007, p. 19) 'It is the strongest weapon or bluntest instrument the mind has at its disposal against the painful, hidden, knowledge of the unconscious' (Rose, 2007, p. 19). Dispelling remnants of any lingering doubt, she notes that 'resistance is not the action of the freedom fighter, the struggle against tyranny, the first stirring of the oppressed; it is the mind at war with itself, blocking the path to its own freedom and, with it, its ability to make the world a better, less tyrannical, place' (p. 21). Complicating the visceral and intuitive meaning of resistance in political vocabularies, Rose is at pains to elucidate how 'tyranny (or un-freedom) and resistance [...] are brothers-in-arms'. And therefore, '[f]ascism is a form of resistance' (Rose, 2007, p. 21), 'nationalism is resistance at large' (p. 23), '[a]utocracy is in itself a form of resisting, a way of staving off internal panic' (p. 23). In this chapter, I will stay with this idea to explore the duality of feminist resistance: resistance *for*, as well as resistance *against* change to explore what is it that impedes social change, despite well intentioned political and legal initiatives which inform the women's movement.

This chapter will be an exposition of the production, constitution and suppression of emotions in the struggles for justice. I will situate my argument in, what I believe to be, the two important moments for the Indian women's movement in the last decade: first, the legal aftermath of the infamous December 16, 2012, Delhi Gang Rape and, second, the not-so-well-known controversy around Leslee Udwin's documentary film *India's Daughter* (2015). I will examine feminist responses (or the lack of them) to the demand for death penalty for the rapists by the victim's parents, and feminist responses (or the surfeit of them) to *India's Daughter*. Listening to the victim, Jyoti Singh's parents in their evocations of the demand for justice which assumed the form of death penalty for all the offenders, including the juvenile accused, I attempt to locate how the feminists spoke and responded or did not speak and did not respond to these mourning parents.[3] We witnessed how the

woman behavior are not unknown that a feeble "no" may mean a "yes"' (Baxi, 2017, September 29).

3 I name the victim of Delhi Gang Rape with self-awareness. The Indian law prohibits the publication of a rape victim's name (S. 228A of the IPC (s. 72 of BNS) and forbids printing or publishing the name or any other information that reveals the identity of a rape victim). In the initial years, many pseudonyms ('Nirbhaya', 'Damini', etc.) were used in the media reports and accounts to refer to her. However, in 2015, her mother, inverting the politics of shame, publicly revealed her

grief of these parents became a political tool for the right-wing conservative groups to advance their own agendas.[4] But in this chapter, I will ask: was this grief of any significance to the feminist politics against retributive justice? Or, was this grief an impediment to feminist justice, and hence, it should have been resisted by feminists? What would such resistance be a *resistance to*? And, at what costs to our sense of justice? And more fundamentally: what kind of feminist politics do we aspire for in order to overcome the resistance that refuses to acknowledge the desire for violence at the heart of our own psyches? How do we resist this resistance to assume a feminist position against violence and retribution? These and some other related issues will be untangled in this chapter.

I will then critically read the feminist responses to *India's Daughter*. I will show that through their interventions, the legal feminists[5] (re)constructed the image of law as a rational, objective system of internally coherent rules, on the one hand, and lost an important opportunity to read the unconscious of the socio-legal culture of rape, on the other. Finally, I will show that *India's Daughter* and the responses to it constitute cultural texts that epiphanically display the unconscious desires that constitute the social/legal script. The question then is whether we can perform the task of decoding these texts. I will conclude by emphasising that we have to engage with positions of difficulty, complicity and contradiction in order to build an idea of feminist resistance to law's immanent desire for retributive punishment which acquires its strength from the sentiment of 'hostile solidarity'.

The psychic economy of 'governance' feminism

The gang rape of 23-year-old physiotherapy student on the streets of New Delhi on December 16, 2012 had triggered wide-spread protests throughout the country. Anger and outrage poured on the streets as women and men shouted with placards saying 'Hang the Rapists', 'Stringent Punishment to Criminals', 'Stop Violence Against Women' (Banerji, 2012; Taylor, 2012). The ruling government responded by setting up the Committee on Amendments to the Criminal Law (hereafter, 'Verma Committee') to make recommendations for legal reforms. The Verma Committee, in a 627-page report prepared within a month, made recommendations which sought to address sexual violence. While the

name in a rally: 'Whoever has suffered should not hide their name. It is the offenders who should be ashamed and hide their name', she said (Angre & Ghosh, 2016, December 16; Safi, 2017, February 16).

4 National Commission of Women and Akhil Bhartiya Vishva Parishad were in "solidarity" with this grief. See Mathur (2015).

5 The expression 'legal feminists' refers to feminists who are trained in law. This category is not homogenous, and the diversity and complexity of feminist positions clubbed under this umbrella term should not be erased.

Verma Committee was a mixed lot of contradictory recommendations – Prabha Kotiswaran called it a site of 'state feminism' (2017, p. 98) – it also made many useful interventions.

The Committee affirmed that the issue of sexual violence must be addressed through woman's right to bodily integrity and sexual autonomy and not conservative honour-based morality governed by notions of 'Indian womanhood' associated with chastity and purity (Baxi, 2014; Kannabiran & Kannabiran, 2002). It recommended granting legal recognition to consensual adult relationships (Verma Committee, 2013, pp. 51, 54, 406), enacting a marital rape law (Verma Committee, 2013, p. 117) and opposed the demand for the death penalty in cases of sexual violence (Verma Committee, 2013, p. 245). The Parliament, however, chose to ignore these recommendations and effected changes to criminal laws which resonated with the popular public sentiment of retributive justice.[6] While some viewed these developments in terms of the dilemma they posed for the feminists who were forced to choose between state power in the form of a heightened security regime, on the one hand, and gender equality, on the other (Kapur, 2013; Dutta & Sircar, 2013), others contended that feminists were able to insert a substantial part of their own agenda into these reforms (Kotiswaran, 2017). For Kotiswaran, the passage of criminal amendments of 2013 reflected that 'Indian feminism has entered a governance mode in the light of three parameters, namely, an increased reliance on criminal law, a deep commitment to a highly gendered reading of sexual violence and a diluted oppositional stance vis-à-vis state power' (2017, p. 78). The demands for legal reform were articulated within fixed categories of gender based on the binary of male and female (Kapur, 2013; Mundkur & Narrain, 2013; Tellis, 2018), adopting a statist approach that focused on criminal justice, stringent sentencing and a strengthened sexual security regime. These political demands and the state's responses only created an illusion that we are in control of our lives. Ratna Kapur maintains that such a 'carceral vision of feminism does not produce a positive future for women nor address the dispersed forms of power that impact on, or constitute, gender' (Kapur, 2013, p. 341). Instead, feminism gets co-opted into the larger agenda of international law that maintains a top-down understanding of state sovereignty (Orford, 2002; Otto, 2009). This kind of feminism – Kapur invokes the category of governance feminism (Halley, 2008) to illustrate her point – is at best a 'technocratic enterprise' that serves the vision of 'neoliberal political rationality' in the guise of securing women's rights. This constitutes a political subjectivity, articulated in terms of sexual

6 Criminal Law (Amendment) Act, 2013 (India) Act No. 13 of 2013. These amendments, besides expanding the definition of rape and introducing an explicit definition of consent, imposed death penalty in cases where rape leads to the death of the victim or permanent maiming, and for repeat offenders. It retained (rather expanded) the marital exception and provisions dealing with outraging the modesty of a woman, took away judicial discretion in the case of sentencing, and increased the age of consent (BNS retains all these provisions).

agency and freedom from patriarchal constraints, but which is 'neither resistive nor counter-hegemonic' (Kapur, 2013, p. 344).

While governance feminism may not be an apt signifier of the contemporary feminist movement as it homogenises diverse strands of feminisms that constitute feminist politics (Barnes, 2015; Menon, 2019), governance feminism, as a subject position (and not an identity) performs the function of describing the subjectivity that uncritically embraces criminal law as a site of justice for women (Halley, 2018, pp. ix–xxi). Even though we may not agree with the expression 'carceral feminism' (this term, coined in 2007 by Elizabeth Bernstein (2010), was uncritically imported to the Indian context (Sethi, 2016; Baxi, 2016; Banerjee, 2017)), the retributive sentiment that emerged post-Delhi Gang Rape needs to be located within the larger debate of carcerality (Kannabiran, 2016; John, 2013). In other words, the dominance of carceral/governance feminism is not to be seen in terms of the real dominance of feminists or feminist agendas, but the 'psychic economy' of carcerality: the psychic investment in retributive/deterrent law reforms which delude us into believing that we are no longer vulnerable. Via expanding criminal law, we come to believe that *now* we are powerful, now we are in-control.

Grief, loss and demands from the law

Besides changes in the criminal laws, the Delhi Gang Rape also incited changes in the juvenile justice law. Media-stirred fury against the juvenile accused was such that there were demands that, like the other convicts, the juvenile should also be sentenced to death (*The Hindu*, 2018). The Juvenile Justice Board found him guilty of rape and murder and had sentenced him for three years in a probation home, the maximum punishment that could be awarded under the then Juvenile Justice (Care and Protection of Children) Act, 2000. Jyoti Singh's mother, Asha Devi was outraged with this verdict. 'There was no need for these proceedings' she had said, 'We have been fooled. I don't accept the judgement' (Perapaddan & Kumar, 2013).

On the eve of juvenile's release, after he had served his sentence, the Delhi Commission of Women (DCW) filed a special leave petition in the Supreme Court to block his release. This petition was rejected (Chopra, 2015; *Times of India*, 2015b)[7], but there were widespread protests at his release (Henderson, 2015), which led to amendments in the Juvenile Justice Act.[8] The revised Act permits

7 It was argued that he continued to be a threat to the society as no mental assessment of his state of mind was done to effect his release, that even during his stay in the provision home, he was unremorseful and in fact was further radicalised.

8 Juvenile Justice (Care and Protection of Children) Amendment Act, 2015 (hereafter, JJ Act).

juveniles between the ages of 16–18 years to be tried as adults for 'heinous offences'.[9] This law came under severe criticism from feminists who argued that women's rights are not better protected by punishing children for offences against women (Kumari, 2017; Kumari, 2014; Pande, 2015). However, neither logic nor debate prevented emotions from permeating into the law. A grieving mother supported by middle-class empathy moved the Parliament such that the law was compelled to respond with a prompt display of 'compassion'. The (then) Union Minister for Women and Child Development, Menaka Gandhi set the affective tone of the debate with the opening words: 'you cannot get more nuanced and more compassionate than this'. Lest the law forget their loss and grief, Jyoti Singh's parents remained present all through the Rajya Sabha (Upper House of the Parliament) proceedings (Panicker, 2015).

The parents' unabated loss was the key instrument to mobilise the juridical process, and the law became the primary site of their mourning (*The Economic Times*, 2018). They *moved* the court several times to secure justice. The commonly used legal expression 'moving the court' – which means to make an application to the court to make any rule or order or to take any other action – bears a close etymological connection with emotion. As noted in the previous chapter, the word 'emotion' comes from the Latin word '*ēmoveō*' which means 'to move out, move away, remove, stir up, agitate'. This *moving* – every time a litigant files an application to the court and sets the process of law in action – reveals what has been repressed in erecting the rational edifice of law. That the foundational moment of judgement and justice is emotion.

The death penalty is seen as complete justice, and closure, in popular imagination. On May 5, 2017, when the Supreme Court upheld the death penalty for the convicted, there were loud cheers and applause in the courtroom (Bagriya & Sinha, 2017; Asian News International, 2017). While it is easy to classify this euphoric celebration at the death penalty verdict as barbaric or as a lynch mob mentality (Asrar, 2017), at the heart of this vengeful and retributive sentiment was utter helplessness and grief. The Supreme Court's decision of the confirmation of death sentence captures this sentiment.[10] While Dipak Misra J noted that this case led to 'devastation of social trust', 'destroy[ed] the collective balance' and thus invited 'the indignation of the society' (*Mukesh* v. *State*, para 363), according to Bhanumati J, justice demanded that punishment reflects 'public abhorrence of the crime' (*Mukesh* v. *State*, para 517). How the court viewed infliction of severe punishment as the only response to the sense of social insecurity and helplessness is encapsulated in the following excerpt:

9 JJ Act, s. 2(33) reads: 'heinous offences' include the offences for which the minimum punishment under the Indian Penal Code or any other law for the time being in force is imprisonment for seven years or more. As per s. 15 and s. 18 of the Act, a child below the age of 18 years, who has the 'ability to understand the consequences of the offence and the circumstances in which he allegedly committed the offence' may be tried as an adult (in what is inappropriately called the 'Children's court').

10 *Mukesh & anr* v. *State For NCT of Delhi & ors*, 2017 SCC Online SC 533.

> We live in a civilized society where law and order is supreme and the citizens enjoy inviolable fundamental human rights. But when the incident of gang-rape like the present one surfaces, it causes ripples in the conscience of society and serious doubts are raised as to whether we really live in a civilized society and whether both men and women feel the same sense of liberty and freedom which they should have felt in the ordinary course of a civilized society, driven by rule of law. Certainly, whenever such grave violations of human dignity come to fore, an unknown sense of insecurity and helplessness grabs the entire society, women in particular, and the only succour people look for, is the State to take command of the situation and remedy it effectively.
>
> (*Mukesh* v. *State*, para 519)

The court took 'command of the situation' and remedied the 'unknown sense of insecurity and helplessness' by ordering that the offenders be hanged to death. On 20 March, 2020, at 5:30 a.m. IST, Mukesh Singh, Vinay Sharma, Akshay Thakur and Pawan Gupta were executed at Tihar Jail. The grieving parents were finally 'at peace' (Dutta, 2020). The sentence of death felt like justice.

When mourning becomes the law

Emotions are at the heart of our political and social struggle, but it appears that we don't know what to do when they turn vicious and demand retribution. The impulse is to either deny their existence altogether or render them irrelevant. When confronted with 'bad' and difficult emotions, tendency is to expunge them intellectually. Consider, Martha Nussbaum's account of anger in her book, *Anger and Forgiveness* (2016). In her cognitivist cosmology, any intensity of emotions which is based on the desire of 'payback' is either cast aside as 'irrational' or 'stupid' (Nussbaum, 2016, pp. 249). For her, 'anger *should* always be promptly transcended in the direction of the Transition' (2016, p. 96, emphasis mine). A rational person will soon realise normative problems with anger and move from anger to 'compassionate hope'. She calls this 'transition'.

The only form of anger acceptable to Nussbaum is, what she calls, 'Transition Anger'. Transition anger neither focuses on status nor does it get involved in the type of 'magical thinking' where the suffering of the offender is a payback for victim's injury. It is forward-looking and focuses on social welfare from the very beginning. Transition anger then is a 'rational emotion' and has 'instrumental roles'. Such transition anger, Nussbaum argues, is seen in parents' relationships with their young children. Parents don't want payback, but their anger is directed towards making things better. This approach resembles the kind of Freudian psychology which took a turn towards strengthening the ego to control instincts (*id*) in accordance with the reality principle (superego). Jacques Lacan reserved his most acerbic diatribes for this form of psychology. This form of ego strengthening psychology, for him, was no less than a perversion of Freudian psychoanalysis. This is because this practical-guidebook-form-of-psychology, what Lacan described as 'pop psychology' discounted something essential to Freudian psychoanalysis – the unconscious.

Besides the ego/pop psychology assumption of a 'rational, coherent ego' (Grosz, 1990) that pervades Nussbaum's oeuvre – that ego can be guided and brought into balance with the *id* and the superego – Nussbaum's faith in the liberal institutions remains steadfast. The romantic view of transition anger based on the platonic view of an ideal parent and ideal family, represses the unconscious hostilities and conscious violence of the family,[11] where violence is explained either as individualised pathology or worse, primitive barbarism. Unfortunately, the feminist normative worldview is not very different from Nussbaum's prescriptivism. This is why, most well-meaning left-liberal activists and feminists, while expressing genuine sympathy with Jyoti Singh's parents, were at a loss to understand the retaliatory form their mourning had taken. A few days before the execution of the convicts,[12] senior advocate and leading feminist activist, Indira Jaising had tweeted: 'While I fully identify with the pain of Asha Devi I urge her to follow the example of Sonia Gandhi who forgave Nalini and said she didn't want the death penalty for her. We are with you but against the death penalty.'[13] 'Even if God asks me, I won't forgive them', Asha Devi had replied (Hindustan Times, 2020). Did Indira Jaising's gesture of support as well as alienation – we are with you, but against (your desire for) death penalty – embrace and reject the victim in the same moment? Does feminism, in resisting bad emotions, make feminist resistance for psychic change stunted? Here, I am not suggesting that we should identify with or accept victims' retributive sentiment. However, by evading, erasing or repressing such emotions, we only end up foreclosing the space for, what feminist critic Gayatri Spivak calls, 'non-coercive rearrangement of desires' (Spivak, 2004).[14]

11 For illustrations of anger at the new-born baby and parents' (honour-based) anger, see Grosz, 2014; Baxi, Rai & Ali, 2006). Also see, Rose (2014) particularly the second section of the book, "The Lower Depths", devoted to three young women killed in the UK and Sweden in so-called 'honour' killings.

12 Several review and mercy petitions were filed by the convicted which were rejected by the Supreme Court and the President of India respectively (Singh, 2020, March 20).

13 Sonia Gandhi is an Indian politician who was the longest serving president of the Indian National Congress. She is the widow of former Indian Prime Minister, Rajiv Gandhi, who was assassinated in 1991. Nalini was one of the convicts in his assassination. She had pardoned Nalini and even filed a clemency petition that led to the reduction of her sentence (Bose, 2022, November 14).

14 Talking about a training in the Humanities classroom, Spivak writes: 'suspending oneself into the text of the other – for which the first condition and effect is a suspension of the conviction that I am necessarily better, I am necessarily indispensable, I am necessarily the one to right wrongs, I am necessarily the end product for which history happened, and that New York is necessarily the capital of the world. It is not a loss of will [...] [it] is a training to learn from the singular and the unverifiable' (Spivak, 2004).

How can we forge a common struggle till desires do not converse – my desire that you forgive and your desire to never forgive? While there are myriad examples of grieving families of victims choosing forgiveness over hatred and revenge, we know that forgiveness does not come easy, especially within the contemporary adversarial legal system which discourages any possibility of healing, forgiving and reconciliation possible (Bibas & Bierschbach, 2004). Forgiveness is something *to be arrived at* through a difficult and demanding psychic journey which works-through the painful process of mourning (Vashist & Bindal, 2023). In feminist politics, where is the process of forgiveness situated?

For Jyoti Singh's grieving parents, their pain was a 'driving force' for justice which unfortunately only acquired the available vocabulary of retribution. The question is: could we stand with them, in their struggle for justice, without acknowledging their mourning? Mourning, we know, is distinct from grieving: grief is an emotional reaction to loss, while mourning is a kind of psychical work that functions 'to detach the survivors' memories and hopes from the dead' (Leader, 2008, p. 168). Mourning, like forgiveness, doesn't come easily. It is a slow and difficult journey with anger as the only constant companion. The *work* of mourning, Freud tells us, is difficult and there is nothing natural about it. In fact, there is a resistance in our minds to mourning (Freud, 1917/1957). Moreover, the process is ridden with guilt and feelings of anger. Mourning 'has to do with an *unwanted transformation* where neither the full shape nor the full import of that alteration can be known in advance' (Butler, 2014b). People often 'find it difficult to mourn a loss when tender feelings jostle with fury at that person for having died' (Leader, 2008, p. 39). There is a simultaneous presence of hatred and love, hostility and affection, along with the unconscious hostility we feel and which we want to forget or ignore in our rational, waking lives. As Freud observed in *Totem and Taboo*, '[i]n almost every case where there is an intense emotional attachment to a particular person we find that behind tender love there is a concealed hostility in the unconscious' (Freud, 1913/1955a, p. 60).

A culture that does not attempt to accept these unconscious hostilities and anger complicates the mourning process severely. Darian Leader writes that as the feelings of general hostility towards the dead are obstructed, this hostility manifests as 'anger with the living':

> We find this obstruction frequently when we are exploring the lives of bereaved people: they become angry with colleagues, friends or lovers without linking this displacement consciously to their loss. Undertakers, doctors or hospital staff may also be recruited as targets, and time and time again we see the emergence of an 'enemy' in that person's circle after a significant loss. *The anger is displaced on to someone else.*
>
> (Leader, 2008, p. 43, emphasis mine)

Victims' desire for retribution is an uneasy reality and a difficult terrain for feminists and their allies.[15] Feminists have unfortunately responded to this difficulty only by resisting retributive emotions. The emotional undertow of the demands for retributive law by most feminists, like Nussbaum, has been relegated to the zone of irrationality or avoided. They have sustained their bonds of solidarity with the victims by either erasing the rage at the centre of their grief or by directing their 'feminist anger' (Woodward, 1996) at the irrational bloodthirsty populace who appear to be exploiting the victims' emotional state to propel the retributive agenda through the law. Consider this sentiment mirrored in the following remarks of human rights lawyer, Sanjay Hegde:

> Driving the agenda of the dead are Asha Devi and Badri Singh Pandey, parents of Nirbhaya, who are now the face of India's response to the tragedy. For the past three years, their public mourning for their brutalised, dead daughter has been a very intense affair. They are present at every court hearing of consequence; they have attended innumerable condolence meetings, commemorations and vigils. They have not allowed their daughter's fighting spirit to die. We feel their sorrow, and share and understand their anger. To them, the release of the juvenile offender, in this case after only three years in a correctional facility, appears to be inordinately early. But *the righteous anger of this couple has become Schadenfreude and worse for a whole mass of citizenry.* Anger is being exploited by TRP-driven purveyors of outrage porn, to strike at all possible newsworthy targets.
>
> (Hegde, 2015, emphasis mine)

While majority of feminists in India have consistently, and rightly, distanced themselves from demands for death penalty and retributivism, we have not been able to transform the 'social' that seeks justice through extreme and cruel form of punishment (Subramani, 2015; Singh, 2011; Mehta & Nigam, 2016). The way in which empathy with the victims organises and solidifies the social is an important question for us, something that cannot be addressed by Nussbaumian suggestion of merely keeping bad emotions outside the legal process. It is important to recognise how the social as well as the legal acquire their own emotions.

Feminists do not endorse the retributive theory of punishment, nevertheless, we need to take the psychic economy of retribution in victims and survivors of crime

15 In the US context, Susan Bandes has argued that Victim Impact Statements (VIS) should not be admitted in capital sentencing because they 'evoke not merely sympathy, pity, and compassion for the victim, but also a complex set of emotions directed toward the defendant, including hatred, fear, racial animus, vindictiveness, undifferentiated vengeance, and the desire to purge collective anger' (Bandes, 1996, p. 395; Bandes, 2009). In contrast, Gabriele Schwab discusses the effects of failure of grieving by perpetrators of violence (Schwab, 2010).

seriously.[16] We need to ask: what is this subjectivity that desires lynching, hangings, castrations? Wouldn't sanitised distancing of feminists from retribution suppress, instead of acknowledging and addressing, the violence that forms our subjectivity? The arguments of false consciousness or hegemony may not be sufficient to understand this grief-rage-revenge complex as anger and grief get 'redistributed in a new economy of the emotions' (Woodward, 1996, p. 111).

Moreover, the feminist response to retributive rage is couched within the problematic reason-emotion binary, characterised by a few scholars as 'rule of law' versus 'rule of sentiment'. Ascribing irrationality to all emotions, Flavia Agnes wondered, in the wake of death penalty awarded in the Delhi Gang Rape case, if we have become 'a nation ruled by emotions, by public sentiment, and not by the rule of law' (Agnes, 2013). Such a binary logic constructs the legal as a space that is free from all emotion and emotions become irrational instincts sans any meaning. Again, if we look at the statement of the Working Group of Human Rights on abolition of death penalty, we find a perfect example of feminist rationality that overlooks the power of victims' grief-rage and fails to reflect on the emotionality of law. The statement reads: 'WGHR empathises with the loss of life and anguish caused to the victim's family [...] WGHR, however, believes that death penalty embodies the idea of retribution, which is as violent as the offence for which one is convicted, and is contrary to all civilised notions of criminology and constitutionalism.' (Working Group on Human Rights in India, 2013). What are the 'civilized notions of criminology and constitutionalism', one wonders. Do we not know that criminology 'was developed primarily as a tool for imperialist domination and it continues to operate largely as a repressive technology' (Agozino, 2003, p. 228), and how criminology 'served colonialism more directly than many other social sciences' (Agozino, 2003, p. 1). Further, are these 'civilised' notions of constitutionalism devoid of affectivity (Bindal, 2020)? Can one empathise without understanding and engaging with the irrationality of payback anger?

It is not easy to free oneself from the fantasy of payback. This phantasy is historically etched into our consciousness through a *belief* in the idea of an

16 I do not intend to homogenise the experiences and psychic responses of victims either empirically or theoretically. I remain aware that victims respond to loss differently and not always with a retributive sentiment. Norrie in this context argues that victims do not demand punishment as their natural right. According to Norrie (2019), victims often seek 'the retrieval of [their] lost humanity after violation'. He shows how victim's engagement with the perpetrator is 'a relational process based upon love: Love for herself that led her to meet [the perpetrator], love for the other so that she might put herself in his place and understand his motivations, love based on a universal nature in humankind [...] love as the wholeness of self to be retrieved through dialogue with the other and love as the means to retrieve the wholeness of the other'. I do not contest Norrie's assertions empirically, but I do not agree with his theoretical formulation of 'love against law'. Love is not a unidirectional force always in the service of securing social bonds; there is ambivalence in love which inheres the risk of destroying what we are most attached to.

equilibrium between pain and suffering (Nietzsche, 2006, pp. 20–48). In his lectures on *The Death Penalty* (2013), Jacques Derrida, tracing the genealogy of the idea of equivalence, discusses how for 'primitive humanity' punishment was not about punishing the wrongdoer, the one who was responsible; it was driven by anger. At a certain moment in history, this idea had changed; anger was contained and repressed by the notion of equivalence, i.e. every injury has its equivalent and thus, can be compensated by inflicting some pain on the author of the injury. This most 'bizarre' equivalence between injury and pain is at the heart of penal law and the framing of the legal subject. The idea of equivalence changed with time: from giving something or someone as a form of payment to a psychic reimbursement in the form of an internal enjoyment, the pleasure of doing violence (Derrida, 2013, p. 155):

> Instead of a thing, instead of something or someone, he will be given pleasure, some enjoyment [*jouissance*], a feeling of well-being or if a greater well-being (*Wohlgefühl*), he will be given a pleasure that consists in the voluptuous pleasure of causing the other to suffer, and cruelly, the voluptuous pleasure [...] of doing harm for the pleasure of it.

Thus, the fantasy of equivalence through payback cannot be dismissed as magical or irrational thinking because the rationality of law itself is constructed through the fantasy of equilibrium between pain and suffering. The force of this fantasy is in the *jouissance* or 'surplus pleasure' it generates (Derrida, 2013; Butler, 2014a; Mladek, 2003). There is a 'voluptuous' pleasure in this incommensurable (for Nietzsche) and foolish (for Nussbaum) payback and law iterates it. How can one just wish it away?

The 'balance' sought through payback also needs to be carefully thought through. In his research on the Ilongot tribe of Philippines and their cultural practice of headhunting,[17] Renato Rosaldo toyed with the idea of payback to understand the headhunter's rage. He writes (Rosaldo, 1993, p. 3):

> One day in 1974, I explained the anthropologist's exchange model to an older Ilongot man named Insan. What did he think, I asked, of the idea that headhunting resulted from the way that one death (the beheaded victim's) canceled another (the next of kin). He looked puzzled, so I went on to say that the victim of a beheading was exchanged for the death of one's own kin, thereby balancing the books, so to speak. Insan reflected a moment and replied that he imagined somebody could think such a thing (a safe bet, since I just had), but that he and other Ilongots did not think any such thing.

17 Ilongots are a tribe who inhabit the southern Sierra Madre and Caraballo Mountains, on the east side of Luzon Island in the Philippines.

The idea of payback and restoration is bizarre to the headhunter. It is the *force of anger in grief* that provides the compulsion to kill. Here, grief and rage are not distinct emotional states. The desire to kill is rooted in the 'need to throw away their anger'- toss it away with the head of the victim. Rosaldo himself could not understand the force of the feelings of bereavement, concomitant rage and the impulse to headhunt. He sought their explanation in thicker descriptions, analytical details or cultural depth till he experienced the loss of his wife. This devastating loss, he concedes, made him see and feel the rage in grief. Writing about the paradox of Anglo-American culture, he notes how '[the upper-middle-class Anglo-American] culture's conventional wisdom usually denies the anger in grief at the same time that therapists encourage members of the invisible community of the bereaved to talk in detail about how angry their losses make them feel' (Rosaldo, 1993, p. 10). This 'anger in grief' is what we need to think and work with.

Transition Anger and its Limits

Nussbaum concedes that payback anger may be 'co-present' with grief as grief often brings along the tendency to blame someone for the loss. Thus, 'anger may function psychically as a way of restoring the lost person or object' (Nussbaum, 2016, p. 47). Anger may manifest from the 'reluctance to grieve' and acknowledge one's helplessness. Nussbaum prescribes 'a Transition from anger to mourning' (Nussbaum, 2016, p. 96) as '*the way to deal with grief* is just what one might expect: mourning and, eventually, constructive forward-looking action to repair and pursue one's life' (Nussbaum, 2016, pp. 95–96, emphasis mine). But again, this prescription is based on the disavowal of the gripping power of grief. If only one could know how to deal with the weight of unbearable grief.

Judith Butler captures this complexity when she remarks that 'grief does not submit to mathematical measures' nor is it 'a straightforward process that comes to an end when a reality principle delivers its verdict' (Butler, 2014b). The unbearability of unbearable grief is such that it impels the 'headhunter' (Rosaldo, 1993), not very far removed from our own psyche, to kill: 'When we lose, we lose our ground and that makes us at the risk of taking our own lives or the lives of certain others'. As if, the killing could kill the grief itself. Like Nussbaum, Butler also asks what is the phantasy at work in the grief-rage knot? But unlike Nussbaum, she does not cast it away as irrational, stupid or magical for that would fall short of fathoming the life-destroying, paralysing power of grief inflicted by loss. The destructiveness of anger in sorrow that seemingly seeks payback is a 'despairing form of egalitarianism according to which everyone should suffer this devastation' (Butler, 2014b). This anger is a way to bring grief to a 'false stop', by 'wantonly distributing the unbearable', believing this might make the unbearable a little bearable.

The nature of sorrow is such that we no longer remain 'masters of ourselves and our motion'. Loss makes us inscrutable to ourselves, the 'I' that was because of 'You' no longer can remain the 'I' when 'You' are gone. Emotions are not personalised, internal thoughts, but emotions are bonds that bring 'I' and 'You' together. Then, how can 'I' fully *deal* with emotions? In this frame, Nussbaum's 'forward-looking' approach is a violent prescription, a *tyranny of shoulds*. Its violence lies in its failure to engage with the subjectivity of the bereaved person for whom the loss is the loss of self, as if something inside has disappeared and needs to be restored and completed to be fully alive again. The image of a self-present subject irons out the complex workings of the mind. Even when the conscious rational self might be suggesting a particular course, the unconscious might conjure up its own varied paths. For 'there are possibilities in our unconscious minds', Jacqueline Rose reminds us 'that we would prefer not even, sometimes, to dream of' (Rose et al., 2010, p. 54). What one asserts in language may be totally incommensurate and 'radical[ly] un-fit' with what the unconscious seems to be hinting at (Rose et al., 2010, p. 55). This unconscious at work explains an individual's fascination with the *talion*, the retaliatory sentiment of the retributive justice. Retributive law appeals because it is in consonance with the violent demands of our/victims' grief laden psyches.[18] Most philosophers of punishment have often grappled with this idea but only to circumvent it to produce rational accounts of law and punishment. In criminal legal theory, revenge/vengeance as a form of retribution is distinguished from punishment. For instance, it is argued that as revenge is executed by a private injured party, it is susceptible to excesses and may take the form of a greater wrong being inflicted by the injured party. Further, and more importantly, revenge, because it is not institutionalised, is seen as raw execution of feelings and passions. Revenge is excessive, disproportionate, but it is argued that (retributive) punishment in its institutionalised form cures the defects of revenge.

Punishment, by virtue of its institutionalisation – the fact that it is not a private party but a sovereign authority which inflicts pain in the name of general will – is seen as a dispassionate (removed from the influence of passions which can make it unjustly cruel) and a rational form of retribution (Primoratz, 1990; Murphy, 1979). However, the contrast between the 'passion of revenge' and the 'dispassion of punishment' seems diluted when we pose the question of the feelings of the state and the sovereign (or the general will that it seeks to reflect). Does the state have revenge-like feelings? Do people sublimate their revengefulness through state punishment and legal enforcement? Is it not a naïve simplistic assumption that mere institutionalisation frees punishment from the passions that reside in, and engulf retribution? If

18 Significantly, the sight of impoverished mothers of the accused in the Shakti Mills gang rape blurs what appears to be a clear defining the line between the 'real' grief of victim's kin and the grief of perpetrators' kin (D'Mello, Agnes & Sidhva, 2014).

the state and the law possess 'the institutional unconscious', then don't we need to re-think our politics and investigate this category as well? (Žižek, 2008, p. 681).[19]

The retributive theory of punishment does not capture or explain the affective power of the institution of punishment. It is important to note that the turn to law is not a turn to 'pure reason' for '[e]ven when [a person] turns to the courts he desires revenge as a private person: *additionally*, however, as a forethoughtful man of society, he desires the revenge of society on one who does not *honour* it. Through judicial pronouncement, private honour as well as the honour of society is thus *restored*: that is to say- punishment becomes revenge' (Nietzsche, 2006, p. 132, emphasis in original). In other words, it is important to acknowledge the 'emotion work' that is at play in framing of the public attitudes as well as the law.

Predominant scholarly engagement on the question of punishment is in terms of the function and utility of punishment. The harm and pain inflicted by punishment is justified only if it serves a larger social purpose. However, the utilitarian approach to punishment often conceals punishment as 'a realm for the expression of social value and emotion as well as process for asserting control' (Garland, 1990, p. 4). Taking forward the idea of *punishment as an expression of emotion*, Henrique Carvalho and Anastasia Chamberlen argue that punishment is believed to be useful 'because we derive pleasure from the utility of punishment' (Carvalho & Chamberlen, 2017, p. 2). In contrast to Emile Durkheim who argued that it is the 'prior existence of group solidarity' that 'provides the basis for a collective will to punish' (Garland, 2013, p. 25; Garland, 1990), the authors contend that 'that the contemporary urge to punish relies primarily on *a desire for* solidarity fuelled by the experience of social insecurity and anxiety' (Carvalho & Chamberlen, 2017, p. 7). In other words, punishment is a 'solidarity-producing process' which 'allows individuals to pursue emotional release together with a sense of belonging' (Carvalho & Chamberlen, 2017, p. 12). The nature of this solidarity, however, is based on hostility as people are brought together in a shared hatred for and aggression towards the criminals (Carvalho & Chamberlen, 2017, p. 9).[20] Feelings of solidarity are a

19 The idea of institutional unconscious, explains Žižek (2008), 'does not concern the "private" unconscious of individuals, but the "unconscious" of the institution itself: it is not something that happens because the Institution has to accommodate itself to the pathological realities of libidinal life in order to survive, but something that the institution itself needs in order to reproduce itself [...] Such an institutional Unconscious designates the obscene disavowed underside that, precisely as disavowed, sustains the public institution. (In the army, this underside consists of the obscene sexualised rituals of fragging etc. which sustain the group solidarity.) In other words, it is not simply that, for conformist reasons, the Church tries to hush up the embarrassing paedophilic scandals; in defending itself, the Church defends its innermost obscene secret'.

20 This, Carvalho and Chamberlen argue, is a 'specific kind of solidarity which differentiates it from other solidarity-producing processes in society such as religion, political association, civil society organisations etc. Punishment defines identity

result of the sentiment of hostility and hatred for crime and criminals (Mead, 1918). As Rose reminds us, 'there is no sociality without violence, that people are most powerfully and effectively united by what they agree to hate' (Rose, 2014b, p. 75).

Why do we seek hostile solidarity? The solidarity fostered by punishment is pleasurable because it allows for self-expression (which is generally prohibited in modern societies),[21] gives a sense of control (a defence mechanism in the wake of feelings of uncertainty and anxiety) (Ainsworth, 2009, pp. 264–266) as well as an illusion of order (about their society as a civilised order all of whose difficulties can be neatly and easily blamed on criminals) (Carvalho & Chamberlen, 2017, p. 10). The pleasure in the hostile solidarity of punishment is on account of the illusion that punishment creates of civic order. The 'psychic economy' of the desire to punish is in the sense of reassurance and order it instils in the wake of uncertainty and anxiety as well as the burdens posed by ineffective legal and state machineries. In the wake of a crumbling criminal justice system, punishment is often pursued to forge solidarities.

Punishment, by building a hostile solidarity, creates a situation of release of otherwise banned emotions and gives a legitimate license to individuals to symbolically engage in acts of aggression mediated through the state.[22] This is at the heart of the retributive theory of punishment. My argument is that feminism needs to critically engage with these lessons of the retributive theory of punishment diagnosed with a psychoanalytic lens. Only by acknowledging this, can the next argument be made: that the repression of hostile solidarity is rarely the answer as it 'tends to self-reproduce', as despite the 'release of feelings of anxiety, insecurity, anger, frustration, etc., it does not concretely address the sources from which these feelings originated' (Carvalho & Chamberlen, 2017, p. 12). As punishment can never address the root causes of crimes and criminality, 'the urge to punish may display a tendency of sometimes becoming pathological' (Carvalho & Chamberlen, 2017, p. 12).

Thus, we first need to ask, what work do retributive institutions do for us, and then only we can work through to abolish them. Butler (2014a) in her essay 'On Cruelty' makes both these moves. Recognising the destructive impulses that co-constitute our psyche – *eros* and *thanatos* – Butler turns to Melanie Klein to suggest that 'the ambivalence of all human bonds is the basis of an ethical

directly through antagonism' (Carvalho & Chamberlen, 2017). The rise of the right-wing forces, based on similar hostile solidarity, can also be explained through the relationship between punishment and identity. It is a punitive sentiment at work in the mob lynching by *gaurakshaks* (cow protectors) (Alam, 2016).

21 This needs to be qualified in today's digital age where the virtual space offers a platform for not only self-expression but also for forging affective bonds with the anonymous internet community.

22 In *Civilization and Its Discontents*, Freud (2002) suggested that the civilising process leads to a suppression of feelings of aggression and hostility in individuals. This produces a sense of guilt as they feel urges which are prohibited.

demand to preserve the life it is in one's power, and sometimes also in one's interest, to destroy' (Butler, 2014a). Shifting from Derridean dialectical inversion where abolitionists of death penalty become implicated in its cruelty, she wonders if there are other ways of building social bonds and accounts of relationality: '[i]f I seek to preserve your life, it is not only because it is in my self-interest to do so, or because I have wagered that it will bring about better consequences for me. It is because I am already tied to you in a social bond without which this 'I' cannot be thought. So, what implications does the thesis of *emotional ambivalence in love* have for thinking about alternatives to the death penalty and for legal violence more generally?' (Butler, 2014a, emphasis mine). We have to work with this 'emotional ambivalence in love' to arrive at the feminist position against death penalty.

Before moving to the next part of this chapter, on *India's Daughter,* let me return briefly to the notion of resistance. It is not that only the legal discipline resists psychoanalysis. In general, there is a bigger resistance to psychoanalysis (Grosz, 1990). In India, far from introducing psychoanalysis to feminist politics, we have not attended to psychology more broadly or to psychoanalysis at any length even in realms such as consciousness-raising or counselling where they fully 'belong'. However, it is my contention that the psychoanalytic concepts and insights are crucial for the feminist project, especially feminist engagement with the law, as they open the scope for imagining legal scholarship and activism beyond the projects of legal reform and policy recommendations (Schroeder & Carlson, 2015). Otherwise, feminism, even in its critique of law, might end up repeating the assumptions on which the law rests.

Jeanne Schroeder, one of the few legal scholars who works with psychoanalysis in legal scholarship, diagnoses the failure of critical legal studies movement in a similar fashion: 'critical legal scholarship failed fully to realise the implications of its position. As a result, it implicitly repeated the basic assumptions about law, rationality and markets adopted by the law-and-economics movement, albeit coming to diametrically opposite conclusions. Consequently, the critics unintentionally strengthened the very legal position they purported to attack' (Schroeder, 2001, p. 6). Because in psychoanalysis 'we, as conscious, speaking beings do not have direct access to the object world' (Schroeder, 2001, p. 81), it is impossible to imagine that the individual has the ability to work on the social and introduce reforms *to* it, as the individual and the social are not separate spheres. The individual and the social are tied to each other in complex ways and therefore, the capacity to 'reform' the social (including the legal realm) is built by recognising the blockages of both the Symbolic as well as our own unconscious. As Peter Goodrich reminds us, the 'legal system [is] not simply [as] an objective system of rules, but also as a symbolic order or imaginary domain [...] The subject of legal authority is bound to law far more strongly by identificatory images or phantasms of a shared substance, by interior and self-imposed limitations, than by the external dictate of positive law' (Goodrich, 1997, p. 1038).

One cannot shift the Symbolic effortlessly by changing laws. It is not changeable as easily as we think in offering recommendations of change in an à la carte fashion. This is because our own unconscious may be invested in the Symbolic far more deeply than we would like to admit. The unconscious comprises of our own fantasies which are deeply etched within the Symbolic. The fantasy of a common enemy, or a nation, or a common brotherhood, all work well to sustain existing legal structures. No outside change can be introduced successfully to laws unless our unconscious fantasies and desires also undergo radical transformation. To engender social change, we need psychic (and self) work on the desires of the inseparable realms of personal-social-political. This change cannot happen if it is top-down or coercive. It instead demands the slow, hard work of re-arranging and re-working our desires. Effecting a change in the legal order requires a corresponding engagement with the legal unconscious and fantasies that support the institution of the law. The work of a feminist lawyer/scholar/activist is to put the law and ourselves on the couch before we embark the work of re-forming the law. This perhaps will require us to engage with, rather than suppress, the contradictions produced by the difficult proposition of our own psychic investment in the violence of the Symbolic. This argument will be taken forward in the next section where I analyse the limitations of feminist imaginations in their responses to the documentary film, *India's Daughter*.

Feminist resistance to *India's Daughter*

The controversial documentary film, *India's Daughter*, directed by Leslee Udwin was part of the BBC's Storyville series. The film is based on the Delhi Gang Rape. It was scheduled to be aired on TV channels round the world on March 8, 2015 but a court order prohibited the broadcast in India. The documentary was an attempt by the media to return telegraphically to the incident of Delhi Gang Rape and converse with the actors/accused involved. The film included an interview with one of the four men convicted and executed,[23] Mukesh Singh, excerpts of which went viral. Generally, it is the orthodox right-wing groups in India that call for bans on films; this time they were joined by a group of left-wing feminists (though for completely different reasons).

23 I wonder what are the ethico-psychic coordinates of my exploration. Analysing the recorded testimony of a condemned man, who was hanged to death, whose memory is etched in our minds on account of his violent words, who spoke, and we heard, but we will never know what he was asked, why he agreed to speak, did he agree for his words to be taken to the public. It is the burden of these gaps in our knowing that makes me unsure of the ethical questions around my analysis of his presence and his words in this documentary.

In this section, I look at *India's Daughter* as an important 'event'[24] that helps us to illustrate the limitations of Indian feminisms. This event was marked by a multiplicity of feminist positions which extended far beyond the stance of pro-ban and anti-ban. Explicitly or implicitly, these responses sought to theorise, resist and change the domains of the social/political/legal orders. However, the discursive unity of these theorisations was marked by a conjoint *resistance* to confront the obscene underbelly of the social and the legal domains. In this sense, *India's Daughter* and the responses to it, I will argue in what follows, provide an opportunity to engage with the repressions and resistances of Indian feminisms.

At the outset, it may be mentioned that many feminists who advocated for the restraining order had watched the film themselves.[25] After viewing the film, Indira Jaising and several other feminists in India expressed their objections and 'legal discomforts' with the film. These objections were first stated in a letter to an English news channel, NDTV and they called for restraining the screening of the film, on the following grounds (Jaising et al., 2015): the accused's right to fair trial and due process, hate speech against women falling under section 153A (1)(a) of the IPC[26] and prejudicing and interfering with the judicial process.[27] All these arguments merit attention and need unpacking to understand not only the relationship legal feminists have forged with the law but also to understand how and why the law, despite feminist critique, continues to present itself as a unified and coherent body of rules and principles to the exclusion of other languages, including the language of the unconscious.

24 Following Wendy Brown, this may be seen as one of the 'banal events [...] that acquire their status not by being part of a larger historical force or movement but precisely by erupting out of the everyday'. While recognizing that 'there is a world of difference between *reading events* and *theorizing the conditions and possibilities of political life* in a particular time' (Brown, 1997), I attempt to read the event such that it can contribute to theorizing the possibilities of feminist politics.

25 For a critique of the feminist position that called for restraining the film, see Kapur, R. (2015).

26 IPC, s. 153A(1)(a) (now, BNS, s. 194 1(a)) punishes anyone who by words, signs or visible representations, promotes disharmony or feelings of enmity, hatred or ill-will between different religious, racial, language or regional groups or castes or communities, on the grounds of religion, race, place of birth, residence, language, caste or community or any other ground whatsoever. It was argued that the 'interview with Mukesh Singh, which is replete with explicit derogatory statements' falls under the above provision of the IPC. It may be noted that the Law Commission Report on Hate Speech (LCI, 2017) explicitly proposed this to be a crime in its recommendation of the insertion of specific provision prohibiting incitement to hatred on the grounds of religion, race, caste or community, sex, gender identity, sexual orientation, place of birth, residence, language, disability or tribe. It is submitted that the commission, driven by what appears to be a populist urgency, has paid little attention to the constitutional requirement of clarity and precision in the drafting of criminal statutes. There is vagueness in the fault element of the proposed crime and many terms (like 'alarm', 'fear') are left unexplained.

27 Contempt of Courts Act 1971, s. 2(c).

The first question that needs to be explored here is: how do we conceptualise the invocation of due process guarantees alongside the widely disputed criminal law provisions? On the one hand, there was feminist insistence on fair application of the law owed to every person accused of a crime – protection of the accused from state police power. On the other, reliance on a deeply contested criminal law provision that vests wide powers in the state. Indian feminists have always opposed the orthodox ban-culture in advocating free speech, adopting the 'more feminist speech to counter sexist speech' position (Kapur, 1996). However, at this moment they invoked the same provision of the law which has been challenged by them as compromising the constitutional free speech guarantee. Can this inconsistency – of embracing the very same law which they stand in opposition against the conservative camps – be explained as a 'strategic tool' (Sen, 2016)? Or, does such instrumental use of the law expose the philosophical incoherence in feminist understanding of the theory and practice of law, its potential and limits?

This 'feminist' move led to a variety of questions on the very concept of 'fair' and 'due' in the context of criminal litigation. What could we infer from this demand for the restraining order couched in the name of accused's fair trial rights, which simultaneously, and paradoxically, denied him the right to speech and expression? Will the accused's trial ever be a 'fair' trial, if he is not completely heard? Can we ever create fissures and disruptions in the popular socio-legal retributive sentiment that has become the dominant response to rape? Can feminism, that now has to fight this sentiment, as much as rape, ever succeed in its struggle without listening, and listening intently, to this man?

I am not rehearsing the argument of countering 'hate speech' with more (feminist) speech (Kapur, 1996, pp. 16–17) but raising the question about listening to the (abject) Other and listening, like a feminist. Which would mean hearing not merely the unheard, but also the uncomfortable. An ear towards the voice, apparently diabolic voice of the 'radical evil'. This would require us to recall, what Gabriele Schwab characterises as a 'dialogical turn' toward the diabolical, writing as a second-generation German, embracing the guilt of being a descendent of a nation whose past invokes horrors of the holocaust. Delving deeply into her personal history of trauma and loss, she calls for a turn that 'look[s] at the dynamic between victims and perpetrators and see that both of them are suffering from psychic deformations of violent histories, albeit in different ways and with different responsibilities' (Schwab, 2010, p. 72).[28] Without working towards 'an archeology of psyche' (Schwab, 2010), without understanding the perpetrator and his denial, lack of shame and guilt, it is impossible to decode the *ressentiment* that surfaces in sexual violence (John, 2013). Again, as Schwab writes:

28 Schwab argues that trauma discourses commonly focus almost exclusively on victims of trauma and therefore do not understand the relationality between generations of victims and perpetrators.

> Only a process of breaking traumatic silence and revealing a buried secret can help to exorcise its ghostly alien presence [...] The exhumation of buried ghosts of the past is also indispensable for trying to avoid the repetition of traumatic history or its displacement onto other people.
>
> (Schwab, 2010, p. 80)

Against this background, I approach the most important argument made in the letter, one on the due process protections. This due process argument appealed to many feminists, including Nivedita Menon and Shohini Ghosh (Menon, 2015). Fair trial demands that rights of the accused are not prejudiced at any stage of the trial. Indira Jaising and Ritu Menon argued that the judicial process could be infected with bias and prejudice and thereby severely affect the appeal against the death penalty (Jaising & Menon, 2015). Isn't this legal argument (which has been strangely distinguished from the ethical argument), complicit with all the facets and contradictions that sustain the ideological legal order? Doesn't the due process claim of feminists, despite their well-meaning intent, end up being a 'cover-up' for the exposed underbelly of the law? The very production and completion of the film in itself has been an exposé of all the shortfalls of the criminal justice system where the 'rights' of the accused/convicts are only platitudes that must be constantly reiterated in theory but violated in practice.[29] When the law has never cared about the 'monsters' who commit 'heinous crimes', whether they die in custody (Shekar, 2013; Nelson, 2013),[30] are lynched in public (Rutsa & Sunil, 2015) or even when they ask for mercy (Tripathi & Singh, 2015), how does the rhetoric of due process remain the most powerful signifier of law? And in this light, wasn't the restraint order, in effect, nothing but a demand to hide what inadvertently became visible?[31]

Having said this, there is no doubt that the cardinal principles of criminal law – presumption of innocence, principle of legality, fair trial – are the foundation of any adversarial legal system (Packer, 1968) and that media influence and popular opinion have adversely affected these principles on many previous occasions (Dutta & Venkatesan, 2015; Venkatesan, 2015). We know the Supreme Court had dismissed Surinder Koli's appeal against death sentence in the Nithari case, calling him a 'serial killer' on the basis of the media coverage

29 The fact that it was huge lapse surfaced with the government alleging that the film was made without any due permissions to gain access to the prison premises (*Times of India*, 2015b).

30 The High Court judgment that pronounced death penalty for all the accused in this case made no mention of the suicide of Ram Singh. It was reported that Ram Singh was disturbed by the hanging of Afzal Guru. His parents believed that he was murdered after weeks of being raped, tortured and forced to eat his own faeces by the police and prison guards.

31 This critique of due process should not be read as an argument of throwing away of the law/due process or supporting 'LIST feminism'. My argument is that we need to continue working with law/due process while accepting and exposing its limits and internal prejudices.

of the case even though no trial court had confirmed that he had murdered all the other people.[32] Even in the case of Afzal Guru, while giving the sentence the Supreme Court had stated that it was satisfying the collective conscience of society.[33]

However, in invoking the due process to protect judicial reason from outside influence (in this case Mukesh Singh's alleged absence of remorse in his testimony given to the tele-media), one may wonder whether feminists re-constructed the dominant image of the law in terms of an objective, self-contained system of rules. The feminist argument was structured on the inside-outside binary: a fair, rational and internally consistent legal order versus the outside hysteria built up by the film.[34] It was argued that the image and its affects may disrupt the workings of the legal order, presuming the rationality and fairness of law as a fair, impartial arbiter of justice, when not affected by outside forces. The hysteria is relegated to the outside while the inside is projected as rational and fair. It appears that the good reason of law could prevail only by keeping the bad emotion away. This formulation mirrors the long history of the programmatic separation of law from non-law.[35] In other words, the law's overt desire of sovereignty, order and compliance is founded on the repression of desire (Schroeder, 2009). Therefore, law's encounter with the image (here, the cinematic image) reminds it of its own self, its own repressions and inconsistencies. The only way, then, to guarantee neutrality and impartiality embodied in *Iusticia* is by blindfolding and protecting it from the seduction of the image (Liang, 2011). The resistance to the image is in fact *resistance* to confront the internal contradictions of law, the *lack* that exists at the heart of the law.

The feminist objection to the dissemination of the documentary presupposes a rational, mechanical legal system which can fairly adjudicate this case (despite the overwhelm in the public sphere regarding this case). Nevertheless, the objection to viewing this film assumes that the testimony (of the accused) televised in the documentary, as opposed to narrated in the courtroom, could radically change its reception. The former (media) testimony could potentially generate an affective charge (presumably in the judge of juridical sphere) which surpasses the logical structure of the law. This overflow of excessive emotion is presumed to be of such an order that it harbours the potential to irretrievably

32 *Surinder Koli* v. *State of UP* (2011) 4 SCC 80.

33 *State (N.C.T. of Delhi)* v. *Navjot Sandhu @ Afsan Guru* (2005) 11 SCC 600.

34 Uncritically endorsing this binary, Jhuma Sen argued that '[t]he rights of an accused to be a beneficiary of fair judicial process must always triumph over a filmmaker's artistic or cinematic license till such point of time the judicial process has concluded' (Sen, 2016).

35 The history of law is its struggle of claiming 'total self-presence and purity' and sieving out 'the non-legal, the extraneous, the other – in particular the aesthetic, the beautiful and the image' (Douzinas & Nead, 1999, p. 4; Goodrich, 1990, pp. 179–184). It is through the othering of the emotional and artistic that the law became the primary actor in the project of modernity.

rupture the rational mind and legal training of the participants of the law, making it impossible for a trial to be fair after the trail of affectivity blazed by the documentary.

From "unknown unknowns" to "unknown knowns"

Pratiksha Baxi said that '[t]he tension between *knowing* and *an active not knowing* is at the heart of the debate on *India's Daughter* (Baxi, 2015). Baxi's formulation revolves around the public secret – that which is generally known but resists articulation. It is useful to recall her analysis of rape trials in which she reads them as 'privileged sites of the production, negotiation and management of public secrets' (Baxi, 2015, p. 117). The question, however, is what is the nature of this 'active not knowing'? What surfaces and what remains hidden in the realm between the knowing and an active not knowing? To what extent do we really know when we think we know? And can we ever actively not know that which we never really know?[36]

It is important to make a distinction between an 'active not knowing' and what Slavoj Žižek has called 'unknown knowns'. 'An active not knowing', for Baxi, refers to the culture of silence that re-negotiates and keeps intact, the public secret, despite discourse and publicity. It is this 'active not knowing' that institutes sexual impunity. The notion of 'an active not knowing' is comparable to the idea of fetishistic disavowal in psychoanalysis. The subject though very aware of something continues to operate in the world as if it does not exist (Žižek, 2016). Countering this politics of silencing, Srila Roy (2015a; 2015b) has argued that we have a lot to learn from the testimony of those who commit rape, their views serve a 'pedagogical function'. Her reading of Mukesh Singh's testimony is instructive (Roy, 2015a):

> In telling us how sexual violence is practiced as sport and 'fun' and making clear that rape is about power and violence (hence statements like "we were teaching her a lesson"), Singh's words provide clues as to how sexual violence is normalised in our societies. When we hear the defence lawyers voice the same logic of normalising rape – primarily by blaming the victim – we understand how pervasive the culture of impunity is.

The reference to the voice of a defence lawyer refers to the documentary. In a strange collapse of vocabulary, a moment in *India's Daughter*, cuts the scene to a defence lawyer's sexist description of women which is uncannily aligned with the sexism displayed by the rape accused, Mukesh Singh. This coalition is significant. It highlights, for Roy, that the 'normal' co-exists with the abnormal,

36 Secrecy does not mean an absence of conscious knowledge of the past; rather there is a silencing of knowledge and removal from public life. Schwab (2010) calls it 'tacit knowledge' which is shared by everyone yet treated as a tabooed subject.

which in turn is normalised. All this is exhibited and erupts in the shape of culture of impunity. In a similar vein, Baxi, drawing on Diana Scully, argues that the vocabulary of rapists can explain how sexual violence against women continues to be seen as socially and culturally acceptable. This vocabulary is 'learnt through a process of socialisation' that limits the capacity of 'reflexive role-taking that produces empathy, guilt, shame or embarrassment.' In other words, networks of male power produce limited circuits for subjectivities: whose life is liveable, whose pain is real, and so on.

At this point, it may be important to pause on this diagnosis that sexual violence as a product of male power, learnt through socialisation. I want to resist the slippage into socialisation, an easy ready-made script that presumes more than it explains. The explanation of 'socialisation' is a rather easy and quick answer to the question why men rape? What I am suggesting is that the argument of male power should not be read in a totalising fashion to erase vulnerabilities hidden in masculinities. As Rose writes:

> [f]or psychoanalysis, sexuality is lawless or it is nothing, not least because of its rootedness in our unconscious lives, where all sexual certainties come to grief [...] This is where I have always parted ways with MacKinnon and, more generally, with radical feminism, which, brooking no ambiguity on such matters, sees masculinity as perfectly and violently in control of itself, whereas for me it is masculinity out of control – masculinity in a panic – that is most likely to turn ugly.
>
> (Rose, 2018a, pp. 3–11)

Most feminist renditions of Mukesh's account rightly demonstrated that rape needs to be understood in terms of structural violence and not individual mindsets or pathologies. It is about the normalisation of male power as well as sexual impunity in the construction of the social as well as legal (MacKinnon, 1987). This power is neither vested in the male sexual organ nor is it an excess that erupts from a sick and perverse non-human form of life.[37] The muted question however remained: what is the psychic life of this power? If it is learnt through socialisation, can we un-learn it by undoing this socialisation? What entails undoing the 'social'? This would depend on the feminist understanding of the category of the 'social'. Is it only a discursive realm of significations or networks of power relations or is also constituted by *desire*?

Lacanian psychoanalytic theorist, Joan Copjec is an important feminist writer who puts the question of desire to a rigorous scrutiny. In *Read My Desire*, Joan Copjec has argued that, contra Foucault, 'some notion of transcendence is plainly needed if one is to avoid the reduction of social space to the relations that fill it' (Copjec, 1994, p. 7). For Copjec, thus, in social relations

37 The judicial discourse is primarily premised on this dual characterisation of rape and the rapist.

something transcends, it moves beyond socialisation or social space. This something which exceeds our grasp needs to be attended unless we are devoted only to partial sociological accounts of a phenomenon. This something in need of attention, is what desire is for Copjec. The social space, if it only 'ground[s] being in appearance', can only offer a partial theory of power. Arguing that the social is not devoid of the psyche, Copjec urges the 'analysts of culture to become literate in desire, to learn how to read what is inarticulable in cultural statements' (Copjec, 1994, p. 14). This desire may be negatively inscribed in speech and the social space and therefore, any construction of reality ought to be informed by repressions, distortions, complicity and denials.

Following this insight, it is my argument that unless we inform our understandings of social with the psychic, feminism will only offer partial accounts of why rapes happen and why the law remains complicit in sexual impunity. In other words, the shift from active not knowing to knowing can only be mediated through the category of 'unknown known', i.e. the unconscious. Žižek describes the 'unknown known' as that which we do not know that we know; it is that which is so much a part of us, yet we end up ignoring it. The *unknown knowns* 'do not reside in some unexplored recesses of the mind but are displayed in all their (dirty) glory in the practices and products of our culture' (Aristodemou, 2014, p. 4). The unconscious in this sense is right there in front of us, inscribed in cultural practices and products as also in legal texts but it remains unknown to us.

With this, if we turn to look at *India's Daughter*, Mukesh Singh's account gives us access to that underbelly which remains ever-hidden in the social. Mukesh has been variously read as reprehensible, remorseless, dangerous, and legally vulnerable.[38] But as Ashley Tellis (2015) argues:

> All of these responses do not really stay with Mukesh Singh's narrative and read it closely for what it says and does not say, for how he says what he says and how he does not say what he does not say. None of them are concerned with the subjectivity of the rapist.

The dominant reading of Mukesh's testimony has served to strengthen the subject position of 'us' and give it a puritanical, sanitised flavour, marking an abject contrast with the 'diabolic' rapist, whereas Tellis argues that Singh's is a deeply damaged, contradictory, remorseful, hurtful and honest narrative which lays bare our wounded attempts at holding on to the Symbolic.

38 Jaising and Menon argue: 'Mukesh Singh's statements are objectionable and troubling for all the reasons already given – unrepentant, self-serving, disgustingly sexist and repugnant – but also because they come across as curiously choreographed. Rehearsed, almost. He is at once absolving himself of criminal conduct ('I was only driving the bus, who says someone else also drove? Only I drove it.') and justifying the rape and brutality' (Jaising & Menon, 2015).

We participated in the viewing primarily as outsiders, by adequately distancing ourselves from 'them' (Nag, 2015). It is the distancing from the criminal that I intend to theorise in the remaining part of the chapter. Why this distancing of us from the diabolic them? Why the necessity of closure of the case into a narrative of socialisation at the very instant when the question of desire surfaces? In what follows, I will pursue this inability to confront the diabolic other. This inability, I will argue, protects the fantasy of our sense of self, allowing us to deny the penetrating reminder of the presence of that within which we most detest.

All our responses to Mukesh Singh were marked by a clear divide between his position and our own – more guilty Mukesh Singh was, more innocent, perhaps, we are. In this sense, the criminal, by becoming the abject hate figure, becomes in an uncanny manner our "redeemer". Consider Freud's reading of Dostoevsky's *The Brothers Karamazov* (Žižek, 2014):

> A criminal to him [Dostoevsky] is almost a redeemer, who has taken on himself the guilt which must else have been borne by others. There is no longer any need for one to murder, since he has already murdered; and one must be grateful to him, for, except for him one would have been obliged oneself to murder.

Freud is offering an insight into how we are incorporated into the legal order through crime and guilt. In the storyline of the novel, all the brothers had the desire to kill the father, but as only one of them committed the murder, others remained (legally) 'innocent'. In this sense, even though the crime may not actually be done by everyone, we are all potential criminals. The criminal is the 'redeemer' for all others who would have committed the act themselves, if it were not for the criminal's act. This leads to the Freudian paradox: '[t]he more you are innocent, the more you are guilty' (Žižek, 2014, p. 84). As we all have the desire and potential to commit violence, the figure of the criminal is reassuring to us as it produces us as innocent and keeps us remote, removed, and guarded from the violence of our own psyche. In other words, the distancing from the perpetrator is a form of our subtle denial or defence mechanism: that he is a part of 'us'; through these denials, we manage to create a safe distance from the shame, guilt and deformations lurking beneath in the psychic depths of the social. Without psycho-social politics that addresses responsibility, complicity, guilt, shame, and the psycho-social deformation of the culture at large, we only end up perpetuating a politics of silencing and denial.

Returning to the law, in this context, law is what we want, more than anything else because legality perhaps protects us from confronting our own excesses and perversions. This point is well illustrated by Maria Aristodemou. Aristodemou contends that '[t]he law [...] is not an agent of prohibition, preventing access to and attainment of our innermost and deeply held desires, but actually the defence against what we do not even dare to want: the Real of *jouissance*' (Aristodemou, 2010, p. 398) The limitless enjoyment that *jouissance* captures is not what the subject can bear. Legality serves to put limits on this limitless enjoyment. In her words, '[a]ccess to unbridled *jouissance* would be too painful for the subject to bear, and thus the law acts as a limit shielding the subject from the horror of the Real and setting limits to limitless *jouissance*'. In other words, law is the limitation the subject imposes on herself to maintain a safe distance from the unbearable 'Thing' (Žižek, 1997, pp. 238–239). The subject imposes this ban because it is far easier to blame the external agency of law than accept our own inherent lack (Aristodemou, 2010, p. 389).

Any feminist critique of the culture of rape can only begin with the recognition and acknowledgement of our own investment in the violence of the Symbolic. We can only make a shift from the current politics of punishing rape effectively to the politics of 'emancipation from rape' by recognising the nature of our desire that remains complicit with the foundational violence of the law. It is this auto-complicity which propelled me to think about resistance in the opening of this chapter. A resistance not toward freedom, but to resist the removal of those very obstacles which are on the way to freedom. A psychic resistance to resist against unfreedom. To grapple this resistance requires an inner scrutiny without a hurry to change the outer (as Upendra Baxi, reversing Antonio Gramsci called, said, 'maintain the optimism of the intellect with the pessimism of will', 2018). This will not resonate with the 'policy scholarship' that drives the project of governance feminism. But feminist futures can only be built with slow and patient work that requires us to pause, to confront the psychic effects of legacies of violence, guilt, shame, and (impossible) mourning. The desire of striking back and payback cannot be undone (in ourselves and legal processes) without acknowledgement of the darkest parts of our psyche.[39]

Summing up

I have shown that the feminist positions in opposing revenge and advocating that it should not be the basis of punishment, end up embracing the evaluative view which is based on moral appropriateness. Feminist positions also get caught in the prescriptivism of the evaluative view and end up reifying the image of rule of law founded upon morally right emotions (undercutting their own critique of law, especially when they have exposed law as complicit with the desires of the community, family and state). Feminism also gets caught in prescriptivism and policy scholarship, rather than seeing how the law actually works.

I have argued that we cannot move – individually, socially, legally – from anger to non-anger, to generosity by any feel-good normative philosophy about good emotions. Such prescriptivism, even in a feminist framework, would only result in a 'feminist tyranny of shoulds'. In order to even begin transformative politics, we need to shift from liberal approaches of human subjectivity and

39 On how *mere* acknowledgement can also be a way of silencing, see Schwab, 2010.

institutional frameworks which are premised on the notion of autonomy and objectivity respectively. From policy scholarship in law and feminism, we need to move towards a *scandalous feminism* (to evoke Jacqueline Rose (2014a)) that confronts the darkness of the human psyche which percolates into the social as well as the legal. This requires the insertion of the question of the psyche in theoretical discourses as well as psychoanalytic feminist praxis of self-work and the long engagement with the Other in all its political as well as emotional differences.

Broadly, I have tried to argue that we need to evolve practices of feminist resistance which not only strive for social and legal change but also for change in our psyches. Hitherto our focus on legal reform has circled around 'justice' and its 'moral content'. What I am suggesting is a psychic content without which we are doomed to an elusive search for moral content. This requires that we engage with the unconscious desires of our own demands, and we learn to read our own desires more critically. It may also institute a more critical way of reading the law and engaging with the irrational fantasies and unconscious drives that form the other scene of the legal system. This turn in feminist politics might provide the tools to really grapple with the Symbolic which, while it is strong, is surely not unshakeable.

References

Agnes, F. (2013, September 18). The Rule of Sentiments. *Asian Age.*

Agozino, B. (2003). *Counter-Colonial Criminology: A Critique of Imperialist Reason.* London: Pluto Press.

Ainsworth, J. (2009). "We have met the enemy and he is us": Cognitive bias and perceptions of threat. In P. H. Robinson, S. P. Garvey & K. K. Ferzan (Eds), *Criminal Law Conversations.* Oxford University Press.

Alam, S. (2016, June 5). Court orders FIR for cow slaughter against family of Akhlaq, who was lynched in Dadri. *Times of India.* https://timesofindia.indiatimes.com/city/noida/Court-orders-FIR-for-cow-slaughter-against-family-of-Akhlaq-who-was-lynched-in-Dadri/articleshow/53210317.cms.

Angre, K. & Ghosh, D. (2015, December 16). My daughter's name is Jyoti Singh': Nirbhaya's mother 3 years after Delhi gang-rape. www.ndtv.com/india-news/my-daughters-name-is-jyoti-singh-mother-of-delhi-braveheart-1255660.

Aristodemou, M. (2010). Does the Letter of Law always arrive at its Destination? A Study in Feminine Psychology. *Law and Literature*, 22(3), 398–420.

Aristodemou, M. (2014). *Law, Psychoanalysis and Society: Taking the Unconscious Seriously.* Routledge.

Asian News International (2017, May 5). Nirbhaya case: Courtroom scenario, first sombre, then applause. *Business Standard.* www.business-standard.com/article/news-ani/nirbhaya-case-courtroom-scenario-first-sombre-then-applause-117050501442_1.html.

Asrar, N. (2017). Celebration of Nirbhaya's verdict reveals India's new-found lynch-mob mentality. *DailyO.* www.dailyo.in/politics/nirbhaya-bilkis-bano-soni-sori-death-penalty-lynch-mob-/story/1/17044.html.

Bagriya, A. & Sinha, B. (2017, July 19). 2012 Delhi gang rape verdict Highlights: SC confirms death to all 4 convicts, says this will set an example. www.hindustantimes.

com/delhi/dec-16-delhi-gang-rape-verdict-live-will-supreme-court-uphold-death-penalty/story-0YzN3eki36Yfmx1221sCwO.html.
Bandes, S. A. (1996). Empathy, Narrative, and Victim Impact Statements. *University of Chicago Law Review*, 63, 361–395.
Bandes, S. A. (2009). Repellent crimes and rational deliberation: Emotion and the death penalty. *Vermont Law Review*, 33(3), 489–512.
Banerjee, T. (2017). 'Carceral' or 'sex-positive'? *Seminar*, 691. www.india-seminar.com/2017/691/691_trina_nileena_banerjee.htm.
Banerji, A. (2012, December 21). Public fury over New Delhi gang-rape sparks protest across India. *Reuters*. www.reuters.com/article/idUSBRE8BK0R6.
Barnes, A. (2015). *Feminisms of Discontent: Global Contestations*. Oxford University Press.
Baxi, P. (2014). *Public Secrets of Law: Rape Trials in India*. Oxford University Press.
Baxi, P. (2015, March 14). *Law, Visuality and Sexual Violence: Leslee Udwin's India's Daughter. Mukta Salve Lecture Series in the memory of Sharmila Rege*. Krantijyoti Savitribai Phule Women's Studies Centre, Savitribai Phule Pune University.
Baxi, P. (2016). Carceral feminism as judicial bias: The discontents around State v Mahmood Farooqui. *Interdisciplinary Law*, 3, 1–30.
Baxi, P. (2017, September 29). When 'No' is Not 'No' in Law. *The Wire*. https://thewire.in/182578/law-no-may-not-actually-mean-no.
Baxi, P., Rai, S. M. & Ali, S. S. (2006). Legacies of common law: 'Crimes of honour' in India and Pakistan. *Third World Quarterly*, 27(7), 1239–1253.
Bernstein, E. (2010). Militarized humanitarianism meets carceral feminism: the politics of sex, rights, and freedom in contemporary antitrafficking campaigns. *Signs*, 36(1), 45–72.
Bibas, S. & Bierschbach, R. A. (2004). Integrating Remorse and Apology into Criminal Procedure. *The Yale Law Journal*, 114(1), 85–148.
Bindal, A. (2020). Violence, desire, and death penalty: Reactions on the foundations of modern legal subjectivity. In L. Vashist & J. Dogra (Eds), *Rethinking law and Violence*. Oxford University Press.
Bose, R. (2022, November 14). Rajiv Gandhi Assassination: Who Were The Killers And Why Were They Released?. www.outlookindia.com/national/rajiv-gandhi-assassination-who-were-the-killers-and-why-were-they-released–news-237411.
Brown, W. (1997). The Time of the Political. *Theory and Event,* 1(1). https://muse.jhu.edu/article/24233.
Butler, J. (2014a). On Cruelty. *London Review of Books*, 36(14). www.lrb.co.uk/v36/n14/judith-butler/on-cruelty.
Butler, J. (2014b). Talk: Speaking of Rage and Grief. www.youtube.com/watch?v=ZxyabzopQi8.
Carvalho, H. & Chamberlen, A. (2017). Why Punishment Pleases: Punitive Feelings in a World of Hostile Solidarity. *Punishment and Society*, 0(0), 1–22.
Chopra, N. (2015, December 19). Nirbhaya Case: SC Won't Stop Juvenile's Release Even As Delhi Commission For Women Ask For Urgent Hearing Post-Midnight. huffpost.com/archive/in/entry/nirbhaya-case-sc-wont-stop-juveniles-release-even-as-delhi-co_n_8846930.
Copjec, J. (1994). *Read my Desire: Lacan Against Historicists*. London: MIT Press.
Derrida, J. (2013), *The Death Penalty* (Vol, I). University of Chicago Press.
D'Mello, A., Agnes, F. & Sidhva, P. (2014). Making of a High Profile, Shakti Mills Rape Trial. *Economic and Political Weekly*, 49(29).
Douzinas, C. & Nead, L. (1999). *Law and the image: The authority of art and the aesthetics of law*. University of Chicago Press.

Dutta, T. (2020, January 8). Family of Delhi bus rape victim feel 'at peace' following hanging order. www.thenationalnews.com/world/asia/family-of-delhi-bus-rape-victim-feel-at-peace-following-hanging-order-1.961732.

Dutta, D. & Sircar, O. (2013). India's Winter of Discontent: Some Feminist Dilemmas in the Wake of a Rape. *Feminist Studies*, 39, 293–306.

Dutta, S. & Venkatesan, V. (2015). Right to Justice at Stake: Interview with Vrinda Grover. *Frontline*. https://frontline.thehindu.com/cover-story/right-to-justice-at-stake/article7002917.ece.

Freud, S. (1913/1955a). Totem and Taboo. In *The Standard Edition of the Complete Psychological Works of Sigmund Freud*, Vol. XIII (translated by J. Stratchey). Hogarth Press.

Freud, S. (1913/1955b). The Claims Of Psycho-Analysis To Scientific Interest. In *The Standard Edition of the Complete Psychological Works of Sigmund Freud*, Vol. XIII (translated by J. Stratchey). Hogarth Press.

Freud, S. (1917/1957). Mourning and Melancholia. In *The Standard Edition of the Complete Psychological Works of Sigmund Freud*, Vol. XIV (translated by J. Stratchey). Hogarth Press.

Freud, S. (2002). *Civilization and its discontents*. London: Penguin Classics.

Gandhi, N. (1990). Indecent representation of Women (Protection Act), 1986: An analysis. *CBI Bulletin*, 16–20 (April).

Garland, D. (1990). Frameworks of enquiry in the sociology of punishment. *British Journal of Sociology*, 41(1), 1–22.

Garland, D. (2013). Punishment and social solidarity. In J. Simon & R. Sparks (Eds), *The Sage Handbook of Punishment and Society*. Sage Publications.

Goodrich, P. (1990). *Languages of law: From logics of memory to nomadic masks*. Weidenfeld & Nicolson.

Goodrich, P. (1997). Maladies of the Legal Soul: Psychoanalysis and Interpretation in Law. *Washington and Lee Law Review*, 54(3), 1038–1065.

Grosz, E. (1990). *Jacques Lacan: A Feminist Introduction*. London: Routledge.

Grosz, S. (2014). *The examined life: How we lose and find ourselves*. Vintage.

Halley, J. (2008). Rape at Rome: Feminist Interventions in the Criminalization of Sex-Related Violence in Positive International Criminal Law. *Michigan Journal of International Law*, 30, 1.

Halley, J. (2018). Introducing governance feminism. In J. Halley, P. Kotiswaran, R. Rebouche & H. Shamir, *Governance feminism: An introduction*. University of Minnesota Press.

Hegde, S. (2015, December 24). Rage of the self-righteous Republic. *The Hindu*. www.thehindu.com/opinion/lead/lead-article-by-sanjay-hegde-on-justice-juvenile-bill-rage-of-the-selfrighteous-republic/article8022373.ece.

Henderson, E. (2015, December 20). Nirbhaya Case: Anger and widespread protests as juvenile Delhi gang rapist freed after three years in reform centre. www.independent.co.uk/news/world/asia/nirbhaya-case-anger-and-protests-as-juvenile-delhi-gang-rapist-freed-after-three-years-in-reform-a6780601.html.

Hindustan Times (2020, January 18). Asha Devi's response to Indira Jaising's request to forgive gang rape convicts: 'Even if god asks me to forgive them, I won't'. www.hindustantimes.com/delhi-news/asha-devi-s-response-to-indira-jaising-s-request-to-forgive-gang-rape-convicts-even-if-god-asks-me-to-forgive-them-i-won-t/story-bcEtnpv5h3il22PEcQBz0N.html.

Hollway, W., Mitchell, J. & Walsh, J. (2015). Interview with Juliet Mitchell – Psychoanalysis and Feminism: Then and now. *Psychoanalysis, Culture & Society*, 20(2).

Jaising, I. & Menon, R. (2015). Ethics and Theatrics. *Economic and Political Weekly*, 50(13).

John, M. (2013). Class Societies and Sexual Violence: Towards a Marxist Understanding of Rape. https://radicalnotes.org/tag/maya-john.

Kannabiran, K. (2016, Sep. 7). The Cure For 'Moral' Panic. *The Outlook*. www.outlookindia.com/opinion/the-cure-for-moral-panic-news-297807.

Kannabiran, K. & Kannabiran, V. (Eds). (2002). *De-Eroticizing Assault: Essays on Modesty, Honour and Power*. Stree.

Kapur, R. (1996). Who Draws the Line? Feminist Reflections on Speech and Censorship. *Economic & Political Weekly*, 31(16/17), WS15-WS19+WS21-WS3 (April 20–27).

Kapur, R. (2013). Gender, Sovereignty and the Rise of a Sexual Security Regime in International Law and Postcolonial India. *Melbourne Journal of International Law*, 14(2), 317–345.

Kapur, R. (2015). India's Daughter May Change Nothing, But India Needs to Watch It. *Huffington Post*. www.huffingtonpost.in/ratna-kapur/indias-daughter-may-chang_b_6891588.html.

Kotiswaran, P. (2017). A Bittersweet Moment: Indian Governance Feminism and the 2013 Rape Law Reforms. *Economic & Political Weekly*, 52(25–26), 78.

Kumari, V. (2014). Juvenile Justice Bill 2014: A Regressive Step. *Journal of Indian Law Institute*, 56(3), 303.

Kumari, V. (2017). *Juvenile Justice (Care and Protection of Children) Act 2015: Critical analyses*. Universal Law Publishing.

Law Commission of India (2017). Hate Speech. Report No. 267.

Leader, D. (2008). *The new black: Mourning, melancholia and depression*. Penguin UK.

Liang, L. (2011). Media's Law: From Representation to Affect. *BioScope*, 2(1), 23.

Ling, C. W. (2011). Private Defence. In W. C. Chan, B. Wright & S. Yeo (Eds), *Codification, Macaulay and the Indian Penal Code: The legacies and modern challenges of criminal law reform*. Ashgate Publishing Company.

MacKinnon, C. A. (1987). *Feminism Unmodified: Discourses on Life and Law*. Harvard University Press.

Mathur, A. (2015, Dec. 19). Nirbhaya case: Unlawful to keep Juvenile Convict in Jail, says Delhi High Court. *Indian Express*. http://indianexpress.com/article/india/india-news-india/unlawful-to-keep-him-in-jail-says-hc-juvenile-convict-free-on-sunday.

Mead, G. H. (1918). The psychology of punitive justice. *American Journal of Sociology*, 23, 577–594.

Mehta, K. & Nigam, C. (2016, Jan. 6). If law permits, I will feel proud to shoot the rapist. *Millennium Post*. www.millenniumpost.in/if-law-permits-i-will-feel-proud-to-shoot-the-rapist-119073.

Menon, N. (2015). Indian feminists, 'India's daughter', and sexual violence: The issues at stake. https://kafila.online/2015/03/08/indian-feminists-indias-daughter-and-sexual-violence-the-issues-at-stake.

Menon, N. (2019). Sexual Violence and the law in India. In R. West & C. G. Bowman (Eds), *Research Handbook on Feminist Jurisprudence*. Edward Elgar Publishing.

Mladek, K. (2003). The Psychic Life of Punishment (Kant, Nietzsche, Freud). In A. Sarat & P. Ewick (Ed.), *Punishment, Politics and Culture* (Studies in Law, Politics, and Society, Vol. 30). Leeds: Emerald Group Publishing Limited.

Mundkur, A. & Narrain, A. (2013, Apr. 19). Betraying a Third Way. *The Hindu*. www.thehindu.com/todays-paper/tp-opinion/betraying-the-third-way/article4632046.ece.

Murphy, J. G. (1979). *Retribution, Justice, and Therapy: Essays in the Philosophy of Law*. Kluwer Academic Publishers.

Nag, S. (2015, March 5). The selective amnesia of 'India's Daughter' – What the film conveniently ignores! *Youth Ki Awaaz*. www.youthkiawaaz.com/2015/03/indias-daughter-bbc-documentary.

Nelson, D. (2013). Mother of rape accused in shock. *The Telegraph*. www.telegraph.co.uk/news/worldnews/asia/india/9947596/Mother-of-rape-accused-in-shock.html.

Nietzsche, F. (2006). *On the Genealogy of Morality* (K. Ansell-Pearson, Ed., C. Diethe, Trans.). Cambridge University Press.

Norrie, A. (2019). Love in Law's Shadow: Political Theory, Moral Psychology and Young Hegel's Critique of Punishment. *Social & Legal Studies*, 28(1), 10–30.

Nussbaum, M. C. (2016). *Anger and forgiveness: Resentment, generosity, justice*. Oxford University Press.

Orford, A. (2002). Feminism, Imperialism and the Mission of International Law. *Nordic Journal of International Law*, 71(2), 275–296.

Otto, D. L. (2009), The Exile of Inclusion: Reflections on Gender Issues in International Law Over the Last Decade. *Melbourne Journal of International Law*, 10(1), 11–26.

Packer, H. L. (1968). *The Limits of Criminal Sanction*. Stanford University Press.

Pande, B. B. (2015). 'Bad' Juveniles and the 'Worst' Juvenile Justice Law? The Second Challenge to Juvenile Justice Law in Darga Ram v. State of Rajasthan. *Journal of Indian Law Institute*, 57(1), 27–47.

Panicker, R. S. (2015, December 22). Juvenile Justice Bill Passed in Rajya Sabha, Jyoti Singh's Parents Watched Debate. *NDTV*. www.ndtv.com/india-news/rajya-sabha-votes-on-juvenile-justice-bill-jyoti-singhs-parents-in-parliament-1257838.

Perapaddan, B. S. & Kumar, N. (2013, August 31). Juvenile gets 3 years in Delhi gang-rape case. *The Hindu*. www.thehindu.com/news/national/juvenile-gets-3-years-in-delhi-gangrape-case/article5079092.ece.

Primoratz, I. (1990). *Justifying legal punishment*. Prometheus Books.

Rosaldo, R. (1993). *Culture & Truth: The Remaking of Social Analysis*. Boston, MA: Beacon Press.

Rose, J. (2007). *The last resistance*. Verso.

Rose, J. (2014a). *Women in Dark Times*. Bloomsbury.

Rose, J. (2014b). Response to Edward Said. In E. W. Said, *Freud and the Non-European*. Verso.

Rose, J. (2018a). I am a knife. *London Review of Books*, 40(4).

Rose, J. (2018b). *Mothers: An Essay on Love and Cruelty*. Farrar, Straus and Giroux.

Rose, J., Lerman, A. & Chaudhuri, S. (2010). *Conversations with Jacqueline Rose*. Seagull Books.

Roy, S. (2015a, March 7). Leslee Udwin's 'India's Daughter' shows you what the government doesn't want you to seagnese. *Firstpost*. www.firstpost.com/living/leslee-udwins-indias-daughter-shows-you-what-the-government-doesnt-want-you-to-see-2140811.html.

Roy, S. (2015b, March 10). Film Review: Understanding 'India's Daughter', in India and in South Africa. *Daily Maverick*. www.dailymaverick.co.za/article/2015-03-10-film-review-understanding-indias-daughter-in-india-and-in-south-africa/#.Voup5rNViko.

Rutsa, X. & Sunil, O. (2015). Nagaland Lynching: Unanswered Questions Haunt Dimapur. *Times of India*. http://timesofindia.indiatimes.com/india/Questions-that-haunt-Dimapur/articleshow/46546167.cms.

Safi, M. (2017, February 16). Delhi rape victim's parents call for her real name to be used to end stigma. *The Guardian*. www.theguardian.com/world/2017/feb/16/jyoti-singh-parents-call-for-honorary-museum-nirbhaya-to-use-her-real-name#:~:text=The%20museum's%20title%20still%20carries,real%20name%20be%20used%20instead.

Schroeder, J. L. (2009). Totem, Taboo and the Concept of Law: Myth in Hart and Freud. *Washington University Jurisprudence Review*, 1(1), 139–154.

Schroeder, J. L. (2001). *Fear of freedom: A polemic against policy scholarship*. Working Paper Series No. 35, Jacob Burns Institute for Advanced Legal Studies, Cardozo Law School. https://ssrn.com/abstract=262349.

Schroeder, J. & Carlson, D. G. (2015). *Improve Yourself; Not the World*. http://papers.ssrn.com/sol3/papers.cfm?abstract_id=2679317.

Schwab, G. (2010). *Haunting Legacies: Violent Histories and Transgenerational Trauma*. Columbia University Press.

Sen, J. (2016). 'India's Daughter' and Some Feminist Legal Concerns. www.cdhr.org.in/freedom-of-expression/feminist-legal-concerns.

Sethi, M. (2016, August). *Why the Mahmood Farooqui Judgment is Deeply Flawed*. www.hardnewsmedia.com/2016/08/why-mahmood-farooqui-judgment-deeply-flawed.

Shekar, R. (2013). Delhi rape case: Main accused Ram Singh commits suicide in Tihar Jail. *The Times of India*. http://timesofindia.indiatimes.com/city/delhi/Delhi-rape-case-Main-accused-Ram-Singh-commits-suicide-in-Tihar-Jail/articleshow/18902304.cms.

Singh, S. (2011, May 1). Castrate child rapists, Delhi judge suggests. https://timesofindia.indiatimes.com/india/castrate-child-rapists-delhi-judge-suggests/articleshow/8130553.cms.

Singh, S. R. (2020, March 20). Four Nirbhaya case convicts hanged to death in Tihar jail. www.thehindu.com/news/national/nirbhaya-case-four-convicts-hanged-to-death-in-tihar-jail/article61960571.ece.

Spivak, G. C. (2004). Righting Wrongs. *The South Atlantic Quarterly*, 103(2/3), 523–581.

Subramani, A. (2015, October 26). Castrating child rapists best solution for sex offenders, says Madras High Court. *Times of India*. http://timesofindia.indiatimes.com/india/Castrating-child-rapists-best-solution-for-sex-offences-says-Madras-HC/articleshow/49531482.cms.

Taylor, A. (2012, December 26). Violent Protests in India Over Rape Case. *The Atlantic*. www.theatlantic.com/photo/2012/12/violent-protests-in-india-over-rape-case/100429.

Tellis, A. (2018). Men in Feminism: LGBT and Feminist Entanglements over Masculinity. In R. Chowdhury & Z. al Baset (Eds), *Men and Feminism in India*. Routledge.

Tellis, A. (2015, March 26–27). Fantasies of Knowledge: Rape as Event since December 16, 2012. Paper presented at Contesting Knowledge: Event, Truth, Politics, Annual Conference organized by English Departments of Ramjas College and Venkateswara Colleges, Ramjas College, Delhi.

The Economic Times (2018, September 11). Approached DCW to look into 'delay' in execution: Nirbhaya's mother. https://economictimes.indiatimes.com/news/politics-and-nation/approached-dcw-to-look-into-delay-in-execution-nirbhayas-mother/articleshow/65768069.cms?from=mdr.

The Hindu (2018, March 12). Juvenile in Dec 16 gang-rape case must be hanged: Victim's mother. www.thehindubusinessline.com/news/juvenile-in-dec-16-gangrape-case-must-be-hanged-victims-mother/article5079014.ece.

Times of India (2015a, March 5). Govt serves legal notice to BBC for airing Nirbhaya film 'India's Daughter'; Cong, BJP spar. http://timesofindia.indiatimes.com/india/Govt-serves-legal-notice-to-BBC-for-airing-Nirbhaya-film-Indias-Daughter-Cong-BJP-spar/articleshow/46468604.cms.

Times of India (2015b, December 20). Delhi Commission for Women moves SC against Nirbhaya juvenile's release. https://timesofindia.indiatimes.com/india/Delhi-Commission-for-Women-moves-SC-against-Nirbhaya-juveniles-release/articleshow/50250378.cms.

Tripathi, R. & Singh, V. (2015, July 30). President rejects mercy petition of Yakub Memon. *Indian Express*. http://indianexpress.com/article/india/india-others/president-rejects-mercy-petition-of-yakub-memon.

Vashist, L. & Bindal, A. (2023). Thinking Through Forgiveness: Towards Post Colonial Criminology. *Indian Journal of Criminology*, 51, 126–141.

Venkatesan, V. (2015). Delicate Balance. *Frontline*. https://frontline.thehindu.com/cover-story/delicate-balance/article7002842.ece.

Woodward, K. (1996). Anger…and Anger: From Freud to Feminism. In J. O. Neill (Ed.), *Freud and the Passions*. University Park, PA: Pennsylvania University Press.

Working Group on Human Rights in India (2013). Capital Punishment Not a Deterrent: WGHR Demands Abolishment of the Death Penalty. http://wghr.org/wp-content/uploads/2013/10/WGHR-Statement-on-Capital-Punishment-in-Delhi-Gang-Rape-Case.pdf.

Žižek, S. (1997). *The Plague of Fantasies*. Verso.

Žižek, S. (2008). Tolerance as an Ideological Category. *Critical Inquiry*, 34(4), 34–61.

Žižek, S. (2014). *Trouble in Paradise: From the End of History to the End of Capitalism*. Penguin Books.

Žižek, S. (2016). Rumsfeld, UNKNOWN KNOWNS, and Psychoanalysis [Video file]. www.youtube.com/watch?v=4SQpczc8mGg.

Chapter 4

Defamiliarising the Sexual

In criminal law, the sexual appears either as disgusting (crime of obscenity) or violent (sexual offences). The legal position *vis-à-vis* the sexual is largely one of sex-negativism secured through mobilisation of the emotion of disgust (Nussbaum, 2004). Disgust, Martha Nussbaum tells us, is associated with objects 'which are seen as contaminants because they are seen as reminders of our mortality and animal vulnerability' (Nussbaum, 2004, p. 93). The core idea behind the emotion of disgust is one of 'policing the boundary between ourselves and nonhuman animals, or our own animality' (Nussbaum, 2004, p. 137). The sexual evokes disgust, as sex itself is perceived as 'something furtive and self-contaminating' (Nussbaum, 2004, p. 137). Significantly, in the encounter of law and sexuality, law emerges as an emotional site (Vashist, 2022) where the emotion of disgust serves a psychic function through which (anti-sex) laws construct a 'hierarchical system of sexual value' (Rubin, 1984, p. 151) and become 'the most adamantine instrument of sexual stratification and erotic persecution' (Rubin, 1984, p. 157).

It is only very recently, particularly with the struggle of sexual minorities, that sexuality has come to be associated with love and pride in the Indian legal discourse. 'The human instinct to love was caged by constraining the physical manifestation of their sexuality', (para 372) remarked Justice Chandrachud in his much-applauded judgment decriminalising homosexuality in India.[1] He goes on to celebrate sexuality in the following terms (para 478, emphasis mine):

> An individual's sexuality cannot be put into boxes or compartmentalized; it should rather be viewed as *fluid*, granting the individual *the freedom to ascertain her own desires* and proclivities [...] Sexuality must be construed as a fundamental experience through which *individuals define the meaning of their lives* [...] Human sexuality cannot be reduced to a binary formulation. Nor can it be defined narrowly in terms of its function as a means to procreation. To confine it to closed categories would result in denuding human liberty of its full content as a constitutional right. The Constitution protects the *fluidities of sexual experience*. It leaves it to

1 *Navtej Johar* v. *Union of India*, (2018) 10 SCC 1.

DOI: 10.4324/9781003387411-5

> consenting adults to find fulfilment in their relationships, in a diversity of cultures, among plural ways of life and in infinite shades of love and longing.

Here, judicial excitement of jubilant inclusion of the once excluded glosses over key conceptual issues that are still unresolved in the terrains of gender and sexuality (Butler, 2015, pp. 57–75; Mitchell, 2015, pp. 77–99; Mitchell, 2008, pp.111–129). The judge (like many gender and sexuality enthusiasts), besides erroneously equating constructivist gender with sexuality in his rendition of human sexuality (in terms of fluidity, self-definition, and infinite shades), creates a rhetorical flourish of all nice-sounding words – fluid, freedom, diversity, plurality, love – to describe non-heterosexual and queer sexualities. Such 'idealisation of the queer', to use Jacqueline Rose's words (Rose, 2017, p. 394), sanitises the sexual to (re)erect the myth of 'psychic and sexual mastery over ourselves' (p. 393). Rose finds 'something amiss' in such descriptions in as much as they leave out 'the agency of the mind that polices our identities, the superego' (p. 394). This superego resists a straight-forward path to freedom which celebratory accounts of sexual emancipation and erotic justice, which are offered on sale in the academic market of ideas, obliterate for their 'lack of honest toil' (Tellis, 2021).

In line with the above psychoanalytic critique, Ashley Tellis in his review of *Navtej Johar* had said, '[t]he honest toil on the question of homosexuality in India remains to be done' (2021). This honest toil is required for the question of sexuality *per se*, especially within Indian feminism. In this chapter, I attempt to pursue this task. I will take a step back and ask, what indeed is the sexual? I undertake this enquiry, exploring the terrain of the Indian women's movement, and tracing the feminist debates around sexual imagery, to explore the meanings, strategies and possibilities around the sexual. The oeuvre of feminist scholarship on this question can broadly be categorised as sex-negative and sex-positive. The sex-negative position views sexuality as a site of violence, whereas the sex-positive position attempts to foreground sexual agency and feminine desire. For sex-positive feminists, the sexual is a domain of pleasure and therefore suppression of the sexual only constrains possibilities of freedom for 'sexual subalterns', those who have been relegated outside the dominant normative sexual order. The sex-positive feminists foreground the subject-in-pleasure in the larger project of rendering erotic supplement to the imagination of justice. While these positions are not strictly mutually exclusive zones as sex-negative feminists do not completely censor erotica and sex-positive feminists do not deny the fact of sexual violence and exploitation, my argument in this chapter is that together they remain united in their under-theorisation of the 'sexual'.

I will argue that the sexual is not just a zone of disgust or violence (the way it is conceived in the law and sex-negative feminism); it is also not just a space of pleasure. It is the liminal in-between which cannot be understood or conceptualised by assuming either side of the sex-negative/sex-positive binary. This binary configuration of the sexual – negative/positive, violence/pleasure, disgust/freedom – gives us an incomplete picture of sexuality and has only worked to sanitise and tame the sexual, stripping it off its uncontainable 'excess' which escapes the structure of rigid meanings. The sexual, as psychoanalytic feminists have shown, is tied to the unconscious where all certainties along with the fantasy of a subject-in-control, on the path towards sexual freedom, collapse. Thus, I will argue for a shift towards a psychoanalytic understanding of the sexual (desire) which transcends the dichotomy of violence/disgust and pleasure, and draw out its implications for criminal law in India. This will not be a nihilistic project where the subject abysmally falls into a dark dungeon of unknowability – the way the unconscious is dominantly understood – instead a project of hope that brings both law and feminist imaginations closer to the 'truth' of our psychic/sexual lives.

Sexual imagery and feminist debates

The sexual in law, when it does not conform to the heteronormative marital community standard, is inherently bad (Vashist, 2014). This sex-negative position of law comes dangerously close to sex-negative feminists for whom sex fundamentally is violence as men dominate women through sexuality. While law censures sexual imagery to protect social morals, sex-negative feminists support censorship to counter objectification of women and to protect them from sexual violence which is seen as a product of proliferating sexual imagery.[2] To explicate this, I will return to a forgotten fragment from the past of the Indian women's movement: feminist debates around the Indecent Representation of Women (Protection) Act, 1986[3] (hereafter 'IRWP').

IRWP was enacted 'to prevent the depiction of the figure of a woman in a manner which is derogatory to women or denigrating women or which is likely to corrupt public morality'. Indecent representation of women, according to section 2(c) 'means the depiction in any manner of the figure of a woman, her form or body or any part thereof in such a way as to have the effect of being

2 (Radical) feminism makes a distinction between obscene and pornographic images; the former pertain to moral considerations while the latter fall within the domain of violence against women. In Indian law, no distinction is made between obscene and pornographic material. In *Ranjit D. Udeshi* v. *State of Maharashtra*, AIR 1965 SC 881, it was contended before the Indian Supreme Court that the test of 'hard-core pornography' be employed for the interpretation of the word 'obscene' i.e. only hard pornographic imagery should be banned under obscenity provisions. But the court had rejected this argument. Statutorily, however, same laws govern both obscene and pornographic images: the Indian Penal Code of 1860, the Indecent Representation of Women Act, 1986, the Cinematograph Act, 1952 and the Central Board of Film Certification Rules, the Customs Act, 1962 and the Cable Television (Network) Act, 1995 and its Rules among others.

3 The Indecent Representation of Women (Protection) Act was passed in 1986 with very little debate. The Bill was introduced by Margaret Alva, the then head of the Department of Women and Child Development.

indecent *or* of being derogatory *or* denigrating women *or* is likely to deprave, corrupt *or* injure the public morality or morals'. This law came into being out of the campaign of many women's groups located across the country in late 1970s and early 1980s (Gandhi, 1990). These groups agitated against sexually explicit, nude images and sexist representations of women in films, advertisements, and hoardings.[4] Not all women's groups were attentive to the distinction between sexual and sexist images. In fact, by focusing on nude or sexual images of women, the women's groups aligned with the conservative idea that respect for women is by treating them as asexual. The law, we can see in the definition of indecent representation, mirrored this category error.

It is important to note that the women's groups whose activism shaped this law did not represent the position of the women's movement on the question of sexual/sexist imagery. Or, one can say the women's movement did not speak in one voice. There were many dissenting voices that criticised both the law as well as 'feminist' activism on diverse grounds (Gandhi, 1990; Jaising, 1986; Jaising, 2006; Jaising & Wolfe, 2006; Kishwar & Vanita, 2006; Agnes, 2006). Ruth Vanita and Madhu Kishwar highlighted the increasing power of the state through the strategy of criminalisation as they argued that the law was 'ridiculously vague' and detrimental to people's civil liberties (Kishwar & Vanita, 2006, p. 107). Many feminists were critical of the myopic vision of the women's groups who in focussing on sexual imagery left out sexist imagery. Flavia Agnes contended that the campaign which led to the Act did not make a clear distinction between obscene and indecent representation (Agnes, 2006). Also, many sexist images remained unchallenged because of the skewed focus of the campaigners on sexual images. In a similar vein, Kishwar and Vanita, argued that the 'equation of indecency with nudity and sex allows all other portrayals of women to pass off as 'decent'' (2006, p. 107). The over-emphasis on portrayals of women as sex objects, ignoring their depiction as servile objects or dutiful house-keepers, they argued, was 'picked up from women's groups in the West, who have usually targeted only the former kind of portrayal for public action' (p. 107).

Significantly, drawing on 1980's feminist legal activism in the US, which was led by Andrea Dworkin and Catharine MacKinnon, some feminists insisted on making a distinction between obscenity and pornography (Gandhi, 1990; Jaisingh, 2006). While obscenity was about public morality, pornography, borrowing from the US Commission on Obscenity and Pornography, was defined as 'the graphically sexually explicit subordination of women, whether in pictures or in words, if it showed them enjoying pain or humility or in positions of servility or submission or display' (Jaising, 2006, p. 126).[5] For Nandita Gandhi, '[f]reedom of expression,

4 For a compilation of the reports on the activism of different women's organisations and groups, see Manushi (n.d.).

5 Jaising approvingly referred to the Indianapolis ordinance, enacted at the instance of feminists, which was stuck down in *American Booksellers* v. *Hudnut*, 777 F2d 323, 330–31 (7th Cir 1985).

in the case of obscenity and pornography, would mean the freedom of men to be entertained and stimulated at the cost of women's humiliation and degradation' (1990, p. 20). Therefore, she argued, the law against pornography should be based on 'the unequal and exploitative relations between the two sexes rather than morality. The pleasure of one cannot be at the expense of the other' (1990, p. 20).[6]

Obscenity approach, feminist critics of the law were clear, was bound to fail when it came to examining the images of women in servility. 'Obscenity law', wrote Jaising and Wolfe, 'proceeds according to the interests of male power, which it robes in the supposedly gender-neutral language of 'good' and 'evil'' (2006, p. 134).[7] They further contended that extreme harm is caused to women by such images and such images continue to promote subordination of women by men (2006, p. 135):

> Such images teach men and women that women are to be subordinated [...] This is how it becomes possible to have women being burned to death by the families of their husbands. This is how it becomes possible to kill female infants. This is why it is possible to live in a world where the burning of women and the murdering of female children and foetuses can coexist with a presumption of equal protection under the law for women.

Furthermore, (2006, p. 137):

> Each time men see images of women being subordinated, presented as though that hierarchy is correct and as if the quality of ignoble servility in women is praiseworthy, they learn to connect pleasure and family and husband in particular, with domination and abuse and the very nature of women with inferiority.

Jaising and Wolfe advocated for the censorship position on the ground that these images produce a common sense about men and women whereby they internalise the gender roles depicted therein, which in turn leads to violence against women.[8]

6 Besides this, Gandhi also urged that sexist stereotyping should be taken seriously and the women who suffer on account of 'visual and other violence' should have the right to legal remedies. The faith that Gandhi and Jaising display in law is not shared by Kishwar and Vanita who 'disagree(d) with a strategy that prescribes punishment as the way of changing societal perceptions of women'.

7 The authors critiqued the Bombay High Court decision in the case on the Hindi film, *Pati Parmeshwar* which was challenged under the S.5-B of the Cinematography Act, 1952 and guidelines enacted by the Central Government. Guideline 2 (iv-a) provided that 'visuals or words depicting women in ignoble servility to man or glorifying such servility as a praiseworthy quality in women are not represented'. Guideline 3(ii) required the Board of Film Censors to ensure that the film 'is examined in light of contemporary standards of the country and the people to which the film relates'.

8 Here, it may be useful to cross-reference the statement of some Indian feminists calling for a restraining order for the screening of the documentary film *India's*

While they distinguished themselves from the pro-censorship right wing groups by extending a critique of Indian traditional values, they, very much like the right wing, saw women as pure victims of pornographic images. In such theorisation, they not only adopted MacKinnon's analytic strategy of using sex and gender interchangeably uncritically, but also her problematic argument of a direct causal connection between pornography and violence against women.

Despite internal disagreements among women's groups and feminists on the meaning of 'indecent' or the strategy of relying on the law, they all aligned with the negative perception of sex couched in gendered, stereotypical roles which invariably makes it dangerous for women. The critique of the law from within the feminist quarters was predominantly couched in sex-negative terms with no articulation of feminine sexual desire or agency. Women appeared as asexual beings, or worse 'fuckees', devoid of any playfulness or imagination in expressing their sexual being.

MacKinnon and Dworkin's variety of feminism had (and continues to have) a strong hold on (Indian) feminists on the question of the sexual (Halley et al., 2018). In the US, MacKinnon and Dworkin had advocated for a ban against all pornography arguing that it incited rape, sexual harassment, and assault. They defined pornography in terms of subordination, anything that represented women as sexual objects or things to use.[9] The truth of pornography was that it 'enslave[d] women's minds and bodies' and 'makes hierarchy sexy' (MacKinnon, 1985; Dworkin, 1985)[10] In *Only Words*, MacKinnon wrote:

> Sooner or later, in one way or another, the consumers want to live out the pornography further in three dimensions. Sooner or later, in one way or another, they do. *It* makes them want to. When they feel they can, when they feel they can get away with it; when they believe they can get away with it, *they* do. Depending upon their chosen sphere of operation, they may use whatever power they have to keep the world a pornographic place so they can continue to get hard from everyday life. As pornographic consumers, teachers may become epistemically incapable of seeing their women students as their potential equals and unconsciously teach about rape from the view point of the accused. Doctors may molest anesthetized women, enjoy watching and inflicting pain during childbirth, and use pornography

Daughter for precisely the same reasons. They argued that the misogynistic speech of one of the convicts of Delhi Gang Rape, Mukesh Singh, amounted to hate speech and could incite violence against women. See, Chapter 3 for a detailed discussion.

9 Subordination of women, graphically depicted, would include situations where women are presented as dehumanised sexual objects, and/or depicted in a variety of other violent circumstances represented in a sexual framework (Dworkin & MacKinnon, 1988).

10 However, dominance feminists do make a distinction between erotica and porn.

> to teach sex education in medical school. Some consumers write on bathroom walls. Some undoubtedly write judicial opinions.
>
> (MacKinnon, 1993, p. 19)

The argument was that watching pornography had a direct effect on men's actions: it caused them to rape women. In such a behaviourist understanding, porn does not reach the mind of the man, it just acts as a trigger for man's body. Men cannot help but rape when they watch porn. For MacKinnon, pornography '[constructs] the social reality of what a woman is and can be in terms of what can be done to her, and what a man is in terms of doing it' (MacKinnon, 1993, p. 25); and thus allows men to get what they want sexually. Within this framework, all possibilities of a 'feminine imaginary', to evoke Drucilla Cornell (1995), are foreclosed to women as they remain eternally trapped in the masculine imaginary of their own selves (Menon, 2000). This version of feminism – which came to be called 'dominance feminism' – presented a dystopic view by unconsciously and wholly accepting the power of the Symbolic which it had set out to critique (Finlayson, 2018; Rose, 2016).

Despite these limits of dominance feminism in the understanding of the Symbolic, Martha Nussbaum carries the brief for MacKinnon-Dworkin worldview. Interestingly, in doing so, she completely brushes aside her own theorisation on the emotive question of disgust of the sexual. She writes (Nussbaum, 2004, p. 139, emphasis mine):

> the serious moral issue posed by pornographic materials is not the issue of sexual explicitness and its alleged disgusting excitingness. Even *if some citizens in a liberal society continue to believe that sex is disgusting*, the presence of sexually explicit materials is no more harmful to them than the presence of texts defending a religion different from their own. They can simply avoid those materials, and, at most, demand that they not be easily available to children, or displayed in public in a way that accosts unwilling viewers.
>
> The issue that a society committed to the equality of its female citizens *should take seriously* is the issue of subordination, humiliation, and its associated harms [...] Much pornography, it is no news to say, depicts sexuality in a way designed to reinforce misogynistic stereotypes, portraying women as base and deserving of abuse, as wanting and asking for abuse, and as outlets for male's desire to humiliate and abuse. It is this that *we should take seriously* as a moral statement that conflicts pretty directly with the equality of women. Pornography is in this sense similar to anti-Semitic literature or racist literature: it makes a statement that directly conflicts with ideas of equal worth and equal protection that are basic to a liberal social order.

The emotion of disgust (which is tied to the sexual) cannot be wished away. By quickly turning away from the unconscious connection between sexually arousing and disgusting to the question of violent sexist pornography, Nussbaum, unfortunately, addresses none of these aspects clearly. If the sexual evokes disgust as it serves as an unconscious reminder of one's mortality and animal vulnerability (which Nussbaum herself uncovers in one of her brilliant moments (Nussbaum, 2004)), then is it so easy to overcome this disgust in a 'liberal society' and adopt a sex-positive stance on the subject? Besides offering a conservative and one-dimensional reading of (violent) pornographic imagery, there is a standard liberal prescriptivism – *tyranny of shoulds*, as I have been calling it, in the way she responds to both the issues: liberal society should not find sex disgusting and we all should be concerned about issues of equality, subordination and humiliation and not be guided by sexual morality. This conclusion totally erases the questions posed by the psychic power networks of disgust around sexuality which block the way towards sexual freedom. Diluting her own diagnosis of the psychic roots of disgust, Nussbaum adopts an easy liberal resolution of the disgust thesis of both obscenity law and pornography. In aligning with dominance feminists, Nussbaum erases the complexity of the sexual and eros which surfaces in its connection with disgust.

In *The Right to Sex* (2021), Amia Srinivasan has made a critical return to the position of anti-porn feminists. Srinivasan asks '[w]hat if they [the anti-porn feminists] weren't hysterical, but prescient?' (2021, p. 40). Her answer to this question, in the chapter titled, 'Talking to my students about porn', is in the affirmative. While Srinivasan concedes to feminism's pro-sex perspective that insists on women's right to sexual pleasure, nevertheless she argues for a circumspect approach to sex, especially in the contemporary moment when sexual experience of most who have come of age in the internet-dominated world has been mediated by the screen. For the young, for whom learning takes place through imitation, 'sexual imagination is transformed into a mimesis-machine, incapable of generating its own novelty' (Srinivasan, 2021, p. 70). She asserts: '[t]he psyches of my students are products of pornography. In them, the warnings of the anti-porn feminists seem to have been belatedly realised: sex for my students is *what porn says* it is' (2021, p. 41, emphasis mine). If Srinivasan's argument is limited to the effects of early exposure to violent/misogynistic forms of pornography from which children should be protected, no one can disagree with her given porn is the primary and the worst medium of 'sex education' globally. But if Srinivasan's claim is about the messages encoded in porn, then one has to ask: what does porn say about sex? Does it only have one meaning? (Also, is Srinivasan's argument about porn only with respect to the young who need to be protected from the onslaught of porn, or is it a broader argument on the messages inherently encoded within porn?)

Like MacKinnon and other sex-negative feminists, Srinivasan traces a direct relationship between consumption of pornography and negative treatment of women by men (Srinivasan, 2021, pp. 42–43). Porn, according to her, mechanistically speaks to the body, bypassing cognitive and reasoning capacities: 'Porn trains. It etches deep grooves in the psyche, forming powerful associations between arousal and selected stimuli, bypassing that part of us which pauses, considers, thinks. Those associations, strengthened through repetition, reinforce and reproduce the social meaning assigned by patriarchy to sexual difference' (2021, p. 64). Srinivasan's concern is the moving picture. Its deep, gripping impact on the viewer is on account of 'the pleasures of ego-identification' it offers. The (male) viewer identifies with the male actor on screen in a situation where the female actor is awaiting sexual assertion of power. But interestingly, according to her, porn does not seem to have the same effect on women viewers, for 'girls don't regard porn as an authority on sex; they really can distinguish fantasy from fiction. But they know that, for boys, porn sets the 'standard' for 'good' sex, grounds their assumptions about 'what it's always like" (2021, p. 45). How girls escape the power of porn and boys don't is not clear. Her female students are presumably already progressive feminists despite being subjected to the same degrading universe of porn where women's bodies are bleeding holes in existence for male desire.

Despite wide divergence between MacKinnon's dominance feminism that repudiates desire, and Srinivasan's that aspires to discipline desire, what brings the two intimately close is their feminist political imagination that, in its powerful explanation of the force of the Symbolic in the construction of sexed beings, is premised on a denial (in MacKinnon)/disavowal (in Srinivasan) of the unconscious. This translates into their respective theories of law/jurisprudence: 'law is male'/'law is simply the wrong tool for the job [of prohibiting the sort of sex that is produced by patriarchy]' (Srinivasan, 2021, p. 29).

Throughout this text, Srinivasan is labouring to break the binary between sex-positive and sex-negative feminist positions, arguing for a circumspect position of sex while holding on to sexual agency and pleasure. However, her thesis on the whole remains caught in an understanding of the sexual as fully knowable and transparent.

Hegemony of sex-negative feminism

In recent years, in the light of many cases where victims of rape reported that they were forcibly shown pornographic images and videos by the violators (Ali, 2013a; Ali, 2013b), the question of pornography has become a pressing concern. It is no longer a question of sexist representations of women in degrading forms. The concern of dominance feminists has become real: it is about actual violence against real women in the real world, owing to easy availability of pornography (Khanna, 2017; Singh, 2016; *India Today*, 2013). Significantly, with dominance feminism as the hegemonic discourse around sexual violence, it is with MacKinnon's understanding that the issue of pornography has entered contemporary legal as well as popular imagination. The debate on the connection between the 'sexual' and 'violence' hijacked as it is by the sex-negative imagination has offered no feminist insight on the category of the sexual in and of itself. In fact, 'sex panic' instilled in the name of protecting the young as well as 'moral spine of the nation', backed by sex-negative feminism, blocks all possibilities of a critical engagement with sexuality.

In 2013, an Indore-based lawyer, Kamlesh Vaswani filed a Public Interest Litigation in the Supreme Court demanding an action plan and an exclusive law on the pornographic websites on the internet.[11] The petitioner, invoking the memory of Delhi Gang Rape, argued that crime against women is increasing because watching porn is not a crime in India, and only production, distribution and sharing of porn is criminalised. He argued that even private viewing of pornographic material should be banned.[12] It was argued that the sexual content that children are able to access today is far more graphic, violent, brutal, deviant, and destructive than ever before. The petitioner further contended that the minds of the offenders are 'fuelled by pornography, as the sexual offender or rapist achieves his gratification, not only from sexual release alone but also from the thrill of domination, control and power' (para 38).[13] He further argued that there is a causal relationship between exposure to sexually violent material and sexual violence against women.

The Supreme Court Women's Lawyers Association (SCWLA) had impleaded itself in this matter.[14] The counsel appearing for SCWLA expressed her agony and described child pornography as 'moral cancer not on the ground of individual morality but on the foundation of obscenity' (para 7). It was also argued that 'freedom of speech cannot create a dent in the national character or the moral spine of the nation which comes within the constitutional morality (para 9)'.[15] This petition is still pending but the proliferation of sexual imagery owing to the technological revolution has resulted in renewed demands (not necessarily feminist) for prohibiting advertisements and other representations that affect youth and morals or depict women in derogatory forms.[16] In these calls of arresting of sexual

11 *Kamlesh Vaswani* v. *UOI*, 2014 SCC Online SC 355; 2016 SCC Online SC 204; 2016 SCC Online SC 860.

12 During the course of this petition, on July 31, 2015, the Department of Telecommunications, Ministry of Communication and IT, Government of India disabled 857 websites invoking powers under s. 79(3)(b) of the Information Technology Act, 2000, on the grounds of morality and decency. This ban was partially lifted (in the August 4, 2015 order, the BJP government lifted the ban on all sites except the ones which contain child pornography) after the government drew severe criticism from all quarters on the violation of the fundamental right to free speech (Barstow, 2015).

13 *Kamlesh Vaswani* v. *Union of India*, Writ petition, available at: http://onelawstreet.com/pornography-ban-kamlesh-vaswani.

14 Some others have also become parties to the case, like a woman who stated that her marriage was breaking down, owing to her husband's porn addiction (Hariharan, 2014; Math et al., 2014; Nair, 2017).

15 2016 SCC Online SC 204.

16 The Indecent Representation of Women (Prohibition) Amendment Bill, 2012, was introduced in the Rajya Sabha on December 13, 2012 by the then Minister of State (Independent), Women and Child Development, Smt Krishna Tirath. The Bill suffers from many infirmities: the definition of indecency is vague and collapses the categories of sexist, pornographic and sexual images; the Bill provides for enhanced penalties and increased

violence by banning pornography, pornography is understood as presenting the reality of a cohesive and rigid Symbolic with fixed gender structure of powerful masculinity and submissive femininity. In different terms, the social structure becomes determinative of all meaning eliding the question of agency but more significantly the unconscious.

Erotic justice: Response to sex-negative feminism

Sex-negative feminism which has acquired a global appeal remains insensitive to the history of sexuality in the postcolonial context. Contesting the hegemony of MacKinnon-Dworkin inspired dominance feminism, postcolonial feminist Ratna Kapur asserts that in order to imagine the contours of feminist jurisprudence in the postcolonial context, 'the history of exclusions and suppression of certain voices during the colonial encounter' needs to be acknowledged (Kapur, 2007, p. 248). Kapur unravels the blindness of dominance feminism to the specificity of the postcolonial context and its own complicity in the (ongoing) colonial project (Finlayson, 2018). Postcolonial (sex-positive) feminists thus contend that law's disgust of the sexual which also resonates in the dominant feminist reforms cannot be dispelled without acknowledging the repressed past of colonialism.

The imaginary domain of feminine sexual desire was elided in the construction of femininity in the 19th century nationalist resolution of the woman's question (Chatterjee, 2003). The Indians unable to challenge the British rule in the public, material sphere sought to challenge it in the private sphere by fashioning an ideal femininity for the Indian woman in contrast to the 'coarse, crass woman'. This norm of ideal femininity in the colonial encounter has been constitutive of the construction of gendered subjectivities in the postcolonial context where women have solely come to recognise themselves as culturally inhabiting the roles of chaste wives and mothers. Against this backdrop of the colonial past and hegemonic ideology of dominance feminism, Kapur (2005) inaugurated the political project of 'erotic justice' to foreground the question of (sexual) pleasure and desire in the postcolonial context. In contrast to the sex-negative feminists, this move marked a discursive shift in the legal terrain by emphasising on 'sexual speech' as free speech.

Kapur argues that erotic justice can only be imagined with the recognition that sexual imagery (and sexual speech as free speech) is *not always* sexist or misogynist. Representations of sexual imagery, including the desire of 'sexual

punishments for repeat offenders; the state officials are again given wide powers. It is a déjà vu for feminists in India as the debates around the 1986 Act reveal. The Bill was withdrawn on July 26, 2021. Details available at: https://prsindia.org/billtrack/the-indecent-representation-of-women-prohibition-amendment-bill-2012#:~:text=The%20Bill%20prohibits%20the%20publication,in%20ancient%20monuments%20or%20temples.

subalterns', play a significant role in challenging the dominant (hetero)normative framework. Insightfully, she shows how all possibilities of sexual imagery that acknowledge women's sexual agency and promote sexual pleasure get lost, if all sexually explicit representation is characterised as obscene (Kapur, 1996). In fact:

> sexually explicit representations have an important role to play in flouting conventional sexual norms. It is not enough to simply focus on the negative dimensions of sexist representations, but also to attempt to create space for more positive representations of women's sexuality. Such a space has enormous potential for women who are confined by the normative understandings of female sexuality as passive, modest and without agency. It is thus important to encourage images that promote women's sexual pleasure, and affirm women's sexual experiences/fantasies.
>
> (Kapur, 2001)

The emphasis of postcolonial feminists on proliferation of free speech (Ghosh, 1999, Kapur, 1996; Menon, 2015), including sexual speech, is particularly important for feminist struggles in this contemporary moment not only because feminist speech itself has been found to be offensive and is being threatened but also to counter the repressive powers of both governance feminism as well as the state apparatus (John, 2016).

Further, Kapur has argued that we need to shift the subject of feminist politics from 'subject of violence' to 'subject in pleasure'. In calling for this shift she devised the category of 'sexual subaltern'. Kapur defines the 'sexual subaltern':

> as a theoretical device derived from subaltern studies [...] giving voice to those who have been left outside of historical narratives produced by colonial or nationalist writers. The term sexual subaltern is intended to bring together, the disparate range of sexual minorities within postcolonial India, without suggesting that it is either a homogenized or stable category. Indeed, the location and politics of the sexual subaltern in postcolonial India is mediated by class, caste and religion, producing a complex and at times even contradictory politics.
>
> (Kapur, 2000, p. 16)

Sexual subalterns, she claims, are challenging dominant sexual and cultural norms and 'recuperating sex as both a political project, liberating it from dominant familial and sexual ideology, as well as a less stigmatized and more pleasurable project' (Kapur, 2000, p. 21). In other words, it is claimed that this pleasure-seeking sexual subject will contest law's disgust for the sexual as well as feminism's association of sex with violence and women's victimhood.

One acknowledges Kapur's useful emphasis on erotic and pleasure as an antidote to dominance feminism. However, it is difficult to imagine that the categories of 'pleasure', 'desire', 'sexual subaltern in pleasure', against which the conception of erotic justice is located, will be able to engage with the *psychic space of subjects* and accord them with the 'minimum conditions individuation' where they are able to explore their own ways of sexual being. After all, '[w]ithout new images and new words in which to express our sexuality, we will be unable to create a new world for women' (Cornell, 1995, p. 138).

Sexuality is always caught up in the field of power mediated through class and caste. To assume a subject position (including sexual subaltern subject) who can liberate sex from familial, social and sexual ideologies would mean a rejection of the intergenerational transmission of unconscious processes at the heart of sexual difference. To critically think about erotic justice, Kumkum Roy's reading of the *Kāmasūtra* is revealing (Roy, 1996, p. 155). Roy shows how the sexual is woven into a web of social relations, mediated by caste, class and gender. Vastayayana's *Kāmasūtra*, a celebrated Indian text on sexuality, is not a celebration of uncontained *eros*. In fact:

> it delimits the contents of *kāma* [desire], in effect, recognising and centralising the heterosexual desires of upper-class men vis-à-vis all women (directly) and lower-class men (indirectly). Desires, thus constructed, are no longer amorphous or inchoate – in fact, we are faced with 'Desire', which acquires definitional status and in terms of which other manifestations are classified as sub-ordinate, irrelevant, or even disruptive. Clearly, then, the definition of desire which is codified in the *Kāmasūtra* was integrated, ideally, into relations of power, so that desire could be viewed as an expression of power.
>
> (Roy, 1996, p. 156)

Structured along the lines of a hierarchical sexual economy, the text unifies powerful (prosperous and 'cultured') men into a homogenous category while women are differentiated from one another based on whether their accessibility to single man, two men or all men. Lesbian sex was either erased or marginalised, and when recognised, it was assimilated within categories of heterosexual intercourse. The sexual here is not a realm of pure *eros* as 'violence within sexual relations was both recognised and structured' (Roy, 1996, p. 160). Violence was considered a legitimate expression of masculine heterosexual desire, the understanding of sex as 'combat' justified beating of the woman by the man where the woman was required to respond with shouts and shrieks. Even the 20th-century commentators in their translations follow the same trope of justifying sexual violence:

> males now definitely know that the manifestation of tears and cries in a female are quite normal ones and inwardly she desires the opposite of what she expresses by tears and cries and her withholding of favours from the male.
>
> (Upadhyaya, 1961, cited in Roy, 1996, p. 167)

When desire itself is historically structured around abjection of the female and determined by caste and class stratification (and these are our psychic legacies in the realm of sexual desire), the path towards 'erotic justice' is more challenging and fraught than what sex-positive imagination believes it to be. What I have arrived at is this: while the law and sex-negative feminists adopt a conservative stance on the sexual and sex-positive feminists appear to take a progressive position, both positions offer limited understandings of the sexual. The dichotomy of these feminist positions translated in the law as theories of subjecthood (as 'subject of violence'/'subject in pleasure') does little to unravel the complexity of the desiring subject whose subjectivity is constituted by psychic continuums of violence and pleasure. The next section develops this argument.

The subject of desire

In *Politics of the Possible* (1999), literary theorist Kumkum Sangari discusses a nineteenth century *qissa* of *Chhabili Bhatiyari,*[17] a 'jealous contest and battle of wits' between Chhabili, a lower-caste woman, water carrier by profession and Bichitra, upper-caste Rajput wife of a Muslim prince. Sangari's reading of this *qissa*, I believe, offers an acute understanding of the sexual that I propose to develop in this section, and hence I start with the rendition of this story. Chhabili and the prince were already a couple when he got married to Bichitra. Chhabili keeps the prince away from Bichitra, duping him into believing that his wife has a demonic gaze. Soon Bichitra realises this and decides to get her husband back and appears before him in disguised appearances. With much effort, she succeeds in attracting her husband and making him realise that he was indeed duped by Chhabili. When the prince finds this out, he sends for Chhabili to punish her. The courtiers recommend throwing her out of the city. But, for Bichitra, this would not be enough. She insists that Chhabili 'be made to embrace a red-hot log in the same way that she used to embrace her husband's body, then be half buried in the ground with it, and finally to have her head battered by the prince' (Sangari, 1999, p. 252). Only such a punishment would pacify her heart. The prince agrees. The spectre of Chhabili's brutal killing is followed by '[t]he immediate celebration and consummation of the marriage' (Sangari, 1999, p. 253).

Sangari in her reading of this *qissa* captures multi-layered narratives of agency and resistance foregrounding the pronounced role of caste, sexual jealousy and rivalry, delineating how the frames of marital love and sexual pleasure woven in and through the normative sexual order 'are built on the battered

17 *Qissa*, Kumkum Sangari writes, is 'a short *dastaan* in which the real and the marvellous interpenetrate, traversed 'downwards' from Persian to *dakhani* Urdu, from royal courts to bazaars, from persianised 'elite' to Fort William College publications and thence to the 'popular' – popular in terms of its mobility and multiple locations and in the sense of being preferred listening, watching, and reading' (Sangari, 1999, p. 247).

and burnt body of a low-caste woman'. (Sangari, 1999, p. 253). Chhabili's fate in this competing sexual jealousy is not only mediated by caste and class but also women's complicity in the 'masculinist ethos' of sexual desire. Sangari writes:

> The pleasure sets up a community of affect that bridges the gap between Chhabili's tortured death and the beginning of a marriage [...] Female jealousy also stands in for a *consent* to male (self)typification: the banal series in which women change but patterns are repeated and repertoires recycled – in the kindling of desire, the constitution of its objects, the confirmation of dispositions of affective vocabularies.
>
> (Sangari, 1999, p. 266)

What I would like to highlight here is a muted yet subtle conceptualisation of the sexual. *Chhabili Bhatiyari* locates the sexual outside the characteristic motifs of 'sexual as violence'/'sexual as pleasure', as the death of the deceitful low-caste woman is followed by 'immediate celebration' of the marital bond and sexual union, as if indicating a psychic continuity, a simultaneity between violence and pleasure. The communal festivity brought about by the gruesome spectacle conjoined with legitimate sexual union commemorates Bichitra's marital love as enmeshed and enfolded into the desire of the violent, cruel murder of the 'other' woman at the hands of her husband. The sexual here emerges as an experience of 'excess' with the potential of destruction as the psychic coordinates of the subject-in-pleasure are contingent on the 'community of affects' produced by 'consensual misogyny'.

'Excess', writes Austrian-Israeli psychoanalyst, Ruth Stein, 'is a crucial part of sexual experience' (Stein, 2008, 43). In her pathbreaking essay 'The Otherness of Sexuality: Excess', Stein seeks to 'defamiliarize' sexuality for which we need 'to "unforget" and recuperate "primitive sensations, bodily and mental hopes that have become illegitimate and unappealing", [...] and to overcome our "shame of excess"' (2008, pp. 44–45). This unforgetting is not Srinivasan's 'negative education' about sex which would 'remind young people that the authority on what sex is, and could become, lies with them' (Srinivasan, 2021, p. 71). This unforgetting, instead is a re-cognition that sex is an 'encounter with what exceeds and undoes the subject's fantasmatic sovereignty' (Berlant & Edelman, 2014, p. 2). A recognition that we are not the masters of our sexual lives. Thus, Srinivasan's feminist hope that '[s]ex can, *if we choose*, remain as generations before have chosen: violent, selfish and unequal. Or sex can – *if they choose* – be something more joyful, more equal, freer', (Srinivasan, 2021, p. 71, emphasis mine) is belied when we recognise manifestations of the sexual 'as non-sovereign, radical incoherence, and a scene both for optimism and subordination' (Berlant & Edelman, 2014, p. 3).

For Stein, sexuality is never a matter of clear choice or certainty. It is intrinsically about the phenomenon of excess 'that denotes *both* liberated pleasure beyond bounds and abominable transgression and destructiveness'. (Stein, 2008, p. 43, emphasis mine). The '*compelling* power of sexual experience' lies in its excess. And this excess is characterised by 'the overstepping of boundaries', 'overbrimming with inordinate arousal', 'excess of physical sensations beyond physical containment', 'excess of desire over sensible judgment', 'excess of meaning over symbolization', 'other's ungraspable excess over me' (Stein, 2008, p. 44). Besides being excessive, Stein insists, sexuality is also constituted by two other strands: it is 'enigmatic' and 'poignant'. The experience of sexuality is 'enigmatic' because it is inevitably about a sense of wonder and fascination for the other traceable to the fantasy of re-finding the (originally and perennially) lost object of desire. It is 'poignant' as it evokes an involuntary arousal for the object of your desire and helplessness before the one whose object of desire you seek to be. These two strands make sexuality compellingly excessive in as much as it is an encounter with one's helplessness which is potentially destructive of the self as well as the other. It is on account of this psychoanalytic insight that Tellis has little time for pro-sex narratives of emancipatory sexuality. In his words, '[sexuality's] excess is not one that we can easily celebrate. It is an excess that often forces us into position we can't get out of, brings out *ressentiment,* sends us scuttling into corners we do not want to creep out of' (Tellis, 2018, p. 177).

What I am arguing is that the sexual in law as well as feminist debates in India has remained largely under-theorised because it is premised on a simplistic account of our psychic lives. Sexuality is always psychosexuality, and it is this account that needs to inform the subject of both law and feminism. The sexual can neither be reduced to a simple understanding of pleasure nor can it be singularly associated with revulsion and violence. Pleasure and violence, fascination and repression co-constitute sexual desire (Freud, 2002). There is an element of disgust in desire, as disgust is not singularly a sign of repression but also fascination: 'disgust is a sure sign of repression [...] we manifest outright disgust – as opposed to simple disinterest or avoidance – at the very things that interested us most, prior to repression' (Fink, 2016, p. 17). In Freudian psychoanalysis, the emotion of disgust is a part of human evolutionary history. The history of upright walking shows how human beings have distanced themselves from animals. In raising the nose high up and away from genitilia, human beings marked their distance from the animal world of excretion, smells and sexuality. While the reminders of our animality are repressed for the sake of civilisation through a learned disgust (young children are fascinated with urine and excreta, which they later go on to find disgusting), there remains an uneasy attraction and fascination towards these objects. This is the nature of the sexual: disgust for sexual arousal exists alongside a strong attraction for the (repressed) sexual.

There is 'something amiss' (Rose, 2017) about the legal as well as feminist accounts in their political self-assuredness of the sexual. 'A fundamental thesis of Lacanian psychoanalysis', writes Jeanne Schroeder (2008, p. 4), 'is that the subject is split – castrated, negative, empty and alienated'. In Lacan, the recognition of 'lack'/absence originates in the mirror-stage where the child recognises the lack of the mother who may gratify her needs. This lack, in Lacan, of the (m)other is constitutive of human subjectivity and is the basis for desire. As Elizabeth Grosz puts it: '[f]or Lacan, desire is always marked by the desire of the Other. It is an ontological lack that ensures the separation of the subject from the immediacy of its natural and social environment, and the impulse of that subject to fill in this space through, in the first instance, the desire of the (m)other; and in the second, through its axis to language and systems of meaning' (1989, p. xvi; also see, Grosz, 1990, pp. pp. 31–35). Thus, sexuality, haunted by the Lacanian axiom 'there is no such thing as a sexual relationship' (*Il n'y a pas de rapport sexuel*)[18] is an impossible negotiation of an incommensurate two of sexual difference. Rose explains:

> Sexuality belongs in this area of *instability* played out in the register of demand and *desire*, each sex coming to stand, mythically and exclusively, for that which could satisfy and complete the other. It is when the categories 'male' and 'female' are seen to represent an absolute and complementary division that they fall prey to a mystification in which the difficulty of sexuality instantly disappears [...] Lacan therefore, argued that psychoanalysis should not try to produce 'male' and 'female' as complementary entities, sure of each other and of their own identity, but should expose the fantasy on which this notion rests.
>
> (1985, p. 33)

Psychoanalytically, desire is not the same as pleasure as desire can never be met with complete satisfaction. It is a realm of ultimate fantasy where '[t]he Other appears to hold the 'truth' of the subject and the power to make good its loss' (Rose, 1985, p. 33). Imbued within desire which will forever remain unrealised, it is an experience of vulnerability and helplessness which brings to it the potential of destruction. A realm of uncertainties and precariousness, it is a 'disruptive, excessive reality and experience' (Rose, 2021, p. 124) where guilt, horror, disgust co-exist with fascination, attraction and desire of the other.

The sexual is never settled, fully assumed and fixed. It is precarious, works at the level of fantasy, 'at the level of the unconscious precisely because it is a question which is never quite settled, a story which can never be brought to a close' (Rose, 1984, p. 4). Any notion of sexuality (feminist or legal) which fails to account for desire will remain steadfast to identity politics of masculine, feminine and now LGBTQ+ identities (Tellis, 2018). In contrast, the insight,

18 For Lacan, 'it [i.e. the sexual relationship or the sexual of the relationship] is based only on the written in the sense that the sexual relationship cannot be written (*ne peut pas s'écrire*). Everything that is written stems from the fact that it will forever be impossible to write, as such, the sexual relationship' (Lacan, 1998, pp. 34–35).

that sexuality is not the 'truth' of the subject but structured around a fantasy, is crucial for feminism and critical scholarship on law as it strengthens the goal of progressive change as well as contests the heteronormativity of the law. For if, masculine and feminine are not fixed, stable categories but signifiers subject to change, 'the system of masculine identity will always fail in its cohesiveness because it depends on the fantasy object' (Cornell, 1995, p. 159). The category 'cis' used by trans people to mark those whose sex and gender identities match and they are settled about their sexuality would itself be destabilised. As Rose reminds us, yet again (2021, p. 108):

> For psychoanalysis, it is axiomatic, however clear you are in your own mind about being a man or a woman, that the unconscious knows better [...] Freud once stated that, given a primary universal bisexuality, sex is an act involving at least four people. The 'cis' – i.e. non-trans – woman or man is a decoy, the outcome of multiple repressions whose unlived stories surface nightly in our dreams. From the Latin root meaning 'on this side of', as opposed to 'across from', 'cis' is generally conflated with normativity, implying 'comfortable in your skin', as if that were the beginning and end of the matter.

Quickly returning to the question of pornography. How do we talk (to our students and our peers) about porn then? It certainly cannot be on the model presented by Srinivasan! Taking seriously Srinivasan's argument – that porn 'bypass[es] that part of us which pauses, considers, thinks', means we are pushed back into the same frame of body-mind dualism which feminists have been critiquing for years now (Fausto-Sterling, 2000). But more acutely we end up mirroring the pornographic world where the man becomes his penis, and he cannot help it. This would be too simplistic a reading of pornography. If the cause-effect relation is true, then all men should identify with pornographic imaginary and all men should act out violently after watching pornography. But this is not so. Psychoanalytic understanding of the sexual – that sexuality works at the level of fantasy and the unconscious – also contests this cause-effect relationship drawn between pornography and violence by sexual conservatives as well as sex-negative anti-pornography feminists. Thus, Cornell, critiquing the 'behavioristic analysis of the structures of desire' (1995, p. 100), had argued for a different discourse where we re-read the script of pornography differently and explore the 'temptation of pornography'.

True, that masculine identification with the male actor is because porn depicts what men desire. But it is not a straightforward expression of desire to exert sexual power over women. Desire always operates at the level of fantasy and therefore the question is what unconscious fantasy is enacted in porn. Thus, Cornell contends that 'mainstream heterosexual pornography does not communicate an idea as much as it graphically portrays an unconscious scene of rigid gender identities played out in explicit sex acts' (1995, p. 100). It 'communicates an unconscious fantasy scene [...] an unconscious mirroring through imagistic signifiers of a repressed phantasmatic structure' (1995, p. 139). While MacKinnon/Srinivasan's contention is that pornography speaks to the penis, which then becomes a weapon against the woman, in psychoanalytic accounts, porn speaks not to the penis, but the unconscious. Pornography is a graphic, more explicit expression of the fantasy that underpins (hetero)sexuality. Instead of male power, pornography presents the image of masculine insecurity about who men are supposed to be and the gap therein:[19]

> it is what some men need to feed their fantasy that there is a compensation for a primary narcissistic wound. It is out of anxiety, and the inability of some men to successfully negotiate their anxiety, that they need to reassure themselves that they have taken up the position of the one who controls the Mother/Other. It is the terror of women that makes the pornographic message arousing to some men because it assuages the fear that has also become the basis their sexuality.
>
> (Cornell, 1995, pp. 142–143)[20]

Implications for criminal law

I have argued that the sex-negative/sex-positive positions of feminism offer no theoretical insights that can complicate the legal construction of sexualities. In fact, sex-negative and sex-positive frames reify the victim-agent binary: the subject is either a victim (of the masculine (state) power) or a transgressive celebrating agent of desire. But sexual subjectivity occupies a liminal position of in-betweenness – of pleasure in violence and violence in pleasure (Dhar, 2017).[21]

19 Cornell's argument is not *status quoist* in terms of letting pornographic depictions continue. Cornell concedes that pornographic images especially if they portray violence against women and reduce women to objects, have degrading impact on women's bodily integrity as well as *the way they imagine themselves*. She argued for imposition of 'zoning' regulations (which look almost impossible in the internet age) but they should not be imposed because sexually explicit material is obscene and disgusting or because it will cause violence but in order to protect *the imaginary domain of women* so that women can invent new images to re-imagine their sex within the Symbolic.

20 Also, see Angela Carter (1978) who argues that there is a progressive aspect of pornography which makes pornography a 'friend' to women, as masculine imaginary about the sexual relationship is depicted in its most explicit form.

21 Dhar (2017) contends that 'one needs to rethink the premise of sexual libertinism and the liberation thesis through the expansion of the pornographic imagination' for there appears to be 'a constant shadow of violence on the sexual'. He argues that the inevitability of violence in pleasure is on account of, what Lacan famously called, the impossibility of the sexual relationship. Therefore, the feminist struggle for erotic justice needs to move away from the paradigm of sexual libertinism and look for other supplements (other than violence) to fill the lack that haunts the sexual relationship. While Dhar wonders if *love* can be that supplement – 'to see

In other words, sexuality is neither a zone of pure violence (with women as eternal victims and men as perpetrators) nor is it normatively progressive. To counter sex-negative law/feminism, many feminists had embraced a sex-positive position but without grounding it in a theory of sexuality which takes *desire* seriously. This was bound to backfire as it did during #metoo when many young women in sharing their sexual experiences wondered if sex positivity had left them more vulnerable (Sharma, 2018; Hinsliff, 2022).

It is my argument that in the absence of a nuanced (psychoanalytic) understanding of the sexual, the law will never be able to adequately and meaningfully respond to the questions around sexuality. The question of child sexuality in Indian law is one such issue which I address in Chapter 6. The question of child sexual desire is muted in not just the discourse of 'best interest of the child' or 'save our children' as advanced by child right activists (Kumari, 2013a; Kumari, 2013b), but also sex-positive feminists (Agnes, 2012). The regulatory sex laws of our culture – increase in the age of consent, the enactment of Protection of Children from Sexual Offences Act, 2012 ('POCSO') with eighteen as the age of sexual consent – completely erase the question of child sexuality.[22] The figure of the child becomes the medium though adult anxieties and cruelties creep into the law.

Consider, for instance, *Supreme Court Women Lawyers Association (SCWLA)* v. *Union of India*[23] where the Supreme Court Women Lawyers Association (SCWLA) petitioned the Supreme Court under article 32 of the Constitution of India for propounding chemical castration as an additional punishment for sexual abuse of the girl child. Aware that the court cannot create a punishment, the women lawyers association sought the court to 'give a suggestion so that the legislature can appositely respond to the collective cry' (para 2). They argued that even though there was a provision to punish rape on a woman who is under sixteen years of age but it was not sufficient as there are many instances where 'tender angelic girls' (para 2) are raped. Therefore, a specific provision for imposing higher and more severe punishment was required. The term 'child', according to the petitioners, needed to be defined and distinguished from a woman below 16 years. The point was that a woman below 16 years is a minor 'but a child, though a minor, may stand in a different category' (para 12). This distinction was argued on the basis that the girl child has no idea about sex or rape, and thus the assault on her is a brutal nightmare. The state, on the other hand, argued that their suggestion 'is more out of passion rather than rational deliberation' (para 4).

The court saw merit in petitioners' arguments and emphasised 'the situation that has emerged compels one to rethink' (para 12). The court also observed

the world from the point of view of *two* rather than *one*' – one cannot sideline the history of the work of love as the reproduction of femininity (Ahmed, 2004, pp. 122–143).

22 These laws do not necessary lead to a culture that is sensitive to the voice of the child, in fact, quite the opposite. See, for example, the chapter on child witness in rape cases in Baxi, 2013.

23 (2016) 3 SCC 680.

that the crimes committed on girl children have no nexus with the economic status of the perpetrator, it rather may have a nexus with 'neurotic behavior' (para 12). The perpetrators, in the court's opinion are 'psychologically and possibly psychographically perverted culprits' (para 1). Conceding that the court cannot prescribe punishment, it urged the legislature to reflect on the issue: 'There can be no doubt that a girl child is a minor but may be a time has come where a distinction can be drawn between the girl children and the minor, may be by fixing the upper limit at ten for the girl children. We are disposed to think so as by that age, a child, a glorious gift to mankind, cannot conceive of any kind of carnal desire in man. Once she becomes a victim of such a crime, there is disastrous effect on her mind. The mental agony lasts long. Sorrow and fear haunt forever. There is need to take steps for stopping this kind of child abuse and hence, possibly there is a need for defining the term "child" in the context of rape and thereafter provide for more severe punishment in respect of the culprits who are involved in this type of crime. In the light of the said decision, we part with the suggestion with the fond hope that Parliament would respond to the agony of the collective, for it really deserves consideration' (para 14).

Significantly, the Criminal Law (Amendment) Act, 2018 provided for stricter punishments for rape on a woman under sixteen years (section 376(3) of the IPC providing mandatory minimum punishment for twenty years which may extend to life imprisonment) and a girl under twelve years (section 376AB of the IPC providing mandatory minimum punishment for twenty years which may extend to life imprisonment or death) respectively. Section 65 of BNS has retained these provisions.

Significantly, concerns around child sexual assault get embroiled with disgust at the very idea of child sexuality. Rose diagnoses adult disgust at child sexuality and claims that such a disavowal only reveals our (adult) own sexual anxieties: '[t]he child is sexual, but its sexuality (bisexual, polymorphous, perverse) *threatens our own at its very roots. Setting up the child as innocent, is not, therefore, repressing its sexuality – it is above all holding off any possible challenge to our own*' (Rose, 1984, p. 4, emphasis mine). Recognition of child's polymorphous and perverse sexuality dismantles all myths of (adult) sexuality that is comfortable in its own skin. I will take up the issues of child sexuality and listening to the child in Chapter 6.

In the legal realm of sexual consent, the adult, in opposition to the child, is constructed as all-knowing with no opacity about her sexual desire. But as Judith Butler reminds us, 'in the time of psyche, childhood does not precisely end at a certain age; it continues to act, time and again, throughout the course of adult life' (Butler, 2011–2012, p. 19). We never become fully mature so as to freely choose and decide upon the unknowable and unconscious aspects of our desire. Writing on sexual consent, psychoanalysis and law, Judith Butler shows how the question of child sexuality not just puts the very idea of categorical and clear consent into question but also exposes the 'fantasy of the liberal subject, the perspicacious and choosing "I"' (Butler, 2011–2012, p. 23). This question of sexual consent is my focus in Chapter 5.

Bringing psychoanalysis into a dialogue with the law will compel us to recognise and acknowledge the complexity of the sexual rather than rushing to paper over its cracks, contradictions and precarity. We will not so easily give in to the myth of abstract liberal individualism. No doubt this acknowledgment can threaten the very foundations of the legal order that continues to preserve the fantasy of the subject-in-control and the realm of the sexual as fully knowable. But, at the same time, it will inaugurate new and compelling directions for the existing legal discourse on sexuality.

Summing up

This chapter explored the limits of imagination with respect to the sexual within the law as well as feminist movement in India. In the legal understanding, the sexual is an excess that needs to be tamed, checked, regulated. The sexual is connected to corrupting arousal or lasciviousness which if left unchecked would either lead to violence or corrupt the moral fabric of society. Such reductionist view of sexuality not only forecloses any imagination of non-heteronormative alternative sexualities but also remains encrypted in pre-Freudian mind-body duality (where sexuality is confined to biology and anatomy). In this view, given its fixity and innateness, there is no possibility of shifting the Symbolic that constitutes the sexual in its conservativeness and in a normalised manner.

Sex-negative feminists end up aligning with the law in seeking legal regulation of the sexual (imagery/pornography) which they believe leads to violence against women. For sex-positive feminists, sexuality being the realm of pleasure offers a carnivalesque escape from the rigidity of the Symbolic. I have argued that both these positions, in as much as they conceptualise the sexual as knowable and transparent, are based on reductionist accounts of the sexual (Lacan, 2006; Mitchell, 2000). Disgust and revulsion are a crucial part of desire and psychoanalysis makes us aware of their proximity in the constitution of the sexual. We, therefore, need a complex theory of the sexual which recognises the precariousness of our sexual lives where we crave for destruction in helplessness and violence in love. This traumatic configuration that marks the sexual, its optimistic negativity (Berlant & Edelman, 2014) that draws us into cycles of repetitions needs a feminism, neither radical nor carnivalesque, but one that is 'capable of imagining what we are in the process of becoming' (Tellis, 2003; Mitchell, 1984). For this, first and foremost, we need to begin the psychic labour of defamiliarising the sexual.

References

Agnes, F. (2006). Indecent Representation of Women. In B. Bose (Ed.), *Gender and Censorship*. Kali for Women.

Agnes, F. (2012). Consent and controversy. *Indian Express*. http://indianexpress.com/article/opinion/columns/consent-andcontroversy.

Ahmed, S. (2004). *The cultural politics of emotion*. Routledge.

Ali, S. A. (2013a). Mumbai gang rape: Accused forced victim to watch porn clip on cell. http://zeenews.india.com/news/maharashtra/mumbai-gang-rape-accused-forced-victim-to-watch-porn-clip-on-cell_873740.html.

Ali, S. A. (2013b, September 2). Mumbai gang rape: Three accused watched porn regularly, cops say. http://timesofindia.indiatimes.com/city/mumbai/Mumbai-gang-rape-Three-accused-watched-porn-regularly-Cops/articleshow_b2/22218702.cms?prtpage=1.

Barstow, D. (2015, August 3). India Blocks 857 Pornography Websites, Defying Supreme Court Decision. *The New York Times*.

Baxi, P. (2014). *Public Secrets of Law: Rape Trials in India*. Oxford University Press.

Berlant, L. & Edelman, L. (2014). *Sex, or the Unbearable*. London: Duke University Press.

Butler, J. (2011–2012). Sexual consent: Some thoughts on psychoanalysis and law. *Columbia Journal of Gender and the Law*, 21(2), 3–14.

Butler, J. (2015). Ideologies of the Super-Ego: Psychoanalysis and Feminism, Revisited. In R. Duschinsky & S. Walker (Eds), *Juliet Mitchell and the Lateral Axis: Twenty-First-Century Psychoanalysis and Feminism*. Palgrave Macmillan.

Carter, A. (1978). *The Sadeian Woman and the Ideology of Pornography*. Pantheon Books.

Chatterjee, P. (2003). The Nationalist Resolution of the Woman's Question. In K. Sangari & S. Vaid (Eds), *Recasting Women: Essays in Colonial History*. New Delhi: Zubaan.

Cornell, D. (1995). *The Imaginary Domain: Abortion, Pornography and Sexual Violence*. Routledge.

Dhar, A (2017). What if, there is violence in pleasure. *Seminar*, 691. www.india-seminar.com/2017/691/691_anup_dhar.htm.

Dworkin, A. (1985). Against the Male Flood: Censorship, Pornography and Equality. *Harvard Women's Law Journal*, 8, 1.

Dworkin, A., & MacKinnon, C. (1988). *Pornography and Civil Rights: A New Day for Women's Equality*. Minneapolis, MN: Organizing Against Pornography.

Fausto-Sterling, A. (2000). *Sexing the Body: Gender Politics and the Construction of Sexuality*. Basic Books.

Fink, B. (2016). *Lacan on love: An exploration of Lacan's Seminar VIII, Transference*. Polity Press.

Finlayson, L. (2018). Can the law be feminist?. *London Review of Books*, 40, 2.

Freud, S. (2002). *Civilization and its discontents*. London: Penguin Classics.

Gandhi, N. (1990). Indecent representation of Women (Protection Act), 1986: An analysis. *CBI Bulletin*, 16–20 (April).

Ghosh, S. (1999). The Troubled Existence of Sex and Sexuality: Feminists Engage with Censorship. In C. Brosius & M. Butcher (Eds), *Image Journeys: Audio Visual Media and Cultural Change in India*. Sage Publications: New Delhi.

Grosz, E. (1989). *Sexual subversions: Three French feminists*. Allen & Unwin Pvt.

Grosz, E. (1990). *Jacques Lacan: A Feminist Introduction*. London: Routledge.

Halley, J., Kotiswaran, P., Rebouche, R. & Shamir, H. (2018). *Governance feminism: An introduction*. University of Minnesota Press.

Hariharan, G. (2014). Our unchained Sexual Selves: A Case for the Liberty to Enjoy Pornography Privately. *NUJS Law Review*, 7, 90.

Hinsliff, G. (2022) 'It stopped me having sex for a year': why Generation Z is turning its back on sex-positive feminism. www.theguardian.com/lifeandstyle/2022/feb/02/it-stopped-me-having-sex-for-a-year-why-generation-z-is-turning-its-back-on-sex-positive-feminism.

India Today (2013). Is watching porn increasing rapes in India?. http://indiatoday.intoday.in/video/is-watching-porn-increasing-rapes-in-india/1/267139.html.

Jaising, I. (1986, October). Obscenity: The Use and Abuse of the Law. *The Lawyers*.

Jaising, I. (2006). Obscenity: The use and abuse of the law. In B. Bose (Ed.), *Gender and censorship*. New Delhi: Kali for Women.

Jaising, I. & Wolfe, A. (2006). The 'Ignoble Servility' of Pati Parmeshwar: Towards Equality for Women. In B. Bose (Ed.), *Gender and Censorship*. Kali for Women.

John, M. E. (2016). This attack on Nivedita Menon. *The Hindu*. www.thehindu.com/opinion/op-ed/This-attack-on-Nivedita-Menon/article14158131.ece.

Kapur, R. (1996). Who Draws the Line? Feminist Reflections on Speech and Censorship. *Economic & Political Weekly*, 31(16/17), WS15–WS19+WS21–WS23 (April 20–27).

Kapur, R. (2000). Law and the Sexual Subaltern: A Comparative Perspective. *Clev. St. L. Rev.*, 48, 15.

Kapur, R. (2001). Sexcapades and the law. *Seminar*, 505. www.india-seminar.com/2001/505/505%20ratna%20kapur.htm.

Kapur, R. (2005). *Erotic Justice: Law and the New Politics of Postcolonialism*. Permanent Black.

Kapur, R. (2007). The Prurient Postcolonial: The Legal Regulation of Sexual Speech. In B. Bose & S. Bhattacharyya (Eds.), *The Phobic and the Erotic: The Politics of Sexualities in Contemporary India*. Seagull Books.

Khanna, M. (2017). Too much exposure to pornography to blame for cases of rape by teens. www.tribuneindia.com/news/ludhiana/too-much-exposure-to-pornography-to-blame-for-cases-of-rape-by-teens/209431.html.

Kishwar, M. & Vanita, R. (2006). Using Women as A Pretext For Repression — The Indecent Representation Of Women (Prohibition) Bill. In B. Bose (Ed.), *Gender and Censorship*. Kali for Women.

Kumari, V. (2013a, April 19). Betraying a Third Way. *The Hindu*. www.thehindu.com/todays-paper/tp-opinion/betraying-the-third-way/article4632046.ece.

Kumari, V. (2013b). Submissions to Justice Verma Committee. http://feministlawarchives.pldindia.org/wp-content/uploads/submissions-by-ved-kumari.pdf.

Lacan, J. (1998). *On feminine sexuality: The limits of love and knowledge (Encore The Seminar of Jacques Lacan)* (J. A. Miller, Ed., & B. Fink, Trans.). W.W. Norton & Company.

Lacan, J. (2006). *Écrits* (B. Fink, Trans.). W.W. Norton & Company.

MacKinnon, C. A. (1985). Pornography, Civil Rights and Speech. *Harvard Civil Rights-Civil Liberties Law Review*, 20, 1.

MacKinnon, C. A. (1993). *Only Words*. Harvard University Press.

Manushi (n.d.). Face to Face: Interaction Between the Media and the Movement. www.ced.org.in/docs/ced/publications/Mirror-Image/chapter-4-face-to-face.pdf.

Math, S. B., Viswanath, B., Maroky, A. S., Kumar, N. C., Cherian, A. V. & Nirmala, M. C. (2014). Sexual Crime in India: Is it influenced by Pornography? *Indian Journal of Psychological Medicine*, 36(2), 147.

Menon, N. (2000). Embodying the Self: Feminism, Sexual Violence and the Law. In P. Chatterjee & P. Jeganathan (Eds), *Community, Gender and Violence: Subaltern Studies* XI. Delhi: Permanent Black.

Menon, N. (2015). Indian feminists, 'India's daughter', and sexual violence: The issues at stake. https://kafila.online/2015/03/08/indian-feminists-indias-daughter-and-sexual-violence-the-issues-at-stake.

Mitchell, J. (1984). Women, femininity, narrative. In J. Mitchell, *Women: The longest revolution: Essays on feminism, literature and psychoanalysis*. Virago Press.

Mitchell, J. (2000). *Psychoanalysis and feminism: A radical reassessment of Freudian psychoanalysis*. Basic Books.

Mitchell, J. (2008). *Siblings: Sex and Violence*. Polity Press.

Mitchell, J. (2015). Debating Sexual Difference, Politics, and the Unconscious: With Discussant Section by Jacqueline Rose. In R. Duschinsky & S. Walker (Eds), *Juliet Mitchell and the Lateral Axis: Twenty-First-Century Psychoanalysis and Feminism*. Palgrave Macmillan.

Nair, V. H. (2017). Fed up of porn, class 12 student knocks on Supreme Court's doors. http://indiatoday.intoday.in/story/fed-up-of-pornography-boy-moves-supreme-court/1/950900.html.

Nussbaum, M. C. (2004). *From Disgust to Humanity: Sexual Orientation and Constitutional Law*. Oxford University Press.

Rose, J. (1984). *The Case of Peter Pan or the Impossibility of Children's Fiction*. University of Pennsylvania Press.

Rose, J. (1985). Introduction – II. In J. Mitchell & J. Rose (Eds), *Feminine sexuality: Jacques Lacan and the école freudienne*. Pantheon Books.

Rose, J. (2016). Feminism and the abomination of violence. *Cultural Critique*, 94, 7–36.

Rose, J. (2017). Something Amiss. In E. Watson & N. Giffney (Eds), *Clinical Encounters in Sexuality: Psychoanalytic Practice and Queer Theory*. Punctum Books.

Rose, J. (2021). *On Violence and On Violence Against Women*. Faber & Faber.

Roy, K. (1996). Unravelling the Kāmasūtra. *Indian Journal of Gender Studies*, 3(2), 155.

Rubin, G. (1984). Thinking sex: Notes for a radical theory of the politics of sexuality. In C. Vance (Ed.), *Pleasure and danger: Exploring female sexuality*. Routledge and Kegan Paul.

Sangari, K. (1999). *Politics of the Possible: Essays on Gender, History, Narratives, Colonial English*. Anthem.

Schroeder, J. L. (2008). *The four Lacanian discourses: Or turning law inside out*. Taylor & Francis.

Sharma, K. (2018, Nov. 17). #MeToo: Understanding consent and sex-positivity in a patriarchal society. *Firstpost*. www.firstpost.com/long-reads/metoo-understanding-consent-and-sex-positivity-in-a-patriarchal-society-5535191.html.

Singh, A. K. (2016). India's sick interest in rape porn is dehumanising. www.dailyo.in/politics/rape-porn-uttar-pradesh-bulandshahr-akhilesh-yadav-voyeurism-nirbhaya/story/1/12192.html.

Srinivasan, A. (2021). *The Right to Sex: Feminism in the Twenty-First Century*. Farrar, Straus and Giroux.

Stein, R. (2008). The Otherness of Sexuality: Excess. *Journal of the American Psychoanalytic Association*, 56(1), 43–71.

Tellis, A. (2003). Ways of becoming. *Seminar*, 524. www.india-seminar.com/2003/524/524%20ashley%20tellis.htm.

Tellis, A. (2018). Men in Feminism: LGBT and Feminist Entanglements over Masculinity. In R. Chowdhury & Z. al Baset (Eds), *Men and Feminism in India.* Routledge.

Tellis, A. (2021). Lack of Honest Toil. *Seminar,* 721. www.india-seminar.com/2019/721/721_ashley_tellis.htm.

Upadhyaya, S.C. (1961). *Kāmasūtra of Vātsyāyana* (transl.). Bombay: Taraporevala.

Vashist, L. (2014). Law and the obscene image: Reading Aveek Sarkar v. State of West Bengal. *Journal of Indian Law and Society,* 5, 248–272.

Vashist, L. (2022). Disgust for the sexual: the emotional side of obscenity law in India. *Oxford University Commonwealth Law Journal,* 22(2), 150–176.

Chapter 5

Theorising Sexual Consent

Consent, perennially, is the zone of feelings and emotions. Meaning 'agreement to do something' or 'permission for something to happen', it is derived from the Latin word 'consentire'. Consentire comes from con- ('together') and sentiō ('sense; perceive; feel') and means 'feel together'. The emotive root of consent – the feeling of togetherness – is repressed in the positivist evocations of the legal register. This is symptomatic of the erasure of the sensual and the affective in the construction of the edifice of law's Reason governed by assumptions of reasonableness, sanity, maturity, adulthood. In the meeting of minds (*consensus ad idem*), the heart is nearly wiped out.

Consent in law seeks to speak about, and bring justice to violated intimate relationalities, but without acknowledging that '[i]ntimate encounters give rise to feelings and emotions which are often not in the realm of the conscious' (Kaul, 2023, p. 7). What would an acknowledgment of (unconscious) feelings and emotions do to the conception of sexual consent in law? What would consent in law begin to look like if we bring back the dimension of 'feeling' and put it into an unhurried conversation with the juridical left-over which unfortunately has come to predominate all socio-legal conceptions of sexual intimacy? Will we get an alternate theory of sexual consent? These are some of the questions that I will stay with in this chapter.

Law is a normative political project with definite and prescriptive aims. Specifically, the domain of criminal law, an emissary of the state, is required to be determinate, not vague or overbreadth. Psychoanalysis, on the other hand, is the domain of desire which by definition is unbounded, uncontainable and excessive. Can law and psychoanalysis – strange bedfellows – ever be in bed with each other? Is this intercourse, between law (consent) and psychoanalysis (desire), possible? Is it even desire-able for the subject of law who holds on to juridical consent as a consolation in lieu of dignity, equality and freedom? I will argue that this impossible conversation between consent and desire is not only possible and desirable but also necessary for a theory of sexual consent which is based on a truer account of our sexual lives.

In doing so, i.e. entering the world of psychoanalytic consent, I will insist that we can neither abandon the field of law, nor the concept of consent, even

DOI: 10.4324/9781003387411-6

as psychoanalysis completely turns law upside-down and inside-out. We need to stay with the law when it comes to sexuality as the 'law enters the most intimate dimensions of human experience and implicitly organizes what can be thought, what can be felt, and what can be done or imagined' (Clark, 2019, p. 279). However, as I have stated before, this invariably will be an alternate account of the law. Law is normative and performs a pedagogic function, but it is amply clear that the legal script is not just of one determinism and positivism. It is both a discursive and affective realm: it affects and is affected by its subjects. There is also an 'other scene' of law, the legal unconscious, where the question of the desire of the subject is/can/ought to be accounted for.

I remain aware that the register of psychoanalysis offers no easy resolutions, yet my desire is to work towards a disciplinary friendship between the sexual and the legal that allows for what Christopher Bollas, in a different context, has called the 'psychic contrapuntal'. Contrapuntal, Edward Said's musical gift for reading literary texts, calls for reading with 'an awareness of simultaneous dimensions' where you enter and traverse a new environment against the memory of the older one (Said, 2001, p. 186). Said's emphasis was on reading 'to include what was once forcibly excluded' (Said, 1994, pp. 66–67). Bollas' proposal of a psychic contrapuntal 'recognizes the benefit of a movement outside of one's primary place, to a new location from which the self, and its others, are seen in a different light' (Bollas, 2014, p. 8). What for Bollas is an ethical-empathic psychic move – 'we may all be exiles of a sort' – I take as a proposal for engaging in inter-disciplinary work, leaving original attachments to our own discipline and moving to new avenues and vistas, where meaning takes form in the contrapuntal play of memory and stability of the old, and excitement and risks unfolded in the encounter with the new.

The chapter begins with an outline of the juridical model of sexual consent, focusing on the definition of consent in section 375 of the IPC/section 63 of BNS. I will then show how the feminist critique of consent aligns with the psychoanalytic critique, resulting in a mutual abandonment of the very concept of consent by both feminists and psychoanalysts. Against these critiques, I would argue that we need to hold on to the concept of consent, but turn it inside-out. Drawing from the psychoanalytic notion of consent, I will prepare the canvas, so that gradually we can draw a sketch of psycho-legal consent.

Sexual consent: the register of penal law

Consent in Indian law was explicitly defined in the provision of rape through the Criminal Law Amendment Act of 2013. Let me extract the exact legislative vocabulary which belaboured to define consent:

> Consent means an unequivocal voluntary agreement when the woman by words, gestures, or any form of verbal or non-verbal communication, communicates willingness to participate in the specific sexual act:

> Provided that a woman who does not physically resist to the act of penetration shall not by the reason only of that fact, be regarded as consenting to the sexual activity.

This definition tells us *what* consent is and *how* it is (to be) communicated. Contrast this with section 74 of the UK Sexual Offences Act, 2003, which says 'a person consents if he *agrees by choice*, and has *the freedom* and *capacity* to make that choice'. Here, the focus is on both what is consent (agreement by choice) but also equally on *when* can a person consent (only when the person has freedom and capacity to consent). The UK's model is close to what Vanessa Munro has called the 'consent plus model' (Munro, 2017) which requires 'procedural insistence on critical reflection about the reasons that underpin, constrain, construct, and motivate our choices' (p. 950). Here, willingness to participate in the sexual act cannot be assessed from the standpoint of an abstract individual and the (liberal) notions of agency and free choice. Instead, willingness will be discerned by examining 'the concrete context in which that choice is framed, selected, and then acted upon' (p. 951). In her later work, Munro (2017) also warned that 'the turn to context has increased space for discourses grounded in amorphous notions of 'vulnerability' and 'exploitation'' (2017, p. 420), which tied to protectionist and surveillance policies of the state 'can be deployed to responsibilize and discipline women' (p. 426). Taking Munro's position as a take-off point beyond the impasse of liberal individualism and structural determinacy, elsewhere I had suggested that 2013 amendment in rape law offers interpretive possibilities such that the judicial enquiry on consent is not totally devoid of the 'concrete context'. To be specific, the amendment opens a space for concrete, grounded and relational idea of sexual consent, ensuring that the woman had the time and space to form and communicate her consent (Vashist, 2020a). Building on this argument, I will shift towards the register of psychoanalysis to explore how the dominant meanings attributed by the consent regime continue to make presumptions which, more often than not, are radically far from the truths of our mental and sexual lives.

But first, let me dig into the essential ingredients of 'consent', the keywords. 'Unequivocal' imposes the requirement of clarity and unambiguity which should leave no doubt whatsoever that the sexual act is desired. While 'voluntary' points towards spontaneity of choice and freedom, 'willingness' – from the word 'will' which refers to the faculty of conscious action which shapes our choices – implies the readiness for sex. Imagining consent as an 'agreement' presumes a harmony or coming together of the individuals with respect to this issue. By couching consent in these terms, the intention of the drafters may have been to ensure that the man does not act on ambiguous expressions of willingness, but in practice, the courts have completely slid over these expressions.[1]

1 The judicial reasoning in both *Mahmud Faruqui* (MANU/DE/2901/2017) and *Tarun Tejpal* (Sessions court of Goa) (Sessions Case (Ors) No. 10/2014) reveals how the

The reason for this is not (just) because judiciary is sexist or misogynistic. There is also something about the nature of the sexual – it is unbound and equivocal – that escapes the law. All the terms – 'agreement', 'communication', 'willingness', 'participate' – that make-up the legal meaning of consent (re) institute the legal subject as one in complete control of her desire. But as I have strived to show in this book, the subject, who is always a sexual subject (Mitchell, 1985; Rose, 1985), is a 'subject of desire' who does not have a transparent access to her inner world. Our desire always exceeds us.

Consent, as defined in law, falls squarely within the realm of that which is conscious – articulable, communicable, comprehensible. This legal concept, perhaps like no other, squarely captures the absurdity of the insistent legal desire for clarity and certainty in the world of sexuality which is inherently one of psychic conflict. Sexual experiences are rarely contingent on verbalising one's desire.[2] We rarely ask: may I play with your hair, may I fiddle with the tips of your fingers, now can I kiss you on your mouth, oh! when can I undress you? In the realm of the sexual, consent-seeking and consent-giving speech can disrupt desire, and in fact, sound absurd, comical, or even repulsive. Sexual desire *needs* fantasy, not a script. That is why the legal register, in its existing form of juridical consent, is incapable of holding sexual desire.

But before I turn to the register of psychoanalysis, it is important to ask whether this is, at all, a worthwhile endeavour (I wonder what is betrayed about my desire that I keep going back to the question of relevance and worth), especially in the wake of many feminists rejecting the concept of consent altogether as a useful category in sexual encounters.

Consent: an intrinsically unequal concept?

'Consent is a pathetic standard of equal sex for a free people' declares Catherine MacKinnon (2016, p. 465) in her recent proposal for redefining rape and sexual assault. For MacKinnon, the concept of consent 'is inherently an unequal one' (p. 440) because there is an impossibility of free choice between the actor and the acted-upon in conditions of gender inequality. Freedom is contingent on

courts have completely given up on their primary function of interpretation. Decisions about guilt and culpability are based on extraneous, irrelevant and illegal considerations about the conduct and identity of the complainant. Here, the mis-delivery of justice is not because of the mindless application of the black letter of law; it is rather on account of complete judicial amnesia and disregard of both the letter and spirit of the law. Simple said, the courts just forgot to read the law! For a critique of the above decisions, see Baxi, 2016; Baxi, 2021; Satish, 2017; Vashist, 2020a.

2 This is not to erect any false binary between the sexual and the verbal/speech (Zupančič, 2017). It is not to downplay the significations tied to verbalising (in the repetitions that take place within the act itself ('oh no', 'oh God') or as the gateway to one's desire (an excessive joke, for instance). I thank Jibraan Mansoor for helping me articulate this.

equality; one can never be (sexually) free without being (sexually) equal. Rape, she asserts, 'is less a question on unwanted sex than of unequal sex [...] equality not autonomy is its primary issue [...] internal psychology is less determinative of these criminal acts than leveraged external conditions and gendered social behaviors' (p. 436). The ineffectiveness of existing rape law is on account of 'its failure to define the legal reality in terms of the social reality' (p. 439). The social context is one of inequality of sexes, and this inequality serves as the 'context' and 'potential content' of sexual interactions (p. 440). But the legal reality never captures the truth of this social reality because the legal standard of consent is itself based on social inequality of sexes where 'active A initiates, passive B acquiesces in or yields to A's initiatives' (p. 440).

MacKinnon in her characteristic style is asking us to move from 'consent theory' to 'power theory'. While the former focusses on what B has in her mind or what B allows, the latter perspective starts with A and what A does with his power. Focus on power means that the inquiry is how A exercises power over B to get her to do what she does *not* want to do or by manufacturing her desire: '*Why* B came to acquiesce in an act on or in her own body that she did not initiate – including why she would yield her will over intimate self, say, to something she did not really want and never would have chosen without A using his power to impose it on her' (p. 442). Here, certainty of meaning – seduction *as* coercion – and the claim to absolute knowledge about B's 'intimate self' is stunningly blocked from any critical reflection. No doubt these are pressing questions – why one acquiesces in an act that one has not initiated, why does one yield one's will to another – but MacKinnon's conclusions, based on a deterministic account of both sexuality and power (Mitchell & Rose, 1985; Foucault, 1978), are painfully reductive of our sexual lives. It indeed is important to ask what is the meaning of *yielding one's will* and further, whether surrender of will necessarily translates as surrender of one's desire (Saketopoulou, 2019)?

MacKinnon is right that consent, the way it is explored in legal cases, disproportionately focuses on what the alleged victim thought/felt and not on what the accused did. However, even here, despite correct diagnosis, her conclusion is deeply problematic. She writes: 'Consent makes the legal case turn on what the alleged victim was thinking and feeling at the time, or on what she said or did as an expression of what she thought or felt, as if the accused can have said and done exactly the same things – used the same amount of aggression, for example – and the interaction could have been sex, not assault' (2016, p. 453). For MacKinnon, aggression equals assault. But I contend that it *is* possible that 'the accused can have said and done exactly the same things – used the same amount of aggression, for example – and the interaction could have been sex, not assault', *if* there it was done with the approval and desire of the other. In MacKinnon's view, force and aggression *per se* make the encounter unequal/unfree/violent/criminal. If, at all, B consented, it was consent to accept force, and hence no consent at all. But is it impossible to imagine B feeling 'free' in the sexual encounter marked by aggression? Can force be a part of the sexual? In her formulation, one may ask, what is her understanding of the sexual? By setting up such binary oppositions between unwanted/autonomy, unequal/equality, internal psychology/external conditions, does she not collapse the sexual with gendered constructions (Rubin, 1984; Mitchell, 2015; Mitchell, 2008), risking the erasure of the 'internal' dimension of sexual life which is marked by unconscious choices.

MacKinnon's concern is that A's criminality is based on how B felt and not on what A did: 'rape occurs in the mind of B if it was non-consensual, or in the mind of A if he wrongly thought B consented, not by or in or on anyone's body in the world. Few victims confine their injuries to this. With nonconsent as an element, or consent available as a defence, A's criminality turns on how B felt, not on what A did' (2016, p. 453). Such a framing, on the one hand, creates an unequal hierarchy between an objective external world of action and the world of feelings and emotions, on the other, problematically re-institutes the mind-body dichotomy that has characterised rape law such that body was made to speak against mind (Baxi, 2014). Like active and passive, 'A' and 'B' are fixed identity positions, unchangeable, unmalleable, immutable. Apart from the fact that this moulding of sexual life into frames of gendered power caricaturises sexual power, the sexual interaction mirrors the linear terms of contractual transactions of offer-acceptance-agreement.

All hierarchies, for MacKinnon, are inequalities: 'Consent is known to become meaningless in *exceptional* hierarchical settings when acquiescence is the only realistic option. The tabooed question is: when is this not the case' (2016, p. 463, emphasis mine). Then her examples abound: adults/children, prisoners/guards, teachers/students, patients/therapists, lawyers/clients and so on. For her, all these categories are self-evident, clear and conceptually same, as all are situations of hierarchy and unequal power. In a sweeping assertion, in the context of statutory rape, she remarks that age is 'an inequality tantamount [ing] to a form of force' (2016, p. 463); there is no space for any questions or contradictions. Even conservative accounts of law offer a more complicated position of children's agency (see, Law Commission of India, 2023)! One wonders if there is any scope for love, care and respect in hierarchical relationships, say of a parent and child or teacher and student, if inequality *as* aggression is the only standard to assess the nature of hierarchical relationships.

We have reverted to the old dominance feminist claim that in conditions of inequality of power, all sex is rape (MacKinnon, 1987). Conversely, 'when a sexual interaction is equal, consent is not needed and does not occur because there is no transgression to be redeemed' (p. 476). No doubt '[t]he presence of consent does not make an interaction equal' but do we seek equality or freedom in our sexual interactions? What kind and form of equality? What is an equal sexual interaction? Will political, social, economic equality make the sexual interaction equal? Will socio-economic-political equality automatically translate into psychic equality? Do we even crave for equality of sexual desire? Can the structure of desire be moulded exclusively in terms of demand of equality? Isn't there an impossibility of equality with an-other, an impossibility which sustains desire for the other? Of course, these are not MacKinnon's question for she already knows the answers. Is it difficult to understand, even now, why Janet Halley (2006) called for a break from (this) feminism? With Halley and all other feminists who have grown tired of such surety and certainty, I would insist that we need to turn our conclusions into hypothesis (Halley, 2006; Cossman, 2015; Rose, 2021; Saketopoulou, 2023; Franke, 2001). In other words, we need to understand, not presume, the content of equality, as it is this promise of equality of power that is offered to us as a hope for a feminist world.

Therefore, we need to ask: is the desire for inequality, the desire to surrender, to be taken over by the other, necessarily anti-feminist? This is a difficult question for the registers of law and feminism, given both law and feminism are normative political projects. However, repressing this question – shying away from the coordinates of sexual desire – would only give politically correct answers about the experience of sexuality (Žižek, 2018, pp. 150–164; Žižek, 2017, pp. 178–224).

My critique of MacKinnon is not to salvage the concept of consent – not at least in this present juridical formulation. Consent is often burdened with the expectation that it will give 'moral magic to sex' (Heidi, 1996; Fischel, 2019). But it invariably fails to meet this expectation because the consent-question is only mapped out as a 'no' or 'yes' enquiry when it actually demands negotiation with ambiguously articulated nos, yeses and silences. In *Tomorrow Sex Will be Good Again* (2021), Katherine Angel remarkably traverses the difficult terrain of sexual consent to show how saying no is tough, but so is saying yes. Women, socialised 'to care inordinately about men's feelings' (Angel, 2021, p. 7), often find it difficult to say no, and not just in situations where they apprehend male violence. 'Feeble no' is actually 'a cautious no' which, we are aware, does not stand the truth of women's desire in the courtrooms. Saying yes is equally difficult because '[p]leasure, and the right to it, are not equally distributed' (2021, p. 8). Despite the clamour around affirmative consent which is based on the ideal of know and speak out your desire, most women are intuitively aware 'that a woman who exposes herself, in a world that both desires and punishes that impulse, is making herself vulnerable', and thus, 'once a woman is thought to say yes to something, she can say no to nothing' (2021, p. 3). But, akin to MacKinnon, for Angel, the real problem with consent is that it is based on the liberal fantasy which presumes an equality of position, self-determination, and access to sexual pleasure between the parties.

While some may think of affirmative/enthusiastic consent as emancipatory (Baker, 2005; Fischel, 2019), Angel emphasises consent's 'conceit of absolute clarity, places the burden of good sexual intercourse on women's behaviour [...] on their ability to perform a *confident sexual self* in order to ensure that sex is mutually pleasurable and non-coercive' (Angel, emphasis mine). It assumes a confident sexual subject who knows what she wants and can express it clearly. She is assertive, empowered, sex-positive.

At the receiving end of Angel's critique are feminists who in her view advocate, what she calls, 'confidence feminism': feminism that expects women to know what they want and be assertive and confident about its expression. Laura Kipnis (2017), for instance, in her exploration of the implementation of sexual harassment policies in the US universities, finds that when an adult woman says 'yes', taken over by the erotics of (male) power or knowledge, this consent cannot automatically be designated as involuntary on account of power imbalance? Kipnis intends to destabilise fixed notions of power and hierarchy: '[y]outh and attractiveness may also offset the weight of institutional standing and higher degrees; so do calculations about who's more likely to end things first' (Kipnis 2017, p. 94). For her, the inability to say a clear and firm no could be the consequence of 'learned compliance of heterosexual femininity' (Kipnis, 2017, p. 220) and 'female passivity' – where women would not want to own up the consequences of their decisions – rather than pervasive male sexual domination over women.

Angel reads Kipnis as privileging 'a robust self-knowledge about desire, and a capacity for vocal expression of it' (Angel, 2021, p. 13), a feminism which empties out desire of tentativeness, ambivalence and risks. Angel is sceptical about such feminism where it is incumbent on women to be assertive, where woundedness is a sign of weakness and bad sex is a 'brute, intractable fact around which women must work' (2021, p. 18). To be fair to Kipnis, she is not advocating for a confident feminist subject. Her focus was on what she saw as cases of 'retrospective retraction of consent' where a '"Yes" Becomes a "No" Years After the Fact' (Kipnis, 2017, p. 91). In my reading, Kipnis is not seeking to empty the sexual of its tentativeness or risks, her project instead is of shared response-ability in sexual relationality because the capillaries of sexual power offset our fixed notions of who is in control of whom (Žižek, 2018, pp. 150–164). Owning up responsibility about one's decisions (half-baked, even stupid) is what Kipnis is after, it is really not a question of being sure, confident and certain.

Having said that, feminism would emerge as 'dominance' or 'confidence' when it shuts its eyes to the risky and complex premise that sexual desire is. By frantically sanitising desire – by denying its uncertainty and unknowability – in order to make our feminist projects whole, we would only end up deluding ourselves into the fantasy of certainty and safety. For how long, will we refuse to concede that '[a] sexual ethics that is worth its name has to allow for obscurity, for opacity and for not knowing' (Angel, 2021, p. 29)?

Taking the risk, accounting for desire

An ethics of sex ought to be based on a theory of desire that acknowledges and accounts for, what I have elaborated in Chapter 4, the excess of sexual desire. Desire, we know, is precarious, uncertain, opaque, risky and thus, unsettling. How do we incorporate this conception of desire in the law of sexual consent? This is no easy task, as I will show through the work of two feminist thinkers –

Katherine Baker, feminist law professor and Nilofer Kaul, a feminist psychoanalyst – both of whom are important interlocutors, as they acknowledge emotional complexity and ambiguity as constitutive of sexual desire.

Almost 20 ago, Baker, in an essay titled 'Gender and Emotion in Criminal Law' (2005), argued that law needed to account for 'woman's thoughtful uncertainty' in matters of sex (p. 453) rather than reading it as her indifference. Emotional intensity and complexity of sex leaves 'women ambivalent about whether to proceed' and therefore, she argued for a model of affirmative consent in rape law. Affirmative consent, she believed, by placing the burden of understanding and clarifying about women's desire on men would *minimise ambiguity* and enhance women's autonomy: 'A system that put the burden of communication on the pursuer would change the cost of miscommunication; instead of unwanted sex being the result of ambiguity, the result would be a missed opportunity for sex' (Baker, 2005, p. 451).

Besides its gender essentialism (women are risk-averse and ambiguous, and men are risk-taking and clear), her position piggybacked on the fantasy of liberalism that affirmative/enthusiastic consent assures guarantee of women's pleasure and safety. Baker's feminist desire was to contain the sexual – minimising its ambiguity and rendering its excess readable – by imagining it could be brought within the fold of contractual law (Baker, 1999). In other words, sexual desire was translatable into the register of liberal law. Even though Baker went on to critique criminal law for its failure of punishing rape despite the affirmative consent standard (Baker, 2015), there is no visible shift in her conceptualisation of the sexual desire. It continues to be based on a social constructionist view of gendered experience and emotional expression of sexual desire, cast in terms of 'male entitlement to sex' versus 'woman's quiet desire not to go forward' (Baker, 2015, p. 278).

Like Baker, Kaul also recognises the sexual as a space of emotional intensity, but she finds it impossible to bring it within the fold of the law of sexual consent. In fact, Kaul is not interested in the law (of consent) at all, as consent can never be voluntary in a world where gender is organised through asymmetric distribution of sexual power. Consent, she argues, makes sense only if the parties are in 'perfect symmetry'. The reality of gender and sexual organisation is one of 'fearful asymmetry' and therefore consent is a meaningless concept. Furthermore, she posits that consent (sexual or not) 'belong[s] to a register that is based on certain rationalist assumptions' (Kaul, 2023, p. 12). Simply put, law/consent belong to the edifice of rationality, which cannot deal or interpret the emotions which shape our sexual desire.

Kaul is clear that consent cannot carry the weight of our sexual lives. For her, what has come to stand for consent in our relationships is actually 'a part of scaffolding belonging to rationality and its unwavering assumption of reasonableness, its goal of happiness, its belief in pleasure, and its premise of equality' (Kaul, 2023, p. 13). All these, she is right, are mere assumptions which belie how irrationality invades our lives, how we compulsively seek out misery, how pleasure is enmeshed with violence and equality is the greatest myth that conceals violent asymmetries of power.

Against this background, Kaul's overarching argument is to shift the terms of debate in matters of intimacy from the register of law to the register of psychoanalysis. Discontented with 'the discursive limits of [the legal register]', she offers psychoanalysis 'as a more flexible alternative – amenable to stretching itself to accommodate warring voices, tolerant of contradictions, inviting of uncertainties and doubts, and demarcating the line between truth and desire' (Kaul, 2023, p. 13). In this turn to psychoanalysis, Kaul's emphasis is on countering the epistemic violence of law's 'stubborn assertion of rationality' in as much as law seeks to expel out feelings and emotions together with all uncertainties, dreams and fantasies that hold our sexual life hostage.

No doubt she is right. Within the dominant conception of law (which this book seeks to interrupt), consent is premised on the fantasy of clear communication between the parties involved. In the legal/contractual register, communication pertains to transmitting, sharing, making common ideas or information from one person to another. There is a presumption of symmetry here – what will be said by one will be received by another in the same way. But if the context itself is one of asymmetry (not just asymmetry of power but even psychic asymmetry), communication is fraught with difficulties. Let me add that the law is not impervious to this difficulty of impossibility of communication; in fact, this anxiety manifests in the law as repetition in the verbosity of the definition of consent: 'when the woman *by words, gestures, or any form of verbal or non-verbal communication, communicates*'. Verbal from Latin '*verbum*' in fact means 'word', so we land in a tautology. The repetition is not just tautological but a symptom that betrays law's denial of the asymmetrical structure of the relationship where the condition of voluntariness is presumed with respect to the flow of information and intent. Kaul captures this all too well (2023, p. 16, emphasis mine):

> The encounter between two minds is always potentially explosive in that it, explicitly or implicitly, confronts us with difference. The communication between them exceeds the verbal, and even the verbalizable. And so it is that the idea of two consenting adults becomes very fraught. The part that 'consents' or 'seeks consent' is usually the conscious, rational, and verbal part of the mind. But this does not mean that *the other parts* are in agreement.

The sexual is not exhausted by the 'conscious, rational and verbal parts of the mind'. It is made up of the 'other parts' – the domain of 'the unconscious, that uncanny reservoir of unknowability' (Kaul, 2023, p. 14). These 'other parts' are not put into a conversation as easily as law imagines (or desires) them to be for they open up a world of contradictions, uncertainties, fantasies and paradoxes. But, let us stubbornly ask, yet again: is the intercourse between psychoanalysis and law an impossible desire?

It is the argument of this book, that even as law and psychoanalysis are different registers, the two when put in dialogue, destabilise one another to produce a fuller picture of their former selves: law reveals its other side, the legal unconscious; and psychoanalysis owns up its foundational laws (taboos against murder and incest, but also the law of not sleeping with the analyst (Freud, 1915/1958; Freud, 1913/1955). There is no law without the unconscious (Goodrich, 1997); there is no psychoanalysis before law (Derrida, 2009, p. 245). If we stay with this formulation, the conceptual tensions in Kaul's thesis are exposed. The shift to the register of psychoanalysis, governed by a disillusionment with law and an abandonment of the concept of consent, solidifies the disciplinary binary of law and psychoanalysis. This belies the hope not just for an inter-disciplinary dialogue but also of reimagining law as a site for 'ethics of sex'.

Consent serves no meaningful purpose, according to her, 'because it really is the baby of rationality and to that extent must be infected with its genetic defects' (Kaul, 2023, p. 14). This is where I lose her completely – not for the constructed binary of law and psychoanalysis, not even for the unintended alliance with MacKinnon's dominance feminist position – but for her determinist assumption of the fate of the baby. A baby, she would know as a psychoanalyst, though tied to the (m)other, can resiliently survive the psychic and genetic defects, it is not ill-fatedly bound into and wholly determined by the transgenerational transmission of trauma. A baby of rationality can exceed, surpass, overthrow rationality, as I will attempt, struggle, hope to show in the rest of this chapter.

Before turning to the next section, it is significant to place Baker and Kaul side by side to see how their radically divergent worldviews end up yielding the same outcome. While Baker imagined the conversation between the sexual and legal as way too easy – which ended up in the subsumption of the sexual into the legal; for Kaul, it was an impossible dialogue where the legal was dwarfed by the sexual which ended up resurrecting a dystopic dichotomy between (juridical) consent and (sexual) desire, thereby delinking consent from the sexual. Just like Baker elevates the legal, Kaul elevates the psychoanalytic, imagining rather naively that *hospitality* to the other – where the host allows the other to enter and also has *responsibility* towards the other – will furnish ground for ethical asymmetry. Here, Kaul relies on Levinasian imagination of ethical relationships as recognition of the singularity of the other. Evoking the maternal, the womb, Levinas noted: 'maternity is the gestation of the other, the groaning of the wounded entrails by those it will bear or has born [...] maternity [...] is responsibility for the other to the point of substitution for the other [...] it is [...] vulnerability, proximity, contact, 'in a way of caress', sensibility' (Levinas, cited in Kaul, 2023, p. 72).

Via Levinas, Kaul reads the maternal as a site for making the shift from fearful to ethical asymmetry. She sees in the womb 'hospitality', the 'ethical situation where the host, allowing the other to enter in this world, is responsible for him' (Kaul, 2023, citing Mier, 1994, p. 73). Without entering the feminist critique of Levinas here (Chanter, 2001), his phantasmatic conception of the maternal as the hallmark of hospitality needs to be situated against the materiality of the maternal: 'the groaning of the wounded entrails' produced by the loving invasion of the other destroys all boundaries, infusing within and without, melting body onto mind, entangling inside with outside, collapsing past with future. To read the maternal response to this loving invasion as yielding only hospitality, without hostility, would be to belittle the terrifying beauty of the other that produces the desire to annihilate oneself for the other, as also the shameful lingering longing for freedom from responsibility. Maternal is not without its own violence (Vashist, 2023; Vashist, 2020b; Rose, 2018; Cusk, 2003).

Even outside the maternal, in fact more so, there is an in-built 'self-limitation' in hospitality. There remains an eternal distance between the host and the guest/one's own and the stranger (Caputo, 2021, p. 110), hence, as Jacques Derrida maintains, there is always hostility in hospitality (Derrida, 2000). But this in-built limit, the aporia in hospitality, the impossibility sustains its possibility. Hospitality happens when the limit is pushed: 'Hospitality really starts to happen when I push against this limit, this threshold, this paralysis, inviting hospitality to cross its own threshold and limit, its own self-limitation, to become a gift *beyond hospitality*' (Caputo, 2021, p. 111). To be hospitable to the other, the host has to act in 'excess', in 'madness' to break all separation between the host and the guest. For Derrida, 'hospitality is not a matter of objective knowledge, but belongs to another order altogether, beyond knowledge, an *enigmatic* "experience" in which I set out for the stranger, for the other, for the *unknown*, where I cannot go' (Caputo, 2021, p. 112, emphasis mine). How evocative this description of hospitality is of the sexual, the realm of excess and enigma (Stein, 2008) and how it opens possibilities of freedom without holding sexuality hostage to violence/pleasure.

To sum up, I just wish to reiterate that psychoanalysis will not allow us easy resolutions, it will not permit us to repress the hostility-in-hospitality which keeps undoing our response-ability in re-orienting gender and sexual asymmetry from a violent repudiation to creative embrace of the other.

The register of psychoanalysis: Towards a psycho-legal theory of consent

Presence of force, aggression and inequality erode possibilities of consent and therefore 'submission', in law, does not amount to consent (Baxi et al., 1979). There is no conceptual distinction drawn between submission and surrender, neither in law, nor in mainstream feminism. But in psychoanalytic territory, submission is not the same as surrender (Ghent, 1990; Saketopoulou, 2023). In surrender, domination and control are not the governing principles. While submission is exacted by the other, one cannot be *made to* surrender to the other; surrender *happens* in the wake of 'facilitative conditions'. Surrender, writes Emmanuel Ghent (1990), 'is experience of being "in the moment" [...] where past and future [...] have receded from consciousness', it takes one in the direction of 'discovery of one's identity' (p. 111).[3] Submission reveals circumstances of inequality where one's powerlessness before the other is used to render the one more powerless, erasing all possibilities of making way for consent. Surrender, in contrast, 'is a sort of transfer of power', 'a giving of oneself over to the other' (Saketopoulou, 2023, p. 60). Some may contend that surrender occurs within, and produces, a state of inequality. But, again, is inequality per se undesirable? Does it completely incapacitate us in the search of ethics of sex? Making equality – an aspiration and a utopia to strive for – our starting point in the search of sexual ethics would only frustrate thinking. We inhabit the present as asymmetrical and unequal, and with, and despite, this asymmetry/inequality, we seek to keep desire alive, else invariably we would slip into 'all sex is rape' dystopia. The quest then is not to destroy asymmetry but, with Kaul, to make it ethical.

What I am suggesting is that the terms of surrender are such that inequality that is (re)produced between the parties – and yes inequality is (re)produced – does not quickly translate as unethical. Submission only has space for the desire of one, while surrender, acceding to an inherent inequality of and asymmetry in gender and sexual organisation, allows the desire of the one and an-other to co-exist. Surrender to the other pushes against the threshold of this inequality, making the other hold power *for you,* by entering the zone of unknowability of what lies ahead for both oneself and the other (Butler, 2011–2012). Unlike affirmative consent or even contractually determined BDSM, where limits need to be set and observed (both parties, it is assumed, retain sexual power), when one surrenders one remains open to or even invites transgression of limits. Psychoanalyst Avgi Saketopoulou (2020; 2023) usefully calls this 'limit consent'.

3 In arriving at this meaning, Ghent transcended the East–West binary and recovered intellectual resources from the Eastern tradition where surrender evokes 'transcendence, liberation' and not defeat: 'In the West surrender has meant "defeat". In the East it has meant transcendence, liberation. In the West "ego", as used in the vernacular, has meant one's strength, rationality, a very close relative, until recently, of one's self. In the East "ego" has meant maya, (dream, the illusion of one's self), a concept close to Lacan's "the Imaginary" or Winnicott's "unit self" world of identifications and projections, or Fairbairn's closed inner world. The goal in all of these systems is the awakening from the "dream world". In the East, to quote Heinrich Zimmer (1954), "the primary concern – in striking contrast to the interest of modern philosophers of the West – has always been, not information but transformation, a radical changing of man's nature and ... a renovation of his understanding both of the outer world and of his own existence". Perhaps we see vestiges of this distinction in the schism between analysts whose emphasis is informational (insight is what cures) as against those for whom the focus is transformational (with cure comes insight). Seen in this light the controversial "short hour" of Lacan acquires new meaning, its intent and sometimes effect being to at least momentarily awaken the analysand from the world of the Imaginary, the dream ... and perhaps provide a glimpse of something closer to the Real' (Ghent, 1990, pp. 111–112). I will refrain from unpacking this long quote here, which will require another book, another project. But I want to flag its importance and applaud its sheer brilliance and courage to tread on dangerous territories where spirituality meets psychoanalysis.

Limit consent is not about 'the assertion of one's sovereign boundaries but, rather, of surrendering to another – risking coming up against one's own and the other's opacity' (Saketopoulou, 2023, p. 64). This surrender, no doubt, risks injury[4] and casts a responsibility on the other to read one's desire empathetically. One may hastily see this, yet again, as an erotic power differential, but this hurried reading would overlook the vulnerability of the one holding power who had 'to assume the risk and the responsibility of safeguarding the other, thereby accepting the possibility that she may fail' (Saketopoulou, 2019, p. 139). Here, we are returning to the maternal but not via Kaul's hospitality/responsibility. The maternal here emerges with *risk*. It is a risky business to take the responsibility of the other. One may fail, one may pass on one's (defective) genetic material, one's (perverted) desire. The maternal is not a guarantee of safety. There is always a risk. But the possibility of hospitality – with its intrinsic hostility (to evoke Derrida's (2000) 'hostipitality') – is impossible without this risk. Limit consent, in enacting a spectacle of hospitality, converging the host and the guest, blurs all boundaries, making the impossible gift of shaping and experiencing one's desire as the desire of the other.

Besides blurring the divide between active and passive, and risking inadvertent, unexpected injury, the idea of limit consent is based on a nonlinear conception of time (Saketopoulou, 2023, p. 59). Psychic time is not linear which implies that 'the passage of time is escorted by experience, which then acts on the past to revise recollection, making psychic events not fully legible to the subject experiencing them' (Saketopoulou, 2011, p. 248). This means that psychoanalytically consent is not temporally frozen, 'its intention and desire are constantly reinscribed with meaning and become continuously relayered, always elaborated by the *next moment*' (Saketopoulou, 2011, p. 248, emphasis mine). Therefore, when one remembers one's own desire and intentionality in the past, it can never be recovered in its originary form. 'As the present reconfigures the past, consent becomes variegated' (Saketopoulou, 2011, p. 248). For law (as it stands today in its liberal manifestation), this has implications of such a magnitude that both legal scholars and feminists would recoil back into the unsatisfactory contractual model of consent. Law works with a linear conception of time – reconfiguring the past is tampering with temporal evidence. Introducing nonlinear psychic time into law would tantamount to reconstructing the past retroactively (what Kipnis recognised as flip-flopping on consent).

4 The risk of injury 'results from infantile sexual urges that have gone too far, gone beyond play, with neither party knowing it until after the fact. That is, the injury is realised only après coup. Limit consent necessarily involves straddling the murky line along which something may go seriously awry. It could go awry because Imani does not "read" Lumi well; because Lumi may be unable to signal; or, more important, because she is unable to know when, on balance, she really wants Imani to stop; or because Imani's infantile sexuality takes over, becoming too inflamed and resulting in Imani's losing control'. (Saketopoulou, 2019, p. 140).

What was sex yesterday, would become rape today. However, the unruliness of this psychoanalytic idea should not intimidate us. I will show how there are two specific provisions in the law of sexual violence in India where psychoanalytic consent – as a methodology of reading – equips us to understand and critique the law of consent more thoroughly. These provisions pertain to the criminalisation of false promise of marriage and seduction in hierarchical relationships. Significantly, in both these provisions, the question of consent is explicitly set aside.

Promise to marry

Promise to marry cases form an astounding percentage of rape cases filed in India (Rukmini, 2021). The Indian courts painstakingly tried to contain the bounds of criminalisation by making a distinction between *false* promise to marry and *breach* of a genuine promise to marry. In 2005, the Supreme Court, in *Deelip Singh @ Dilip Kumar* v. *State of Bihar*,[5] declared that if the accused had no intention to marry the complainant *from the inception*, this promise would be false and would vitiate the consent of the complainant (amounting to rape). But if the accused had a genuine intention to marry the complainant at the time of making the promise, based on which she had given her consent, this would not be rape, but mere breach of the contractual obligation arising out of the promise to marry.

The feminist position on this issue is clear. Even if the accused had no intention to marry but suggested marriage and the woman agreed owing to her own associations between sex and marriage, this is not rape. Calling it rape would be regressive: amounting to endorsement of patriarchal normative choices made by women; it would take us back into the dreaded man-woman, reason-emotion tropes, reducing her subjectivity to passive helplessness while seeing the man as the responsible agent for the act; criminal liability would be imposed on men because of women's choices (Partners for Law in Development, 2015; Menon, 2019; Basu, 2011).[6]

The question that interests me here is what explains the wide divide between the feminist position on this issue and the fact that resounding number of

5 2005 (1) SCC 88.

6 Feminist lawyer, Flavia Agnes based on her experience with victims of domestic and sexual violence refuses to reduce every invocation of the promise to marry provision to be patriarchal or sexist. A large number of complainants in these cases are from socially disadvantaged groups, who see marriage as an escape from drudgery but are left to fend for themselves by their former lovers, many times with a child born out of the affair to look after. For these reasons, Agnes had contended for a separate offence under the rape law. She imagined that 'a combination of civil and criminal remedies can be woven into the legal provision to include a lesser punishment but damages, maintenance and future security for the child' (Agnes, 2016).

women continue to take recourse to rape law when the promise of marriage is not kept? How do we understand the actions and desires of the complainants in these cases? Are all these women who file rape cases, believing themselves to be violated, vindictive and revengeful? Are they deliberately abusing the law? Or, do they really believe that they had been raped all along?

It is no revelation that all complaints based on (false/breached) promise to marry are the work of psychic time. A past event – which was experienced as intimacy and love *at that moment* – is reconstructed as rape/violence. A *false* promise made in the past, the falsity of which was discovered in the present, and experienced as betrayal by the complainant, re-casts the past yes into a no, and sex into rape. 'I thought it was love/sex. Actually, it was manipulation/rape'. Similarly, a genuine promise of love made in the past, when broken in the present, leads to hurt which re-casts the promise of love into manipulation and violence (exposing how the idea of sexual love is wedded indelibly with, and indistinguishably from, the institution of marriage). This return to the rosy past from the broken present turns the yes into a no and sexual desire into violence. A promise unkept, in the present, turns love into hate, and a lover into a rapist.

The courts were called upon to deal with psychic time in these cases. And interestingly, despite the predominantly linear conception of legal time, judges – without really intending to do so – not only acknowledged and responded to psychic time but brought psychic time into the fold of consent law. In 2019, the bench of Justices D. Y. Chandrachud and Indira Banerjee in *Pramod Suryabhan Pawar* v. *State of Maharashtra,*[7] reiterated the settled position on this matter: 'The promise of marriage must have been a false promise, given in bad faith and with no intention of being adhered to *at the time it was given*. The false promise itself must be *of immediate relevance* or *bear a direct nexus to the woman's decision* to engage in the sexual act' (para 18). The judges emphasised that 'failure to keep a promise made with respect to a *future uncertain date*', when the initial promise was genuine, does not amount to misconception of fact. In other words, consent given by the complainant to have sexual intercourse with whom she is in love, based on a promise of marriage *in future*, is not vitiated under law. It is valid consent. In order to come within the meaning of the term 'misconception of fact', which in turn would vitiate consent, the promise must have been of 'immediate relevance' to the complainant.

It is important to note that, in construing false promise cases as non-consensual, the courts are theorising consent from the vantage point of psychic time, i.e. complainant's consent gets vitiated when we *retrospectively* examine the events and discover that the accused had made a false promise. Even though the complainant, in the past, had no knowledge about accused's false intentions, and she had agreed to, and perhaps had even liked the sexual intimacy, today the meaning of *that act* has changed.

7 2019 (11) SCALE 209.

Unlike false promise to marry cases, in breach of promise, the courts do not see the act(s) as non-consensual, even though the complainant herself must be feeling exactly as the 'victim' in false promise case. When psychic time reformulated the past in cases when the promise, at the given moment, was genuine, the court (rightly) stayed with the inherent temporal fluidity of the idea of promise, and on ethical grounds, rejected the incorporation of psychic time into consent. Law censures reformulation of the past in these cases. Consensual sex in the past was not reinterpreted as non-consensual. Remarkably, the judges do not endorse a spatio-temporal fixity of a promise in these cases – they remain open to the possibility that promise may not be fulfilled – past does not freeze the promise – because of changed circumstances and emotions (Goodrich, 1996).

The above split in judicial recognition of psychic time in promise to marry cases – though never explicitly acknowledged in law – is papered over by the newly enacted section 69 of BNS.[8] The newly enacted deviates from the settled judicial position to the extent that enquiry into consent is foreclosed:

> Whoever, by deceitful means or making by promise to marry to a woman *without any intention of fulfilling the same*, and has sexual intercourse with her, *such sexual intercourse not amounting to the offence of rape*, shall be punished with imprisonment of either description for a term which may extend to ten years and shall also be liable to fine.

The expression 'deceitful means', and we find this legislative clarification in the provision, includes 'the false promise of employment or promotion, inducement or marrying after suppressing identity'. The act is criminalised, *despite* the presence of woman's consent to sexual intercourse; the expression 'not amounting to the offence of rape' requires attention. This legislative fiat is categorical that the act is not, was never, cannot be construed in past or present, as non-consensual. In other words, the law would no longer concede to the complainant's version of the act of the accused based on psychic time. The law has recoiled to affirm the liberal juridical notion of consent within linearity of time, by completely taking consent outside the discussion on promise to marry. The complainant cannot say, I was violated then, or that it was not my free consent, if *at that point in time*, she had not felt violated. Now psychic reconstruction of past from the present knowledge about falsity of promise would not vitiate consent.[9]

8 This section completely deviates from the long-standing position of Indian feminists on this issue. Even Flavia Agnes who has a nuanced approach towards promise to marry cases, remarked that the new law is vague and will 'give more power to the police to act arbitrarily' (Barnagarwala & Bhalla, 2023, August 18; Ali, Vashist & Ghose, 2024).

9 These cases throw open another issue about the very meaning of the promise of love. Lovers make all kinds of spoken and unspoken promises to one another, and to themselves. Starting from the promise of being, and remaining in love with each

I want to clarify, before I am misunderstood, that I am not advocating for promise to marry cases to be viewed as rape cases. I am not taking any normative position on this issue – important as it may be. My objective here is only to show how (false) promise to marry cases were decided based on a conception of consent which accounted for psychic time. These cases, generally seen as cases of misuse of law, create an important opening for dialogue between law and psychoanalysis, enabling a psycho-legal construction of sexual consent.

Seduction

Section 376C of the IPC (now section 68 of BNS) criminalises seduction. Whoever in a position of authority or a fiduciary relationship:

> abuses such position or fiduciary relationship *to induce or seduce* any woman either in his custody or under his charge or present in the premises to have sexual intercourse with him, *such sexual intercourse not amounting to the offence of rape*, shall be punished with rigorous imprisonment of either description for a term which shall not be less than 5 years, but which may extend to ten years, and shall also be liable to fine.

Section 376C, introduced in 2013, encapsulates erstwhile 376-B to 376-D which were inserted in 1983 to hold certain persons in authority (public servants, superintendent of jail, remand home or any other place of custody and member of the management or staff of a hospital) criminally liable for inducing or seducing any woman for sexual intercourse (Gangoli, 1996). However, in 2013 the scope of criminalised seduction was expanded to any person 'in a position of authority or in a fiduciary relationship'. While this provision seeks to consider situations of power asymmetry which render consent meaningless, it is not difficult to see the inherent logic of sexual infantilisation of women (Kumari, 1999), as also 'legal paternalist denunciation of women's sexual choices' (Kotiswaran, 2018, p. 102).

The legal assumption is that seduction and power are a bad cocktail, which turn yes into a no (in fact, make it impossible to imagine a yes). Rather than proceeding with the assumption of impossibility of consent, I want to bring consent back into the matrix of power and seduction, and re-frame the above provision thus: in situations of power asymmetry between the two sexes, seduction is criminal, even if the sexual encounter was consensual. Seduction in situation of power asymmetry automatically turns into abuse. Seduction, in

other, most promises of love seek a permanence, a territory, a finality to their desire. Woven in a crochet of conscious and unconscious wishes, both this-worldly and supernatural, these promises that make love and loving contingent on factors beyond one's control, making love, what ought to be immutable, reassuring and certain, the most precarious thing. Does love's precarity, because it rests on fragile promises, explain its proximity to hate?

other words, is dangerous and one has to guard oneself against it. What is seduction, one may ask? Seduction comes from Latin 'sēdūcō' which means 'to lead apart or astray (*sē*, i.e. 'aside, away, astray' + *dūcō*, i.e. 'to lead'). It assumes a model of relationality where one is passive, *lacking* agency and the other is in control, *having* the power to lead the other astray. But does 'being led astray' only conjure an image of powerlessness? Does getting derailed from one's path – surrendering in other words – necessarily mean a damaging loss of self but can it lead to discovery of another, an-other, self? In what follows, instead of assuming that seduction negates consent, I would like to propose that seduction is essential for the emergence of consent.

In an important essay, where the idea of consent in therapy sessions is juxtaposed with sexual consent, psychoanalyst Ginna Clark, remarks that 'seduction involved a psychological state where we come to know otherwise unknown parts of ourselves' (Clark, 2019, p. 276). This possibility of knowing 'unknown parts of ourselves' is on account of seduction being intrinsically intersubjective and empathic: an empathic ability to enter the inner being of the other, allowing the other to move away from their already determined ways of inhabiting the world, by encountering an-other, another within the self. Seduction in this sense means 'relinquish[ing] certainties, perhaps moving away from a more rigid organization *toward something that creates space for the less active dimensions of consent*' (p. 276, emphasis mine). Clark in a way is suggesting that seduction makes consent possible: not juridical, affirmative consent but consent which is closer to 'feeling together', 'the less active dimension of consent' which is worked out together 'quietly and underground' (2019, p. 276).

Defining consent solely in the background of sexual power invariably translates it into terms of inequality (and ensuing violence) forever foreclosing the possibility of imagining a relationality where one is held by the other, where divergent *and unequal* desires meet. Against the backdrop of sexual desire, consent cannot be reduced to nought, it rather comes alive when the reticent and unsure one borrows from the 'yes' of the (relatively) certain and (marginally) confident other. Even in this situation there is no clear 'yes' but the 'no' has loosened up without being overridden by other's desire. As Clark sums it up, '[w]here divergent desires meet – one tentative and reticent, the other more confident and determined – it seems that seduction is what tips the scale' (p. 276).

This obviously does not mean that seduction cannot align with the field of power and inequality. It can and it does. But the point is that in that case seduction will turn into coercion – a forcible extraction of yes. It will not remain seduction. What makes seduction an art is the quality of slow work and patient waiting for the sublime to emerge, making space for other's surprising and challenging differences, allowing time for dormant desires to assume fresh life and always remaining ready to retreat, slow down and may be start afresh, another time. Seduction is contingent on empathy towards other's inner world where one comes together *and* is undone by contradictory desires: excitement and fear, ecstasy and reluctance, fascination and revulsion. Negotiating these contradictory impulses and desires by reading subtle, non-verbal clues, communicated through the body is the idea of psychoanalytic seduction (and consent). It also requires overcoming the fear of exposing one's own desire before another and then waiting for the other 'to register her own desire in a real, undeniable, and body-based way' (Clark, 2019, p. 278).

Where are we now?

Do we have a theory of psycho-legal sexual consent? No, not yet.

There is an aporia that I am up against. On the one hand, we recognise that the liberal idea of consent is so limited and skewed in its representation of the realities of sexuality that law itself abandons the concept in hard cases: promise to marry, seduction and statutory rape. On the other hand, a realistic exposition of sexuality and desire through a psychoanalytic lens threatens to damage the normative ideals of both the legal and feminist project. We know that contractual model of sexual consent is one of biggest lies of the liberal order, yet we cannot (yet) give up on this legal lie especially to safeguard situations where sexuality is contracted and managed in advance (for instance, sex work).

Today when the struggle is to secure convictions, foregrounding the unknowability of desire with respect to the concept of consent can seriously derail the feminist dream of making rape 'extinct' (MacKinnon 2016, p. 477). It can result in (more) misogynistic judgements where courts would rule that rape was either desired by the victim, or she took the risk of being raped. So, is there a way out? How do we settle against this aporia, neither slipping into liberal law's abstract individualism nor abandoning the normative political project? How do we imagine a feminism that refuses to deny the unsettling and dangerous aspects of sexuality to secure safety and pleasure? What would the contours of psycho-legal sexual consent look like, such that both law's promise of respectful dignity and desire's uncontainable and formidable excess are enfolded in it?

For now, there are no answers. As a non-answer, I will stay with the hope that 'psychic contrapuntal' reading will allow us to pose and diagnose the problem from different vantage points – all equally important – and enhance our capacity to bear the weight of contradictions and accept the limits of knowledge.

References

Agnes, F. (2016). What makes up the majority of cases of rape under promise of marriage? Here's a reality check. Times of India. https://timesofindia.indiatimes.com/blogs/toi-edit-page/what-makes-up-the-majority-of-cases-of-rape-under-promise-of-marriage-heres-a-reality-check.

Ali, S. M. A., Vashist, A. & Ghose, A. (2024). Bharatiya Nyaya Sanhita and the False Promise to Marry. *Economic and Political Weekly*, 59(18).

Angel, K. (2021). *Tomorrow Sex Will be Good: Women and Desire in the Age of Consent.* London: Verso.

Baker, K. K. (1999). Sex, Rape, and Shame. *B.U. L Rev.*, 79, 663.

Baker, K. K. (2005). Gender And Emotion in Criminal Law. *Harvard Journal of Law & Gender*, 28, 447–466.
Baker, Katharine K. (2015). Why Rape Should Not (Always) Be a Crime. *Minnesota Law Review*, 100, 221.
Barnagarwala, T. & Bhalla, V. (2023, August 18). Why legal experts are criticising new clause to punish sex by false promises. https://scroll.in/article/1054438/why-legal-experts-are-criticising-new-clause-that-punishes-sex-gained-by-making-false-promises.
Basu, S. (2011). Sexual Property: Staging Rape and Marriage in Indian Law and Feminist Theory. *Feminist Studies*, 37(1), 185–211.
Baxi, P. (2014). *Public Secrets of Law: Rape Trials in India.* Oxford University Press.
Baxi, P. (2016). Carceral feminism as judicial bias: The discontents around State v Mahmood Farooqui. *Interdisciplinary Law*, 3, 1–30.
Baxi, P. (2021). For the Judge, It Was a Feminist Who Was on Trial, Not Tarun Tejpal. https://thewire.in/women/for-the-judge-it-was-a-feminist-who-was-on-trial-not-tarun-tejpal.
Baxi, U., Sarkar, L., Kelkar R. & Dhagamwar, V. (1979). *An Open Letter to the Chief Justice of India.* 4 SCC *(Jour) 17.*
Bollas, C. (2014). Introducing Edward Said. In E. W. Said, *Freud and the Non-European.* New York: Verso.
Butler, J. (2011–2012). Sexual consent: Some thoughts on psychoanalysis and law. *Columbia Journal of Gender and the Law*, 21(2), 3–14.
Caputo, J. D. (2021). *Deconstruction in a Nutshell: A Conversation with Jacques Derrida.* Fordham University Press.
Chanter, T. (Ed.) (2001). *Feminist Interpretations of Emmanuel Levinas.* Pennsylvania State University Press.
Clark, G. (2019). Yes-saying, no-saying, and the places in-between: Seduction and the psychoanalytic exploration of sexual consent. *Studies in Gender and Sexuality*, 20(4), 274–284.
Cossman, B. (2015). Feminism in Hard Times: From Criticism to Critique. In A. Barnes (Ed.), *Feminisms of discontent: Global contestations.* New Delhi: Oxford University Press.
Cusk, R. (2003). *A Life's Work: On Becoming a Mother.* Picador.
Derrida, J. (2000). Hostipitality. *Angelaki*, 5(3), 3–18.
Derrida, J. (2009). *Beast and Sovereign: Volume I* (M. Lisse, M.-L. Malet & G. Michaud, Eds & Trans.). University of Chicago Press.
Fischel, J. J. (2019). *Screw Consent: A Better Politics of Sexual Justice.* University of California Press.
Foucault, M. (1978). *The History of Sexuality: The Will to Knowledge* (R. Hurley, Trans.). Vintage.
Franke, K. M. (2001). Theorizing Yes: An Essay on Feminism, Law, and Desire. *Colum. L. Review*, 101, 181.
Freud, S. (1913/1955). Totem and Taboo. In *The Standard Edition of the Complete Psychological Works of Sigmund Freud,* Vol. XIII (translated by J. Stratchey). Hogarth Press.
Freud, S. (1915/1958). Observations on transference-love. In *The Standard Edition of the Complete Psychological Works of Sigmund Freud,* Vol. XII (translated by J. Stratchey). Hogarth Press.
Gangoli, G. (1996). The Right to Protection from Sexual Assault: The Indian Anti-Rape Campaign. *Development in Practice*, 6(4), 334–340.

Ghent, E. (1990). Masochism, submission, surrender—masochism as a perversion of surrender. *Contemporary Psychoanalysis*, 26, 108–136.

Goodrich, P. (1996). Gender and Contracts. In A. Bottomley (Ed.), *Feminist Perspectives on the Foundational Subjects of Law*. Cavendish Publishing.

Goodrich, P. (1997). *Law and the Unconscious: A Legendre Reader*. Macmillan Press.

Halley, J. (2006). *Split Decisions: How and Why to Take a Break from Feminism*. Princeton University Press.

Heidi M. H. (1996). The Moral Magic of Consent. *Legal Theory*, 2, 121–146.

Kaul, N. (2023). *Consent: Fearful Asymmetry*. New Delhi: Zubaan.

Kipnis, L. (2017). *Unwanted Advances: Sexual Paranoia Comes to Campus*. Harper.

Kotiswaran, P. (2018). Governance Feminism in the Post Colony: India's Rape Law Reforms of 2013. In J. Halley, P. Kotiswaran, R. Rebouche & H. Shamir, *Governance Feminism: An Introduction*. University of Minnesota Press.

Kumari, V. (1999). Gender Analysis of Indian Penal Code. In A. Dhanda & A. Parashar (Eds), *Engendering Law: Essays in Honour of Lotika Sakar*. Lucknow: Eastern Book Company.

Law Commission of India (2023). Age of consent under the Protection of Children from Sexual Offences Act 2012, Report No. 283.

MacKinnon, C. A. (1987). *Feminism Unmodified: Discourses on Life and Law*. Harvard University Press.

MacKinnon, C. A. (2016). Rape redefined. *Harvard Law & Policy Review*, 1, 431.

Menon, N. (2019). Sexual Violence and the law in India. In R. West & C. G. Bowman (Eds), *Research Handbook on Feminist Jurisprudence*. Edward Elgar Publishing.

Mitchell, J. (1985). Introduction – I. In J. Mitchell & J. Rose (Eds), *Feminine sexuality: Jacques Lacan and the école freudienne*. Pantheon Books.

Mitchell, J. (2008). *Siblings: Sex and Violence*. Polity Press.

Mitchell, J. (2015). Debating Sexual Difference, Politics, and the Unconscious: With Discussant Section by Jacqueline Rose. In R. Duschinsky & S. Walker (Eds), *Juliet Mitchell and the Lateral Axis: Twenty-First-Century Psychoanalysis and Feminism*. Palgrave Macmillan.

Mitchell, J. & Rose, J. (Eds). (1985). *Feminine sexuality: Jacques Lacan and the école freudienne*. Pantheon Books.

Munro, V. E. (2008). Constructing consent: Legislating freedom and legitimating constraint in the expression of sexual autonomy. *Akron Law Review*, 41(4), 923–956.

Munro, V. E. (2017). Shifting Sands? Consent, Context and Vulnerability in Contemporary Sexual Offences Policy in England and Wales. *Social & Legal Studies*, 26 (4), 417–440.

Partners for Law in Development (2015). *Marriage, sexuality and the law: Roundtable on exploring the continuum between sexuality and sexual violence*.

Rose, J. (1985). Introduction – II. In J. Mitchell & J. Rose (Eds), *Feminine sexuality: Jacques Lacan and the école freudienne*. Pantheon Books.

Rose, J. (2018). *Mothers: An Essay on Love and Cruelty*. Farrar, Straus and Giroux.

Rose, J. (2021). *On Violence and On Violence Against Women*. Faber & Faber.

Rubin, G. (1984). Thinking sex: Notes for a radical theory of the politics of sexuality. In C. Vance (Ed.), *Pleasure and danger: Exploring female sexuality*. Routledge and Kegan Paul.

Rukmini, S. (2021). *Whole Numbers and Half Truths: What Data Can and Cannot Tell Us About Modern India*. Westland Publications.

Said, E. W. (1994). *Culture and imperialism.* New York: Vintage Books.
Said, E. W. (2001). *Reflections on exile and other essays.* Cambridge, MA: Harvard University Press.
Said, E. W. (2014). *Freud and the Non-European.* Verso.
Saketopoulou, A. (2011). Consent, sexuality, and self-respect: Commentary on Skerrett's "Beyond consent". *Studies in Gender & Sexuality*, 12, 245–250.
Saketopoulou, A. (2019). The Draw to Overwhelm: Consent, Risk, and the Retranslation of Enigma. *Journal of American Psychoanalytical Association*, 67(1), 133–167.
Saketopoulou, A. (2020). Risking sexuality beyond consent: Overwhelm and traumatisms that incite. *The Psychoanalytic Quarterly*, 89(4), 771–811.
Saketopoulou, A. (2023). *Sexuality Beyond Consent: Risk, Race, Traumatophilia.* New York University Press.
Satish, M. (2017). The Farooqui Judgment's Interpretation of Consent Ignores Decades of Rape-Law Reform and Catastrophically Affects Rape Adjudication. *The Caravan.* https://caravanmagazine.in/vantage/farooqui-judgment-consent-ignores-rape-law-reform-catastrophically-affects-adjudication.
Stein, R. (2008). The Otherness of Sexuality: Excess. *Journal of the American Psychoanalytic Association*, 56(1), 43–71.
Vashist, L. (2020a). Law, violence and sexual consent. In L. Vashist & J. Dogra (Eds), *Rethinking law and violence.* Oxford University Press.
Vashist, L. (2020b). Anxiety and everydayness. *Seminar*, 733. www.india-seminar.com/2020/733/733_latika_vashist.htm.
Vashist, L. (2023). Encountering the maternal body. *Seminar*, 764. www.india-seminar.com/2023/764/764-07%20LATIKA%20VASHIST.htm.
Žižek, S. (2017). *The Courage of Hopelessness.* Penguin Books.
Žižek, S. (2018). *Like a Thief in Broad Daylight: Power in the Era of post-Humanity.* Allen Lane.
Zupančič, A. (2017). *What is Sex?.* MIT Press.

Chapter 6

Sexuality and the Figure of the 'Child'

CHILD (FIVE-YEAR-OLD BOY): *Pitaji, mere pet mein baccha hai*
[Daddy, there is a baby inside my belly]
FATHER: *Accha* [okay]
CHILD: *Aapke pet mein hai?*
[Do you have [a baby] in your belly?]
FATHER: *Nahin, mere pet mein nahin hai.*
[No, I don't have in my belly]
CHILD: *Kyun nahin hai?*
[Why don't you have?]
FATHER: *Jis tarah raat main din nahin hota, waise hi nahin hai*
[The way there is no morning in the night, in the same way I don't have]
CHILD: *Accha* [okay]

This exchange between a curious five-year old boy and his father, at the risk of being contained or forgotten by its humour-evoking quality, gives a glimpse into the impenetrable and fascinating psychic life of children. This world of curiosity and imitation, even when it throws challenges, like the one in this conversation, we would like to believe is one of 'innocence', far removed from the domain of the sexual. But is it so? In the above snippet, what was this five-year old conveying through the baby in his belly? What all does the belly store? What did he wish to know from the father? What is the import of the questions posed by this five-year old? How does one make sense of this curiosity, this 'instinct for knowledge or research' (Freud, 1905/1953, p. 194)?

In 1915, ten years after the publication of his *Three Essays on the Theory of Sexuality,* in which he had claimed all infants and children are sexual in nature, Sigmund Freud added a new section titled 'The Sexual Researches of Childhood' to the second of his *Three Essays* in the fresh edition of the book. He opened this section by drawing an interesting link between sexual life and instinct for knowledge. 'At about the same time as the sexual life of children reaches its first peak, between the ages of three and five', wrote Freud, 'they also begin to show signs of the activity which may be ascribed to the instinct for knowledge or research' (Freud, 1905/1953, p. 194). The child's yearning to

DOI: 10.4324/9781003387411-7

know – most significantly about its own origins and its sexual identity – is connected to its sexual life which, for Freud, was not focused on the genital drive but on achieving gratification in any way it can. Significantly, this Freudian move was a turn away from biology toward the realm of fantasy.

This century-old psychoanalytic discovery of infantile sexuality has made little inroads within the discipline of law which continues to uphold a fictional image of an innocent child and a mythical asexual childhood. Even as macro-level decisions taken to 'protect' children from sexual abuse create an elongated legal machinery of carceral governance, foundational questions about the child are never posed. To begin with, let us put some questions to the law: who is a child? Is the figure of the child asexual? Does the child possess any agency? What is the meaning of 'childhood'? When does childhood end?

This chapter seeks to raise the fraught questions of age, consent and sexual agency within the contemporary discourse on childhood and sexuality in Indian law. I will examine the implications of the presumption of irrelevance of sexual consent in cases concerning 'children' in Indian criminal law. The category of the 'child', anyone below 18 years, is excessively broad and encompasses infants, toddlers, pre-puberty children and adolescents. The signifier 'child' comes to stand in and speaks for both a five-year-old and a 17-year-old evaluating them with the same yardstick: both lack rationality, are not competent to decide for themselves and need protection by the family and the state. In law, the absurdity of this equation keeps surfacing time and again – the age of consent being its most potent site – but the lawmakers continue to remain fixated on their fantasy images of the child and childhood.

My concern in this chapter is not that we (adults) could make better laws for children (of course we can, if we try), or that involving the child, with sensitivity, as a subject in the process of law-making would yield a better law (certainly it would, if we care). I am also not embarking upon the task of determining what kind of law the child wants. Or, as some commentators have written on how such desire ought to be reflected in the process of law-making (Jain, 2020). Instead, my enquiry, following feminist and psychoanalyst Jacqueline Rose, is around 'what the adult desires – desires in the very act of construing the child as the object of its speech' (Rose, 1984, p. 2).

I will focus on the age of consent law in India. Age of consent is the site where fears over childhood sexuality shroud both the figure of the child and the idea of the child's voice, rendering both impossible. Rose uses the word 'impossible' in her account of children's fiction – her book is called *The Case of Peter Pan or the Impossibility of Children's Fiction* (1984) – to indicate that the child's voice is impossible because it is drowned out by adult anxieties on behalf of the child and that adults project their own fears onto the child, especially around the sexual. The child in 'children's fiction' is always an adult fantasy. Staying with Rose, I will attempt to enquire, via the age of consent law, whether her argument about children's fiction remains valid for 'children's laws'? Are 'children's laws', specifically, the age of consent law, an adult fantasy? What is that fantasy? Do children's laws exist for children, or do they serve some other societal, superordinate (adult) goal?

In this chapter, I will start by exploring who a child is, a question rarely asked within law. This is an enquiry into the meaning of age and the sexual nature of the child, both these facets being erased in law's presentation of the child. The law disciplines the figure of the child with mythical assumptions which belie the realities of childhoods, and childhood sexuality gets entrapped and collapsed into abuse/violence. Focusing on the issue of the legal impossibility of consent, I will show how this fictional incapacity to consent is taken to absurd limits in cases of adolescents[1] who have willingly entered into consensual romantic and sexual relationships. In these cases, the law becomes the instrument through which adult fantasies about societal institutions and relationships are projected onto children who are made to carry the weight of adults' desired worldview. However, from (adults') experience, as much from psychoanalysis, one learns that childhood sexual innocence is a myth constructed by notions of temporal morality and adults' anxiety about pathological deviations from the normative image of the child. I will try and show in this chapter that psychoanalysis offers important lessons for the law, the most important one being, not to discover the 'best interest of the child', but embarking on the impossible task of listening to the child.

The figure of the 'child': questions of age and sexuality

Within the framework of the law, we find a prompt (and often unthoughtful) response to the question who a child is: 'a child means *every* human being below the age of 18 years, *unless under the law applicable to the child, majority is attained earlier*'. Article 1 of the UN Convention on the Rights of the Child (CRC) lays down a universal standard and provides the common goal of humanity, against which childhood should be evaluated. Contained within the dictates of 'the law applicable', the child is caught between contradictory legal objectives and impulses. Why, one may ask, under the Indian law in sexual matters, is the age of consent 18[2], but when the question is of imposition of criminal culpability, it can be 16?[3] If a 16-year-old can be punished, like an

1 In Indian law, an adolescent is defined as a person who is between the age of 14 and 18 [section 2(i) of The Child and Adolescent Labour (Prohibition and Regulation) Act, 1986]. However, in matters of sexuality, adolescent is subsumed within the overarching 'child'.

2 S. 2(d) of the POCSO; S. 375 (Sixthly) of the IPC; S. 63 (d)(vi) of BNS. S. 2(3) of BNS defines a child as 'any person below the age of eighteen years'.

3 Juvenile Justice (Care and Protection of Children) Act, 2015, S. 15. The amended juvenile justice law (as discussed in Chapter 3) in case of a 'heinous offence' committed by a child who is above 16 years, requires the juvenile justice board to conduct 'a preliminary assessment with regard to his mental and physical capacity to

adult, for rape, how can the law paradoxically presume him to be devoid of the capacity of sexual consent? Why is it that the law denies (sexual) agency to a desiring child but affixes criminal responsibility upon a delinquent child? Why is the age of freedom to contract affixed at 18,[4] but age of employment is much lower at 14?[5] If a 14-year-old cannot enter into a contract, how will she determine the terms of her employment? These contradictions around the legal age do not just inflict the law but also sneak into the position of law's critics who, for instance, would seek to retain 18 years as the age for affixing criminal responsibility but will argue for reduction of age of sexual consent (Kumari, 2014a; Kumari, 2015; Kumari, 2016; Sheriff & Ghosh, 2019).[6]

We have not reached any satisfactory answer, leave alone a semblance of a resolution, on the contradictions that persist around the legal age of the child. Perhaps this is because the question of 'age' (intrinsically tied to the question of childhood framed as a developmental stage in a person's life) has not been thought carefully within, or even outside, the law. What do we mean when we talk about the age of a person? Is it chronological age that is adopted as the frame for legal age? Or, 'mental' age – the age connected to cognitive capacities? Or, do we mean 'social' age which is based on societal norms and cultural expectations that define inter-personal and interactional skills of an individual? French philosopher, Jacques Derrida stretched the question of age to even the 'unconscious' age, the age of the unconscious which knows no time.

commit such offence, ability to understand the consequences of the offence and the circumstances in which he allegedly committed the offence'. In such assessment, the board 'may take the assistance of experienced psychologists or psycho-social workers or other experts'. This provision, by way of an amendment, was added after the Delhi Gang Rape which I have discussed in Chapter 3. This change in the law was done because of the political debate which surfaced after the incident as one of the accused persons was a juvenile. This raises complex questions on what is age of culpability and how political, historical assessments and even feelings of resentment can determine the legal age/capacity for guilt determination.

4 S.11 of the Indian Contract Act,1872; S. 3 of the Indian Majority Act, 1975.

5 S. 2(ii) of the Child and Adolescent Labour (Prohibition and Regulation) Act, 1986.

6 According to Ved Kumari, children aged between 16 and 18 can distinguish right from wrong. However, their 'ability to control risk and pleasure-seeking behaviour' is extremely weak. Relying on studies of adolescent brain imaging and monitoring, she notes that for adolescents, 'the part that promotes risk-taking behaviour is much more developed than the part that controls those instincts'. Children are more vulnerable because of the constitution and limited development of their brains and hence require 'social guidance and supervision from parents as well as from the state'. Adolescents cannot be dealt with like adults as their 'brains at that age are not like adults'. Besides problematically relying on brain science, Kumari (in contrast with Agnes) views parents' and state's 'guidance and supervision' as benign, not controlling or regulatory. Again, a conceptual argument for reduced age of sexual consent on the one hand, and higher age of responsibility on the other, is absent. Reliance on brain science does not tell us why adolescents who are exploring their sexuality should be left outside the control of the family and state. Kumari, 2014b; Sheriff & Ghosh, 2019.

Law appears to remain impervious to these complexities. As Derrida remarks: '[u]p until now, the law has forbidden itself or has been unable to integrate into its essential axiomatic a logic of the unconscious or the symptom: above all, [...] *another thinking of age* (that is, of the time of life and the multiplicity of heterogeneous measures, orders, or ways of counting); law has not reckoned with this other thinking of age' (Derrida, 2016, p. 9). How will the law reconcile with multiplicities of age – biological, mental, social and unconscious – when the legal age dominates and eclipses these alternate conceptions of measuring time and being? Into these questions how do we introduce the 'sexual age' (of consent)? Lawyers might be tempted to reject these questions as philosophical musings but at their own peril. The question of age perpetually haunts the law. It came up squarely before the Supreme Court of India in *Ms. Eera through Dr. Manjula Krippendorf* v. *State (Govt. of Delhi)*.[7]

In *Ms. Eera*, the court faced the question of distinguishing between biological and mental age of the victim. In terms of statutory interpretation, the court had to ascertain whether the numerical figure of 18 years in section 2(d) of the Protection of Children from Sexual Offences Act, 2012 (POCSO Act)[8] refers to chronological/biological age or 'mental age' of the victim. The context in which this vexed question originated before the court was the following. In 2017, mother of a 38-year-old rape victim who had cerebral palsy moved the Supreme Court of India. She pleaded that her daughter's case should be transferred to the Special Court under the POCSO Act because her daughter's mental age was between six to eight years. The impetus of this plea arose from the fact that under POCSO she would be governed by a different, sensitive procedure and would also be entitled to compensation. A purposive construction of the Act, the petitioner argued, required that the word 'age' includes biological as well as mental age. The argument was couched, not unproblematically, in terms that completely infantilised the disabled victim. The petitioner's argument was that POCSO aims 'to protect the class, that is, child', however, the legislation elides the question of the mentally disabled, '*though they are worse than the children of the age* that is defined under the POCSO Act' (para 10, emphasis mine). It was further argued that a person with intellectual disability 'is incapable of understanding what is happening to her' and is therefore 'equal to a child' (para 13).

Justice Dipak Misra, the then Chief Justice, remarked that the intention of the legislature must be respected which has always maintained a difference between 'mental illness' and 'mental retardation'. The judge sought to distinguish children from the persons with mental disability by emphasising that the latter possess the capacity to consent which is absent in the former. Relying on *Suchitra Srivastava's case*,[9] the court

7 (2017) 15 SCC 133.
8 S. 2 (d) of POCSO Act defines 'child' as any person who is below the age of 18 years.
9 *Suchita Srivastava* & another v. *Chandigarh Administration* (2009) 14 SCR 989. In this case, the court had held that, for medical termination of pregnancy, the requirement of consent of the woman suffering from any 'mental retardation', cannot be diluted since that would amount to an arbitrary restriction on the reproductive rights of the 'mentally disabled' woman.

observed that there cannot be any dilution of the consent of persons with 'mental retardation': '[i]f a victim is mentally retarded, definitely the court trying the case shall take into consideration whether there is a consent or not. In certain circumstances, it would depend upon the degree of retardation or degree of understanding. It should never be put in a straight-jacket formula. It is difficult to say in absolute terms' (para 83).

In a separate and concurring judgment, Justice R.F. Nariman, relying on the doctrine of separation of powers, noted that 'we would be doing violence both to the intent and the language of Parliament' if the word 'mental' was read into the section. He provided a close reading of various other provisions of the POCSO (sections 5(f), 13(a), 27(3), 39) to categorically conclude that 'the Act's reach is only towards the protection of children, *as ordinarily understood*' (para 30, emphasis mine). In the Rights of Persons with Disabilities Act, 2016 (sections 2(s), 4, 9, 18, 31), children with disabilities are treated differently from persons (above 18 years of age) with disabilities. The National Trust for Welfare of Persons with Autism, Cerebral Palsy, Mental Retardation and Multiple Disabilities Act, 1999 also makes it clear that 'whatever is the physical age of the person affected, such person would be a "person with disability" [...] Conspicuous by its absence is the reference to any age when it comes to protecting persons with disabilities' (para 41).

This decision affirmed the distinction between persons suffering from cerebral palsy and children, and refused to infantilise women with mental disabilities, under the pretext of state protection. It rather emphasised legal agency and choice-making capacity of persons with disabilities. Treating them as children within the framework of POCSO would have resulted in an erasure of their capacity to consent as well as their right to sexual agency. However, it does not ask why the child is only defined with respect to biological age? Where does this idea originate? Why does childhood *need to* end at a given age? Does it *actually* end?[10] Taking the discussion away from the context of disability in which the case came up, the idea of biological age became the determinative category which creates binaries of child/adult, irrational/rational, dependent/independent, asexual/sexual. Are these binaries, hinging on the biological age, really fixed? Can we ask if/when/which adults, like children, slip into states where they lose their capacity of understanding and consenting? Conversely, can/do children (like adults) function and perform as actors who know what they want and what is good for them – what is in their 'best interest' if you like – and can/do make decisions accordingly? In other words, what are the terms on which the line is drawn between a child and an adult, if not the fictions of non-malleable, unalterable capacity of 'rationality' – a concept which gets attached to certain subjectivities in uninterrogated ways – pinned onto a biological conception of age?

10 It is also important to ask: are answers to these questions ahistorical, atemporal and universal or are they based on cultural variants, social values, perceptions around normality and abnormality?

Even as the figure of the child is guaranteed stability by defining it in universal and ahistorical terms of chronological age,[11] the category of childhood, the way we understand it today as a distinct phase of human development, only emerged around the 17th century. In *Centuries of Childhood* (Ariès, 1962), Philippe Ariès (not uncontroversially) claims that the (Western) concept of childhood, and relatedly of age, was very different in the period before 1700s in France and England. Unlike in the present times, when young children are taught their age, people in the 18th century did not (bother to) remember or record their age. Thus, the changing notions of chronological age had a bearing on the emerging idea of childhood. Ariès contends that till the 17th century, 'the child under the age of puberty was believed to be unaware of or indifferent to sex' (Ariès, 1962, p. 106). This changed under the influence of modern educational system of the age of Enlightenment and the child came to be seen as sexually innocent whose sexuality had to be protected from immoral influences.

In the (Western) history of childhood, one sees shifts in the portrayal and understanding of the child – from the child seen as 'natural wicked and corrupt' because of the original sin (prior to 18th century), to the child whose sexual innocence needed to be protected (18th-century Enlightenment). During the 18th century, there were anti-masturbation campaigns aimed at protecting the children from dangers of masturbation so that they could be brought up into healthy, moral adults. The sexual child was not just morally but also physically and mentally diseased. The idea was that the child was distinct from the adult and thus, sexually innocent and unaware of shame. Thus, to ensure preservation of their innocence, children needed to be kept under the close supervision and surveillance of their parents and moral educators.

Around the 1900s there was a shift in the (Western) conception of childhood sexuality from a pathology to being a part of child's normal development (Sauerteig, 2012). While Sigmund Freud has been credited with the introduction of sexuality as central and natural in childhood, his psychoanalytic ideas were part of a much wider general discourse about childhood sexuality during that period (Sauerteig, 2012). Unlike his contemporaries, Freud conceptualised infantile sexuality in significantly broad terms. While researchers like Albert

11 Besides the ahistorical notion of childhood, the dominant ideal of childhood presented in the CRC has also come under critique. The ethnocentric bias of CRC has been a matter of serious concern since its inception (Nieuwenhuys, 1998; Barnes, 2015). The argument is that there is no single childhood. '[T]he instrument is not culturally neutral', remarks social anthropologist, Olga Nieuwenhuys, 'but is grounded in the assumption both of the superiority of the childhood model as it has evolved in the North and of the need to impose this model on a global scale' (Nieuwenhuys, 1998, p.270). Drawing on her anthropological inquiry into the work of children in India in the coastal village of Poomkara, Kerala in 1980s, she argues that the model of global childhood 'denies the possibility of diverse childhoods, it not only underscores the superiority of the Northern ideal but also condemns "other" styles of upbringing as a "lack", or, to use the popular expression, of being "outside childhood"' (Nieuwenhuys, 1998, p. 270).

Moll and Ellis looked for sexual activities and behaviour in children that were akin to adults and as early forms of adults' sexual feeling, for Freud children's sexual experiences were of a polymorphous nature but triggered by the same libido as in adults. In the second of his *Three Essays on the Theory of Sexuality* Freud challenged the idea of an asexual child by arguing that infantile sexuality was natural. However, unlike his contemporaries, he claimed that infantile sexuality was not focused on the genitals rather it was polymorphous, unfocussed and diffuse. A polymorphous sexual child seeks pleasure from wherever it can, in all sensual interactions, including sucking, touching, exhibiting, rocking, defecating, urinating.

Freud presented three characteristics of infantile sexuality: it followed vital bodily functions (eating), it was not focused on one sexual object and hence was autoerotic, and it was governed by erogenous zone (Freud, 1905/1953, pp. 179–185). Freud's distinction was that he detached sexuality from biology or anatomy and took it to the realm of fantasy. Rose aptly states: '[b]y describing the child's development in terms of a *query*, Freud moves it out of the realm of an almost biological sequence, and into that of fantasy and representation where things are not so clear' (Rose, 1984, p. 16). This meant focusing not just on sexual acts but emphasising upon distinct *meanings* of children's experiences. This focus on meanings of children's sexual acts was a significant development within psychoanalysis, and it is precisely from this insight, I argue, that the law can learn a lot about children's encounter with the sexual, not just in terms of abuse.

In our contemporary cultural moment, there is a staunch denial of childhood sexuality despite pervasive 'evidence' of its existence (Bromberg & Donohue, 2013; Robinson, 2013; Saria, 2017; Taha et al., 2021; Butalia, 2013). This denial co-exists despite a long-standing historical acknowledgment and celebration of childhood sexuality both in the mythological tradition as well as cultural practices of the Indian sub-continent (Kakar, 2008; Kumar, Dhar & Mishra, 2018).[12] Despite this common knowledge, we all participate in the myth of sexual 'innocence' of the child through an induced forgetfulness (Freud called it 'infantile amnesia' [1905/1953]) of this part of our own childhoods: a 'sexual'

12 The myths of Hindu god, Krishna's *bal leela* (childhood sexual play) with *gopis* (village maidens) have co-existed with an acceptance towards child marriage which is not void ab initio in India. Historically, the child bride of 11 years in India was considered as capable of sexual intercourse (Sarkar, 2001, pp. 226–249)! We remain in denial about childhood sexuality despite common knowledge of most parents and child educators who can tell that children are naturally drawn to exploration by touching, feeling, hugging etc. They derive pleasure from touch. They are curious and playful. In their early years, children touch themselves to self-sooth, but also their care-givers and peers to draw a sense of comfort. Healthy sexual behaviour in child between 0–4 years includes kissing, hugging, showing curiosity about private body parts, talking about private body parts, touching, rubbing or showing off their genitals or masturbating as a comforting habit. Aarambh India, 'Understanding Healthy Sexual Behaviour in Children', http://aarambhindia.org/understanding-normal-sexual-behaviour-children.

child (even if it were you, yourself) has to be muted because the sexual invokes disgust and shame. Silencing this (individual and collective) past,[13] enacted on the myth of the child's innocence, simultaneously produces us (the adults) as 'normal': *I do not have a perverse past, therefore, I am not a pervert.*

For Melanie Klein, the first analyst of children, '[o]ne of the important achievements of psycho-analysis is the discovery that children possess a sexual life which finds utterance both in direct sexual activities and in sexual phantasies' (Klein, 1960, p. 164).[14] In her experience, it was a 'regular thing for quite young children to enter into sexual relations with one another' (Klein, 1960, p. 166). She recognised that masturbation in children is common up to the latency period, when it subsides, only to re-surface in the period before puberty and during puberty. However, during the latency period, 'the child's struggle against masturbation is at its height' (Klein, 1960, p. 164) and 'a moderate amount of masturbation of a non-obsessive kind is a normal occurrence in every stage of its life' (Klein, 1960, p. 166). Klein also wrote that it was 'highly doubtful' if such relations could be prevented 'without causing a good deal of harm in other ways' (like keeping the children under regular surveillance and curtailing their liberty). While in some cases such early experiences 'can do a lot of mischief', in other cases 'their effect upon the child's general development can be a favourable one' (Klein, 1960, p.174). It will be useful to quote her at length here, not to advocate for the Kleinian method of analysis of young children (Pontalis, 1998) but to understand how the sexual is the realm where the child's forbidden fantasies and fears play out:

> For besides gratifying the child's libido and his desire for sexual knowledge, relations of this kind serve the important function of diminishing his excessive sense of guilt, and for this reason: the phantasies the child introduces into these relations are based, as we know, upon sadistic masturbation phantasies round which are centred his most intense feelings of guilt; therefore the knowledge that his forbidden phantasies against his parents

13 This silencing of the child is not peculiar to the law but is evident in feminist scholarship in India. See for instance, Sarkar (2001, pp. 226–249) where the child is totally muted and overtaken by the colonial/nationalist voices. This is visible even in the submissions of feminists on age of consent. The maximum that the feminists ask for is the reduction in age of consent from 18 to 16; the question of child sexuality is again muted (Grover, 2013). As Vrinda Grover recently said: 'We have made a mistake in the articulation of the law, by focussing almost entirely on the specific acts that constitute the crime, and ignoring the behaviour that goes into a long period of grooming, which is why the child keeps quiet' (Rukmini, 2017, June 8).

14 Juliet Mitchell usefully notes that English analysts made a distinction between the term *phantasy* with a 'p' and *fantasy* with a 'f'. The word *phantasy* was used to refer to unconscious phantasy whereas the term *fantasy* was reserved for a conscious *fantasy*. However, Mitchell shows (especially while commenting on Kate Millet) how American writers never maintained this distinction (Mitchell, 2000, pp. 351–355).

are shared by another gives him the feeling of having an accomplice and this greatly lightens the burden of his anxiety. On the other hand, a relation of this kind gives rise to anxiety and a sense of guilt on its own account. Whether its effect will ultimately be good or bad whether it will protect the child from anxiety or increase it seems to depend upon the quantity of sadism present in him and more especially upon the attitude of his partner. From my knowledge of a number of cases, I should say that where the positive and libidinal factors predominate, such a relationship has a favourable influence upon the child's object relations and capacity for love; but where [...] destructive impulses, on one side at any rate, and acts of coercion dominate it, it is able to impair the whole development of the child in the gravest way'.

(Klein, 1960, pp. 174–175)

Thus, rather than censoring or disavowing the sexual, it is important to create an opening that allows readability of sexual behaviour in/among children. The disgust for the sexual child blocks the possibility of empathy towards those childhoods that are trapped in neglect and abuse, or as Nilofer Kaul says, neglect as abuse (Kaul, 2013, p. 163). In a poignant reading of childhood and childhood sexuality in the face of brutal impoverishment and neglect, Kaul offers a reading of the shockingly high rates of addiction among street children. The prevalence of addiction to substance – shoe polish, whiteners, glue, sex, pornography – 'may be seen in that they allow the momentary sensations that must compensate the community of children for the unredeemed bleakness of their existence' (Kaul, 2013, p. 163). 'Sexuality', writes Kaul, 'thus becomes a balm that provides temporary relief' (Kaul, 2013, p. 164).

'Age of consent' in law

In 2012, with the enactment of POCSO, sex with any child under 18 years is made punishable.[15] To ensure uniformity, the 2013 criminal law amendments to

15 Since the enactment of the IPC, the age of consent, originally fixed at ten years for the girl child, has gradually increased. In 1890, the age of consent was increased to 12, following the death of a ten-year-old girl because of violent sexual intercourse by her husband. Her death was not considered murder since the husband had the legal right to have sex with her (Sarkar, 2001). In the early 20th century, the social movements against child marriage which now included women's organisations contributed to the enactment of the Child Marriage Restraint Act, 1929 (CMRA) and the resultant increase in the age of marriage for girls from 12 to 14. The issue was framed within the discourse of advancing girl's education, young women's health and their protection from early pregnancies (Sinha, 2006). In 1949, the age of consent in rape law was raised to 15 years which was followed by the Hindu Marriage Act in 1955, which laid down a minimum age of marriage of 15 for girls and 18 for boys. In 1978, the Hindu Marriage Act,1955 was amended to again increase the age of marriage; for girls the age was raised to 18 while for boys to 21

the IPC increased the age of consent from 16 to 18 years in rape law (Section 63(vi) of the BNS replicates the provision of the IPC with respect to statutory rape). The *proviso* to the rape law provision that granted judicial discretion to reduce the sentence below mandatory minimum in the case of 'special and adequate reasons' was taken away by 2013 statutory amendments. The courts were left with no discretion whatsoever to reduce the sentence or show mercy. This has a significant implication in situations where the minor was a willing party to the sexual act. With the 2018 amendments, if a man committed rape on a woman when she was under 16 years of age, he was entitled to aggravated punishment of mandatory minimum of 20 years which may extend to life (section 376(3) of the IPC, now section 65(1) of BNS).

Age of consent laws, in their presumption of absence of consent, construct the minor as 'incapable of thinking rationally',[16] turn all 'Yes' – even unequivocal, affirmative and enthusiastic – into 'Nos'. Feminist (as well as various other) supporters of an increased age of consent are driven by the desire to protect the (girl) child who, they believe, lacks the requisite agency to take decisions about her sexuality. In this rigid frame, the possibility of any harm to men is completely effaced. Such politics and such feminism 'can't see injury to men. It can't see injury to men by women. It can't see other interests, other forms of power, other justice projects' (Halley, 2006, p. 33). Calling for a 'break' from such a feminism, Janet Halley observes:

> there are many, many reasons to worry about this kind of political consciousness. Not seeing the productive effects of one's purposive actions can cause one to intensify them. If, for instance, you don't think that young men approach heterosexuality with fear and trembling and suffer the inevitable failures of intimacy with deep pangs, you might end up imagining that male-disadvantaging statutory rape laws – which you might be advocating in your effort to protect adolescent girls – have no social costs at all, and so you might proceed, once you've got male-disadvantaging statutory rape laws, to intensify them through the addition of rape shield rules, shifts in the burden of proof, pro-prosecution presumptions, and so on. You could keep doing this until the tolerated residuum of abuse had shrunk to its practical minimum and the number of false-positive convictions of perfectly lovely, sexually animated young men had ballooned to what would be [...] intolerable levels.
>
> (Halley, 2006, pp. 342–343)

(s. 5 (iii)). The Prohibition of Child Marriage Act, 2006 (PCMA) which replaced the CMRA, retained 21 as the age of marriage for boys and 18 for girls. In 2021, the Central government introduced a bill to amend the PCMA with the aim of increasing the age of marriage of women to 21 and thereby bringing it on par with that of men. This Bill is pending in the Parliament.

16 *Satish Kumar Jayanti Lal Dabgar* v. *State of Gujarat*, 2015 (3) SCALE 344.

In the Indian context, the age of consent has been historically tied to the age of marriage. This has rendered sexual agency outside marriage impossible. Statutory rape laws have indeed led to 'number of false-positive convictions of perfectly lovely, sexually animated young men'. For many years now, Indian feminists have been arguing for lowering the age of consent (Agnes, 2013; Kotiswaran, 2018).[17] The issue however is that even feminist critics of increased age of consent have not raised the issue *conceptually*. Even when the argument in favour of recognising sexual agency of adolescents is advanced, it is substantiated with the evidence to rescue adolescents/young adults who have fallen in love and eloped to get married.[18] This juxtaposition of sex leading to marriage elides the conceptual issue of asking how age of consent ought to be framed without eclipsing the child/adolescent as a desiring being. The child and the adolescent are sexual beings – putting a lid on their sexuality through paternalistic measures only leads to unfair outcomes in the real world.

There is no serious reflection on the consensual capacities which determine the age of consent. The debates and discourses around age of consent have failed to raise the question of what children desire, and when they acquire the capacity of understanding and dealing with their desire (Waites, 2005). Even as the age of consent is part of a broader penal policy that seeks to protect vulnerable populations (innocent children) from dangerous predators,[19] the discussion proceeds without reflecting on the figure of the child. Often the child

17 The Verma Committee Report on rape law reforms suggested the reduction of age of consent in POCSO from 18 to 16 years. The committee however did not provide any clear reasoning for its preference of 16 years as the appropriate age for sexual consent ('Verma Committee', 2013, p. 443 [fn 1]). To what extent the Verma Committee was feminist, and which feminism was endorsed by it (Kotiswaran, 2018), are questions beyond the scope of this paper. The committee proposed removal of judicial discretion in punishment (leaving no scope for leniency even in cases of consensual sex), and heightened punishment for under-age rape. Proposed section 376B(1), in cases of sexual intercourse below 16 years with or without that person's consent, recommended minimum punishment of ten years which may be increased to life imprisonment. The committee was thus operating with the unquestionable presumption of an asexual (female) child below 16 years.

18 Agnes's work is significant in this regard. Reflecting on elopement and marriage cases involving minor girls, Agnes asks: 'since the girls were minors, were they juridical persons invested with the power to exercise free choice, and would the consent given by the girls to the marriage be deemed legally valid? Examining these judgments through the prism of women's rights, could these judicial interventions in aid of minor girls be termed regressive and the demand to declare these marriages null and void be termed progressive? Could the curbing of the freedom of these minor girls to express their sexual choices by their natal families, with the aid of the mighty power of the state, in a sexually repressive society, be termed a progressive intervention?' (Agnes, 2013).

19 The proposals of creating sex offenders' registry, petitions for increased punishments in sexual crimes against children, and legislative amendments to this end, are driven by the same objective.

himself becomes a predator to be hunted down when he[20] commits an offence that shocks the 'collective conscience' of the society. In a blanket denial of sexual agency to the young, no distinctions are made between different age groups even though, as already discussed, other laws recognise varying vulnerability of different age groups within the category 'child'.

Far from raising the question of the child as a desiring subject, legal reason remains unaffected even by the evidence of sexual agency of adolescents. This turns law into a governance tool trying to tame erring adolescents and preserve the established social order. Flavia Agnes points out that in statutory rape cases, consent is pitted against agency, especially in the context of elopement marriages (Agnes, 2013). The choice and desire of a girl, when it goes against parental authority and familial/community norms, is contained by reframing the terms of consent.[21] In such cases, '"consent" gets embedded in assumptions about rational choice and parental authority, rather than choices made by women' (Agnes, 2012). In other words, consent is no longer about women's agency, autonomy or self-determination. It is instead determined by larger social and community-based goals.

In a significant number of cases, the eloping couple is hunted down and terrorised because the prosecution piggybacks on the sentiments of the violated parents/family members.[22] The judges, who are supposed to protect the best interest of the child take upon themselves the task of responding to the emotions of parents/family 'wronged' by their daughter who has merely exercised her freedom of sexual choice.[23] One finds that in such cases, the law openly assumes a retributive and vengeful form to discipline defiant minors (and their sexual/romantic partners). Law is enforced, as if, to avenge the 'honour' of the parents.[24] The legal discourse makes it plainly clear that the age of consent laws, despite their claims, are never about the children but about the protection and preservation of some other social goals (decency, sexual governance) and institutions (family, marriage, community). This consequentialist logic of larger good of the community confuses the distinction between the question of *utility* and the question of

20 The juvenile is generally a 'he' – both empirically and in law's imaginative fold.
21 A study showed that of the cases fully tried, over 40 per cent dealt with consensual sex, usually involving the elopement of a young couple and the girl's parents subsequently charging the boy with rape. Another 25 per cent dealt with 'breach of promise to marry' (Rukmini, 2014, July 29).
22 *Sk. Sajid @ Sk. Sagir @ Pancha* v. *State of West Bengal*, C.R.A./718/2014 (High Court of Calcutta; Date of judgment: 04.03.2021); *Laxmibai Chandaragi B.* v. *State of Karnataka*, 2021 (2) SCALE 579; *Aversinh @ Kiransinh Fatehsinh Zala* v. *State of Gujarat*, 2021 (1) SCALE 572.
23 *Satish Kumar Jayanti Lal Dabgar* v. *State of Gujarat*, 2015 (3) SCALE 344.
24 *Sk. Sajid @ Sk. Sagir @ Pancha* v. *State of West Bengal*, C.R.A./718/2014 (High Court of Calcutta; Date of judgment: 04.03.2021); *Laxmibai Chandaragi B.* v. *State of Karnataka*, 2021 (2) SCALE 579; *Aversinh @ Kiransinh Fatehsinh Zala* v. *State of Gujarat*, 2021 (1) SCALE 572.

justice. This utilitarian reasoning is visible even in the judgments which are considered progressive. Let me turn to one such case which grappled with the legislative perplexity relating to age of sexual consent for married couple.

On October 17, 2017, the Supreme Court of India in a celebrated decision of *Independent Thought* v. *Union of India*[25] declared that sexual intercourse between a man and his wife who is less than 18 years is rape. This pronouncement stems from a bizarre confusion which emerged in the Indian rape law after the 2013 amendments. The 2013 amendments had increased the age of consent (in the rape law provision) to 18, bringing it in conformity with POCSO Act, 2012. However, no change was made to the marital rape exception which continued to read as: 'Sexual intercourse or sexual acts by a man with his own wife, the wife not being under fifteen years of age, is not rape.' Thus, in law, consensual sex by an unmarried girl below 18 years was deemed to be without consent, but if the girl was married, even when she did not consent to sexual acts with her husband, it was presumed to be consensual. In other words, a girl below 18 years, otherwise unable to give consent, was presumed to have consented to her husband for all sexual acts, at all times. The larger issue underlying this specific question was the absurdity of marital rape exception which was retained even after criminal law amendments in 2013 (and yet again in BNS).

The decision, prospective in effect, read down the marital rape exception and declared that the exemption for non-consensual sex will not be available to the husband if the wife is below 18 years. The state defended the exception on the grounds that child marriage, though illegal vide Prohibition of Child Marriage Act (PCMA), is a stark reality in present day India, and that the sanctity of the institution of marriage must be preserved. The Supreme Court rejected these arguments and declared the exception as arbitrary and discriminatory. This discrepancy, the court held, was preposterous given the 'interest of the child', especially the girl child. However, the court refrained from making any comments on the larger issue of marital rape exception; instead, it framed the issue in reference to the ill-effects of the practice of child marriage. It emphasised that child marriage violates the human rights of a child and is particularly detrimental to the rights of the girl child, the right to bodily integrity, reproductive choice and 'the right to develop into a mature woman', among others.

This decision is applauded for making a dent in the marital rape exception. However, it remains committed to the larger objective of regulation of female sexuality. It is noteworthy that in all its talk of the rights of the girl child, there is no mention of the right to sexuality, within or outside marriage. In fact, the court yet again consolidated the notion of a child/adolescent as an asexual being, and the girl/woman as mere object of male sexuality. There are

25 MANU/SC/1298/2017.

glaring slippages and contradictions in the court's understanding of the figure of the (girl) child. While on the one hand, Justice Madan Lokur stated that '[m]inor girls have not achieved full maturity and capacity to act and lack ability to control their sexuality' (para 16), on the other hand, concurring Justice Deepak Gupta emphasised that '[t]he girl child must not be deprived of her right of choice...[and] her right to develop into a mature woman' (para 70).

Both the judges subscribed to the age of sexual consent as postulated in POCSO. In their zeal to save the girl child from the oppression of marital sex, they sidetracked the issue of familial violence, through the age of consent laws, on adolescents who sexually express themselves. The slippages between lacking 'the ability to control their sexuality' (which admits to sexual desires below 18 years) and the question of 'choice' (which does not specify choice of what and surely must include the right to sexual expression before and outside marriage) are smothered by the rhetoric of victimisation. No serious thought was given to the sexual agency of the young. This further strengthened the idea that a girl under the age of 18 years is incapable of giving consent. In this imagination, there is no space for sexuality outside marriage. By collapsing all sexual intercourse into intercourse within heterosexual marriage, the court left no space for non-procreative, out-of-marriage sex between young people: 'There is a plethora of material to clearly indicate that sexual intercourse with a girl child below the age of 18 years (even within marriage) is not at all advisable for her for a variety of reasons, including her physical and mental well-being and her social standing – all of which should ordinarily be of paramount importance to everybody, particularly the state' (Lokur J, para 25). Sexual intercourse even within marriage is reduced to the economistic logic of a burden on the nation (Lokur J, para 26):

> The social cost of a child marriage (and therefore of sexual intercourse with a girl child) is itself quite enormous and in the long run might not even be worth it. This is in addition to the economic cost to the country which would be obliged to take care of infants who might be malnourished and sickly; the young mother of the infant might also require medical assistance in most cases. All these costs eventually add up and apparently only for supporting a pernicious practice.

The court neatly sidestepped both the issues of the mental and physical costs of marital rape that are borne by women above 18. An artificial distinction is created between marital rape victims above 18 years and those less than 18 but, more importantly, the question of any sexual agency both within and outside of heterosexual marriage is denied and certainly not below the age of 18.

At best, this decision was a step towards a utilitarian abolition of heterosexual child marriage (the court called upon all state legislatures to follow the example of the state of Karnataka and declare child marriages to be void *ab initio*). However, it would be fallacious to conclude that it created any serious dent in the marital rape exception, even though the exception in criminal law was read down in the specific case of child marriages. The question of the 'just' was sacrificed in the rhetorical flourish of utility.

The reading down of the spousal exemption clause was not driven by the desire to accord minor wives equal rights as subjects or partners in the marriage. But because the minor wives were not *really* wives in the first place (Justice Gupta always used the terms wife and husband in quotation marks to refer to marriages of girls less than 18 years, suggesting they are not really wives and husbands). They are sexless children on whom sexual intercourse will be an act of violence with the possible unfortunate effect of malnourished children.

Despite the vocabulary of choice, this is not about choices before the girl as an independent subject. She is merely an object of male sexuality, not ready for sexual activity and the reproducing of children just yet. What the court naively termed as mere inconsistencies in different legislations on the age of consent and marriage, actually reflect the state's overt interest in the preservation of the institution of heterosexual marriage as the only vocation for the girl/woman, on the one hand, and the regulation of all young, especially female, sexuality on the other.

While the marital exception (even for child marriages) is crafted to safeguard the patriarchal and sexist logic of the institution of heterosexual marriage,[26] the increased age of consent only reflects the anxiety of the state around adolescent and child sexuality and not any concern for the choices or sexual agency of the young, especially girls/women. The discussion on the age of consent has been tied to adulthood in relation to marriage, completely erasing questions of the sexual agency of the young, especially girls and women who turn or are turned into objects of the law, both within and outside marriage.

In 2023, the Law Commission of India (LCI) in its 283rd Report attempted to respond to the profound crisis that is unfolding in the Indian criminal justice system, owing to silencing of the issue of childhood sexuality. The two cases that led to this reference to the LCI[27] revealed how the POCSO Act which is

26 BNS retains the marital rape exception. As per S.63 (Exception 2) of the BNS, a man who engages in non-consensual sexual acts with his wife who is above the age of 18 is exempted from the charge of rape. The marital rape exception was challenged before the Delhi High Court in the case of *RIT Foundation* v. *Union of India* (2022) 3 HCC (Del) 572. The Delhi High Court delivered a split verdict. The matter is pending before the Supreme Court of India.

27 *Veekesh Kalawat* v. *State of M.P.*, Misc. Criminal Case No. 4521 of 2023 (Madhya Pradesh High Court, dated Feb. 28, 2023); *State of Karnataka* v. *Basavraj*, Criminal Appeal No. 100515 of 2001 (A) (Karnataka High Court, dated November 4, 2022).

meant to protect children from sexual violence is indeed used against 'children' (who are sexually active) by labelling them as criminals. In both these cases, minor girls had voluntarily left their parents and entered into sexual relationships with the (accused) boys. They eventually got married (in both cases without the permission of the girl's parents which led to the filing of criminal complaints against the boy) and had children by the time the case came before the respective courts.

The commission recommended that the age of consent should remain 18, however, in cases of intimacy where the girl is between 16–18 years and the age difference between the parties is not more than three years, discretion should be granted to the court to give a sentence lower than the prescribed statutory mandatory minimum. The commission specified a set of guidelines for the concerned court, to ensure that there was a 'tacit approval' of the child and there was no element of fraud, coercion or undue influence. Among other factors, the commission also recommended that the court may ascertain whether the parties are now leading a 'happy married life' and that family members of either or both parties have given their approval for the marriage (Law Commission of India, 2023, pp. 116–121).

It was an opportunity for the LCI to take up the issue head on but unfortunately the commission settled with a smug recommendation that retains the myth of the asexual agencyless (girl) child even when the age of the child is more than 16 years; the child is yet again displaced by the adult desires of 'happy married life', approval of family members and socially legitimate terms of intimacy that accommodate 'tacit approval of the child, though not consent in law'. The commission in aligning with the protectionist rhetoric of the POCSO Act and the statutory rape provision premised on saving the children from the dangers of sexuality, has tightened the noose of 'sexual governance' (Baxi, 2009) by family, community, the police, the law and the state, stripping minors off all sexual agency and turning young boys in consensual sexual relationships with minor girls into rapists who deserve no mercy. In failing to attend to the issue conceptually, the commission failed to do justice to the 'child' on whose behalf it speaks. The behalfism of the commission stifled all possibilities of achieving the 'best interest of the child', establishing once again that the laws about children have very little to do with what children want. Rarely concerned with the well-being or agency of the child, these laws are, as Butler says, 'instrumentalized for the purposes of maintaining certain social institutions, like marriage, or they can be used to rationalize the working of certain kinds of economic and legal systems' (Butler, 2011–2012, p. 19).

Listening to the child

So far, I have argued for a shift in the terms of the age of consent debate. While the law casts all children as agencyless and in need of protection from adult sexuality, Indian feminist critics, in making the argument for adolescent sexual agency, sidestep the idea of child sexuality altogether.[28] Feminists also end up endorsing the problematic liberal assumption that sexual consent is a direct expression of freedom and autonomy.

Now let me ask: how can the law fathom the sexuality of the child? Can it? This is indeed a challenging question that first and foremost requires an acknowledgment that in the current legal system, the child is erased, violently mocked and rendered mute. The child is heard and understood, if at all, only through adult categories and experience. We do not have a vocabulary where the child is not written from the perspective of the adult. In fact, adults constantly produce the child in their own terms, for their own purposes. Legally as well as culturally, the emphasis on child sexual abuse is at the cost of disavowing child sexuality. As if addressing abuse necessarily requires repressing desire. The question of child sexuality is only understood in terms of child abuse where the child appears as a victim without agency or voice. Tragically, despite the zeal of protectionist rhetoric (or perhaps as a result of it), the law fails the abused child by burdening it, as Pratiksha Baxi shows, with the contradictory demand of speaking in adult courtrooms, using adult categories, in adult time while simultaneously retaining child-like appearance and innocence (Baxi, 2014, pp. 117–165).

Narratives of abuse demand clarity and precision in a language where the child speaks in terms consonant with adult idioms and conceptions. This not only implies construction of the child as asexual, innocent (without any desire) but also places huge demands on the child to establish the factum of abuse. Any trace of 'play, fantasy or ambiguity' negates abuse, again denying the realm of the sexual for what it is: 'liberated pleasure beyond bounds' but also 'abominable transgression and destructiveness' (Stein, 2008, p. 43). Law and culture appear to tread upon a singular path that neatly segregates pleasure and pain. However, its frames get distorted to complex narrative presenting a difficult irresistible fusion of the two domains.

The impulse towards producing the child as free of sexual desire serves many psycho-social purposes. In the words of Rose:

> The child victim is de-sexualised – necessarily – for there does not seem to be a readily available language in which one can talk of childhood sexuality

28 Even as I will argue against utility-driven protectionism of law and, in favour of the child's voice, it is not to suggest even remotely that the child is not in need of protection. Children need to be protected. The impact of an abusive relationship on a child is unimaginable. Abuse invades into child's sexual world and translates into bizarre unconscious messages which keep playing out into child's future relationships. Contrary to the assumption that we can hear, know, understand a child who has suffered violation, it is as difficult to listen to sexual abuse as it is to sexual play. In both there is a reluctance to speak, owing to the guilt and shame that constitutes the realm of the sexual. But an abused child invariably suffers from self-loathing, self-blame and 'an irrational sense of complicity which is out of place in the register offered by rationality' (Kaul, 2013, p. 157). S/he recoils inward into silence, the weight of which a little child certainly cannot bear.

> and insist on the reality of child sexual abuse at the same time. Language itself is made innocent – since children can only be made to talk of abuse with great difficulty, it is essential to believe them when they do (in cases of alleged child sexual abuse, the idea that there might be play, fantasy or ambiguity in language is almost invariably used to discredit the child). It is essential, too, that the child's voice be clear and unequivocal in order to lift the adult burden of disbelief. More important still, if damage to children can be shown to stem from lone abusers, then the wider culture – with its responsibilities, trials and dangers in relation to children – can be absolved. Thus childhood returns to a pre-Freudian state of sexual innocence and families, that is families without abusers, revert to the ideal.
>
> (Rose, 1984, p. xi)

The rhetoric of protectionism, in as much as it seeks to save the child from sexual predators in the outside world, solidifies the illusion of family as a safe space without any abusers. The challenge is to foreground all these aspects while thinking of laws for and about children. As Ashley Tellis observes: 'Child agency and child sexuality are extremely complicated issues and demand debate and discussion, not loud claims of abuse, the demonising of figures (the paedophile out there) and protection of the bulk of abusers (the family members in here) or the silencing of the child at the very moment when it seems to confer agency on him/her/it' (Tellis, 2015).

Returning to the fundamental question posited by this chapter: how must the law engage with child sexuality? In 1977, a petition addressed to the French Parliament called for repeal of age of consent laws (the age of consent in France was 15 then).[29] The arguments behind the petition were elaborated by the signatories to the petition in a broadcast: philosopher Michel Foucault, paediatrician and child psychoanalyst FranÇoise Dolto and gay activists, Guy Hocquenghem and Jean Danet. Foucault argued that age of consent laws were part of a new penal regime, designed for a 'society of dangers', with the objective of protecting the most vulnerable population from dangerous predators. He made a two-fold argument challenging both the popular as well as psychiatric/psychoanalytic understanding of a child's desire. Despite his emboldened position towards liberating the sexual in the child, he problematically collapses psychiatry and psychoanalysis, Foucault argued that psychiatrists/psychoanalysts construct their own discourse around child sexuality where the

29 As per Article 227–25 of the French Penal Code, the age of consent has been set at 15. Before this change was made, in 2021, proof of coercion had to be established for the act to be prosecuted as rape. The change was made after the #MeToo movement. In case of relatives, the age of consent is set at 18. However, a teen can engage in sexual activity if the age difference with the partner is not more than five years. Reuters in Paris (2021, Apr. 15).

intervention of any adult will always lead to trauma and thus, they end up supporting repressive legal regimes around sexual consent. Foucault noted:

> [Psychiatrists/psychoanalysts would argue] that children's sexuality is a specific sexuality, with its own forms, its own periods of maturation, its own highpoints, its specific drives, and its own latency periods, too. This sexuality of the child is a territory with its own geography that the adult must not enter. It is virgin territory, sexual territory, of course, but territory that must preserve its virginity. The adult will therefore intervene as guarantor of that specificity of child sexuality in order to protect it. And, on the other hand, in each particular case, he will say: this is an instance of an adult bringing his own sexuality into the child's sexuality. It could be that the child, with his own sexuality, may have desired that adult, he may even have consented, he may even have made the first moves. We may even agree that it was he who seduced the adult; but we specialists with our psychological knowledge know perfectly well that even the seducing child runs a risk, in every case, of being damaged and traumatized by the fact that he or she has had sexual dealings with an adult. Consequently, the child must be 'protected from his own desires', even when his desires turn him towards an adult.
>
> (Foucault, 1988, pp. 276–277)

Foucault argued for total abolition of age of consent in favour of listening to the child. For him, the language of consent was 'an absurdity' to understand the erotics of a child's relationship. Rather, he insisted on listening sympathetically to what the child has to say about the relationship:

> Listening to a child, hearing him speak, hearing him explain what his relations actually were with someone, adult or not, provided one listens with enough sympathy, must allow one to establish more or less what degree of violence if any was used or what degree of consent was given. And to assume that a child is incapable of explaining what happened and was incapable of giving his consent are two abuses that are intolerable, quite unacceptable.
>
> (Foucault, 1988, p. 284)

While Foucault's suggestion of 'listening to a child, hearing him speak, hearing him explain what his relations actually were with someone' is instructive, Rose would argue that Foucault had been reading the wrong Freud: first, in attributing to psychoanalysis a conception of child sexuality as a 'virgin territory' that must remain untouched by adult intervention; and second, in offering a simplistic, rather naïve, view of 'listening' to the child made possible with 'enough [adult] sympathy'.

Rose clarifies that a psychoanalytic understanding makes it impossible to bifurcate child and adult sexuality to set them in a 'developmental sequence at the end of which stands the cohered and rational consciousness of the adult mind' (Rose, 1984, p. 13) – child as the point of (virgin and innocent) origin who will gradually mature into adulthood. In sharp contrast to the dominant invocations of Freud on the question of childhood, Rose instructively points out:

> It is relatively easy to acknowledge in the child a sexuality different from our own, if we can see this sexuality as something which is simply grown out of (rather like a set of clothes). In fact, Freud uncovered in the sexual life of children the same perverse sexuality that analysis revealed in the symptoms of his patients and which was expressed indirectly in their dreams.
>
> (Rose, 1984, p. 14)

This does not imply that there is no difference between child's and adult's desire. Nor does it mean that children experience sexuality as adults or that there is no danger of abuse if the child 'consents'. It means that in creating the myth of child's (sexual) innocence, we (i.e. adults) only seek to confirm and consolidate our own ideas of sexual development, unified identity and subjective cohesion. Psychoanalysis, by disrupting the myth of originary innocence and pointing to a continuity between child and adult sexual identity tied through the unconscious, challenges the firm ground of certitude, 'throw[ing] into question the idea of our subjectivity as something which we can fully know, or that ultimately can be cohered' (Rose, 1984, p. 15).

Foucault's reductive reading of psychoanalysis in as much as he fails to recognise the challenge that Freud presents to the self-assured idea of a stable, coherent sexual identity, blunts the edges of his own argument of listening to the child to understand her/his/its experience of (sexual) relation with someone. While Foucault undoubtedly was questioning the protectionist assumptions which constitute the figure of the child (that child's sexuality can never be directed towards an adult and that a child is incapable of talking about him/herself and his/her feelings), his argument slips into 'a kind of libertarian presumption that the child has a reserve of sexual freedom available at all times' (Butler, 2011–2012, p. 14) that can be excavated by the act of 'listening' to it.

Rose warns us against the lure of the idea of listening to and hearing the child; she instead points to the difficulty, rather the impossibility, of adults listening to and understanding the child. The act of listening will always be marred by 'the adult's desire for the child'. Here desire does not mean the adult sexually desiring the child; rather it 'refer[s] to a form of investment by the adult in the child, and to the demand made by the adult on the child as the effect of that investment, a demand which fixes the child and then holds it in place' (Rose, 1984, pp. 3–4). By fixing the child into a primitive state of innocence, the adult sets herself as distinct, evolved, rational, stable. Or, as Rose puts it:

> Freud is known to have undermined the concept of childhood innocence, but his real challenge is easily lost if we see in the child merely a miniature version of what our sexuality eventually comes to be. The child is sexual but its sexuality (bisexual, polymorphous, perverse) threatens our own at its very roots. Setting up the child as innocent is not, therefore, repressing its sexuality – it is above all holding off any challenge to our own.
>
> (Rose, 1984, p. 4)

Listening will always be an adult listening to the child. It cannot be an unmediated representation of child's voice (if there is ever such a thing) and will invariably project the fears and anxieties of the adult onto the child. This obviously does not mean that the adults can never understand the child but only points to the difficulty of that process. Psychoanalytically, listening practices can only be developed with immense patience and hard work that resist the urgency to find clear truth at the risk of flattening the child's narrative by reducing it into a linear account of acts and events that happened to the child with neatly spelled out emotional responses.[30] Listening is possible only with the courage of imagining language, meaning, time in different ways: acknowledging 'play, fantasy and ambiguity' as opposed to certitude, finitude and stability as guarantors of truth. In other words, the pre-requisite of listening is the acknowledgement of a desiring child.

The practice of listening, for Butler, is neither based on the liberal idea of consent nor on a simplistic libertarian understanding of desire as an act of choice. Her position, arrived through a psychoanalytic understanding of child sexuality, acknowledges the trauma of sexuality for the child: 'the psychic repercussions of ambivalence, shame, and unknowingness, and the particular tensions that can and do emerge when one wants that one does not choose, or one chooses what one comes not to want very much, or when sexuality is itself animated without knowing precisely what or how one wants' (Butler, 2011–2012, p. 14). This cosmology of listening does not assume the child to be 'a tiny liberal, epistemologically equipped with a translucent window that opens upon the domain of true desire and choice at a very young age' (Butler, 2011–2012, p. 18). Instead, with care one ought to receive and hold the child's speech, with the knowledge that 'the speaking of the child is one way of trying to make sense of desire and choice *on the condition that someone else is actually listening*' (Butler, 2011–2012, p. 18, emphasis mine). The speech is conditional on listening. Speech, marked by a real lack of grammar of the sexual in case of the child, 'is given over to someone else, and that someone else must receive it'. That is the response-ability of the listening adult in such settings. 'Only within the

30 Structurally, we might have to re-think the very foundations of children's laws, the architecture of children's courts and the logic of procedures and expertise that currently occupies the thinking around child victims. For now, these issues are beyond the scope of this chapter.

context of this scene of listening' writes Butler, 'does something begin to be fathomed and articulated'. This requires a process for carving out a listening space which neither assumes complete lucidity and transparency with respect to one's desire nor mutes the subject by making the law speak on her behalf. Can the scene of law transform into this scene of listening?

Returning to the forgotten child

French philosopher and psychoanalyst Jean-Bertrand Pontalis had said that '[a]ny discourse on the child purporting to speak the child's language for him is questionable' (1998, p. 82). This chapter is no different.

As I am writing the closing lines, I am beginning to become aware of my own appropriation of the child I had mentioned in the opening quote. The behalfism of this chapter, even though I have sought to make a plea for listening to the child, is not lost on me. How my own agenda took over – silencing the voice of the child, reducing it to decorative epigraph – only betrays the protectionist zeal of my own position, my own anxious desire to save the child, my child, from the law, the state, the adult world.

But who am I striving to save by saving the child? Who is saving whom?

I close by returning to my five-year old, pregnant with ideas, hope and dreams that fly in the face of the deadness of the constricted, already fully formed, adult world, a world that is crashing down under the weight of its own rationality. Without burdening the child with the demand of saving our world, of making the future bearable, can we let the child give birth to its own world of possibilities? Can we start by taking on the impossible task of listening to, and even writing for, the child?

References

Agnes, F. (2012, May 12). Consent and Controversy. *The Indian Express.*

Agnes, F. (2013). Controversy over age of consent. *Economic and Political Weekly*, 48 (29), 10.

Ariès, P. (1962). *Centuries of childhood: A social history of family life* (R. Baldick, Trans.). Vintage Books.

Barnes, A. (2015). A genealogy of the UN Convention on the Rights of the Child. In A. Barnes (Ed.), *Feminisms of discontent: Global contestations*. New Delhi: Oxford University Press.

Baxi, P. (2009). Habeas Corpus juridical narratives of sexual governance. *Working Paper Series*, Centre for the Study of Law and Governance, Jawaharlal Nehru University, New Delhi. www.jnu.ac.in/sites/default/files/u63/09-Habeus%20%28Pratiksha%20Baxi%29.pdf.

Baxi, P. (2014). *Public Secrets of Law: Rape Trials in India*. Oxford University Press.

Bromberg, D. S. & O'Donohue, W. T. (Eds). (2013). *Handbook of child and adolescent sexuality: Developmental and forensic psychology*. Academic Press.

Butalia, P. (Ed.) (2013). *Dark Room: Child Sexuality in India*. Harper Collins.

Butler, J. (2011–2012). Sexual consent: Some thoughts on psychoanalysis and law. *Columbia Journal of Gender and the Law*, 21(2), 3–14.

Derrida, J. (2016). *The death penalty (Vol. II).* University of Chicago Press.

Foucault, M. (1988). Sexuality, morality and the law (A. Sheridan, Trans.). In L. D. Kritzman (Ed.), *Michel Foucault: Politics, philosophy, culture: Interviews and other writings.* Routledge.

Freud, S. (1905/1915). Three essays on sexuality. In *The Standard Edition of the Complete Psychological Works of Sigmund Freud*, Vol. VII (translated by J. Stratchey). Hogarth Press.

Grover, V. (2013). *Submissions to Justice Verma Committee on law, policing and related matters to ensure justice and curb impunity for sexual violence against women.* http://feministsindia.com/women-and-law/justice-verma-submissions/vrinda-grover.

Halley, J. (2006). *Split Decisions: How and Why to Take a Break from Feminism.* Princeton University Press.

Jain, K. (2020). Negated agency, silenced voice, and the continued negotiations in the spaces within. In L. Vashist & J. Dogra (Eds), *Rethinking law and violence.* New Delhi: Oxford University Press.

Kakar, S. (2008). *The Inner World: A Psychoanalytic Study of Childhood and Society in India.* Oxford University Press.

Kaul. N. (2013). The Long Shadow of Guilt: An Afterword. In P. Butalia *(Ed.), Dark Room: Child Sexuality in India.* Harper Collins.

Klein, M. (1960). *The psychoanalysis of children.* Grove Press.

Kotiswaran, P. (2017). A Bittersweet Moment: Indian Governance Feminism and the 2013 Rape Law Reforms. *Economic & Political Weekly*, 52(25–26), 78.

Kotiswaran, P. (2018). Governance Feminism in the Post Colony: India's Rape Law Reforms of 2013. In J. Halley, P. Kotiswaran, R. Rebouche & H. Shamir, *Governance Feminism: An Introduction.* University of Minnesota Press.

Kumar, M., Dhar, A. & Mishra, A. (Eds) (2018). *Psychoanalysis from the Indian Terroir: Emerging Themes in Culture, Family, and Childhood.* Lexington Books.

Kumari, V. (2014a). Juvenile Justice Bill 2014: A Regressive Step. *Journal of Indian Law Institute*, 56(3), 303.

Kumari, V. (2014b). Not a grown-up debate. *Indian Express.* https://indianexpress.com/article/opinion/columns/not-a-grown-up-debate.

Kumari, V. (2015). Juvenile Justice in India. In F. E. Zimring, M. Langer & D. S. Tanenhaus (Eds), *Juvenile Justice in Global Perspective.* NYU Press.

Kumari, V. (2016). The Juvenile Justice Act 2015-Critical understanding. *Journal of the Indian Law Institute*, 58(1), 83–103.

Law Commission of India (2023). Age of consent under the Protection of Children from Sexual Offences Act, 2012, Report No. 283.

Mitchell, J. (2000). *Psychoanalysis and feminism: A radical reassessment of Freudian psychoanalysis.* Basic Books.

Nieuwenhuys, O. (1998). Global childhood and the politics of contempt. *Alternatives: Global, Local, Political*, 23(3), 267–289.

Pontalis, J.-B. (1998). The question child. In L. Stonebridge & J. Phillips (Eds), *Reading Melanie Klein.* Routledge.

Reuters in Paris (2021, April 15). France toughens age of consent laws to define sex with under-15s as rape. *The Guardian.* www.theguardian.com/world/2021/apr/15/france-toughens-sex-laws-on-sex-with-under-15s.

Robinson, K. H. (2013). *Innocence, knowledge and the construction of childhood.* Routledge.

Rose, J. (1984). *The Case of Peter Pan or the Impossibility of Children's Fiction.* University of Pennsylvania Press.

Rukmini, S. (2017, June 8). When an adult looks back, and sees a dark crime in her childhood. *Huffpost.* www.huffingtonpost.in/2017/06/08/when-an-adult-looks-back-and-sees-a-wretched-crime-in-her-child_a_22132468/.

Rukmini, S. (2014, July 29). The many shades of rape cases in Delhi. *The Hindu.* www.thehindu.com/data/the-many-shades-of-rape-cases-in-delhi/article6261042.ece.

Saria, V. (2017). The ungovernable and dangerous: Children, sexuality, and anthropology. In T. Meyers (Ed.), *The ways we stretch toward one another: Thoughts on anthropology through the work of Pamela Reynolds.* Langaa RPCIG.

Sarkar, T. (2001). *Hindu wives and Hindu nation: Community, religion and cultural nationalism.* New Delhi: Permanent Black.

Sauerteig, L. D. H. (2012). Loss of innocence: Albert Moll, Sigmund Freud and the invention of childhood sexuality around 1900. *Medical History*, 56(2), 156–183.

Sheriff, M. K. & Ghosh, A. (2019, April 30). Explained: What Madras HC suggested on age of consent & age gap, and the implications. *Indian Express.*

Sinha, M. (2006). *Spectres of Mother India: The Global Re-Structuring of an Empire.* Duke University Press.

Stein, R. (2008). The Otherness of Sexuality: Excess. *Journal of the American Psychoanalytic Association*, 56(1), 43–71.

Taha, G. R. A., Gad, G. I., Khamis, M. E., Ali, Z. M. A. & Ali, K. A. (2021). Sexual behavior in preschool, school and preadolescents children: A sample from outpatient's clinic of pediatric hospital. *QJM: An International Journal of Medicine*, 114 (Supplement_1).

Tellis, A. (2015, July 4). Understanding child sexuality. *Fountain Ink.*

Verma, J. S., Seth, L. & Subramanium, G. (2013). *Report of the Committee on Amendments to Criminal Law.*

Waites, M. (2005). *The age of consent: Young people, sexuality and citizenship.* Palgrave Macmillan.

Afterword

On July 1, 2024, the 'new' criminal laws have come into force in India: Bharatiya Nyaya Sanhita, 2023 (BNS), Bharatiya Nagarik Suraksha Sanhita, 2023 and Bharatiya Sakshya Adhiniyam, 2023 have replaced the Indian Penal Code, 1860 (IPC), Code of Criminal Procedure, 1973 and Indian Evidence Act, 1872 respectively. In his speech at the time of introduction of these laws before the Lok Sabha (the House of People), the Minister of Home Affairs, Amit Shah observed that this 'paradigm shift' is done to address 'the concerns of the people who care for Indianness, the Indian Constitution and the people of India' and 'to add soul to our criminal justice system'. The laws, he added, will assure '[e]ase of Justice', 'victim-centric justice', 'single type of justice system in the entire country', and 'incorporate Forensic Science in law with [...] severity and firmness'. 'These [laws]', he claimed, 'are going to be entirely Indianised versions of laws by doing away with all the footprints hitherto in existence [...] overtly indicative of the British colonial System and serving as reminders of our subjection during the British period [...] the Indian concept is founded on the award of punishment and dispensation of justice' (Shah, 2023).

The Indianised version appears to be based on ideas of efficiency, uniformity and severity, and an amalgamation of 'award of punishment and dispensation of justice'. There is much to be said on this, but for now it is not my purpose to call the bluff of this so-called 'epochal shift' from British colonial system to 'Indianness' – that has already been done by Indian commentators in law and social sciences (Tundawala & Choudhuri, 2023; Satish, Dash & Pandey, 2024; Uma, 2024) – but to reflect on the encrypted desire of the 'new' laws: the desire of 'doing away with all the footprints hitherto in existence', the desire to erase the trauma of the colonial past, the desire for 'de-colonisation', the desire of recovering 'Indianness' beyond, to the exclusion of British colonialism. This overt desire of expunging the 'old' laws – 'reminders of our subjection' – in order to discover our 'true' self, is structured on the deceptive promise of ego-psychology driven 'therapists' who sell the lie that one can be 'cured' of one's trauma simply by strengthening the ego or ego affirmation of the type prescribed by such models of psychology. But what is the 'legal unconscious' of this desire?

DOI: 10.4324/9781003387411-8

The unconscious, we know, can be parsed through dreams, and parapraxes. Parapraxes refer to events such as forgetting words that one is familiar with, forgetting what one intends to do, slips of the tongue and pen, misreading, losing things, and also '*making mistakes against one's better knowledge*' (Freud, 1913/1955b, p. 167). Parapraxes have 'a meaning and an intention' even though it may be hidden, and 'involve a *psychical conflict* which prevents the underlying intention from finding direct expression and diverts it along indirect paths' (Freud, 1914/1955a, p. 167). Writing on slips of pen in *The Psychopathology of Everyday Life*, Freud (1901/1960, p. 125) notes how often 'the most insignificant slip in writing can serve to express a dangerous secret meaning'. In law, what are seen as instances of 'shoddy drafting', which are far too many, are perhaps 'the royal road to the legal unconscious' and reveal the unconscious attachments and motivations of the law(-makers). Take for instance, the very last provision of the BNS, the 'Repeal and savings' clause (section 358) clause. This provision explicitly repeals the IPC (section 358(1)), and makes the applicability of BNS prospectively applicable (section 358(2) &(3)). Thus, from July 1, 2024 BNS is applicable throughout the Indian territory; all cases and proceedings up until June 30, 2024 would continue to be governed by the IPC. Interestingly, with the repeal (of IPC) and saving (of settled and ongoing transactions under the old IPC), another provision (section 358(3)) is squeezed in, which reads as: 'Notwithstanding such repeal, anything done or any action taken under the said Code shall be deemed to have been done or taken under the corresponding provisions of this Sanhita'. To paraphrase, in spite of the repeal of IPC, anything *done* or an *action* taken under the old IPC must be deemed as a thing done or action taken in the provision of the new Sanhita. The thing done or action taken must find itself transposed or transmigrated to the new enactment. This odd juxtaposition of the past and present or past-present appears to have strange consequences.

The temporal scope of this provision is an incongruous mystery. If this provision is to be applied to pre-July 1 cases and proceedings, it would result in retrospective application of the Sanhita, which is unconstitutional (article 21(3) mandates no *ex post facto* application of criminal law). It can also not apply post-June 30, as the IPC stands repealed. Then, considering IPC stands repealed and cannot be evoked, we are compelled to ask: what is the meaning of 'anything done or any action taken under the said Code'? Can *still* – after its repeal – things be 'done' and 'action taken' under IPC? The legal fiction created by this deeming provision – (if and when) the old law continues, it should be read as the new – has grave implications. By giving an impression that the 'old law' survives and its invocation ought to be read as invocation of the 'new' law, it may allow for a reading that cases registered under the old law, now can be converted into BNS cases. This not only undoes the repeal clause [section 358 (1): 'The Indian Penal Code (45 of 1860) is hereby repealed'] but also allows for the continuity of the 'old' IPC into the 'new' Sanhita.

This 'mistake against one's better knowledge', and the contradictions it is bound to produce may be dismissed as hasty drafting. Alternatively, if one is not too quick to dismiss the textual errors, it gives a rare insight into the unconscious desire – concealed beneath the overt desire of 'doing away' with the colonial law. In expunging, or pretending to expunge the 'old' law, the 'new' law reveals its love and fascination for the old, colonial order which, despite the repeal, it cannot let go off; cannot let go even if an entirely superfluous provision gets imprinted and inscribed in the new script of the Sanhita. In *Totem and Taboo* (1913/1955a), Freud told a similar story about the origin of the new legal order. In this myth of the 'primal horde', the band of brothers killed the primal father who had a monopolised access to all the women and unbrindled access to pleasure. But after the murder of the father, the brothers are taken over by remorse who then institute the prohibition against murder and incest. Introducing the letter of the law, the 'Name of the Father' to replace the real father. Etched as the Law, the dead father becomes more powerful than the living one. In Freud's words: 'The dead father became stronger than the living one had been [...] What had up to then been prevented by his actual existence was thenceforward prohibited by the sons themselves, in accordance with the psychological procedure so familiar to us in psychoanalysis under the name of 'deferred obedience" (Freud, 1913/1955b, p. 143). Simply put, what Freud was suggesting was that the father's murder did not liberate the sons. To the contrary, the murder was followed by 'the son's identification with the father which installs itself in the subject's ego and gradually as the superego' (Aristodemou, 2014, p. 40). The dead father returns as the all-powerful being, whose authority is no longer external but resides within the sons which makes it difficult for them to disobey him. Now, the dead father is 'loved' more than ever before.

One wonders if, with the repeal of the colonial law, in this decolonised moment, the colonial law has become more powerful than ever before. The civil rights groups have already answered this with a yes, but what is truly revealing is not that the 'new' law is 'more draconian', but that BNS, through what looks like a superfluous, absent-mindedly drafted provision, has *acknowledged and revealed* the existence and persistence of the old order.

This impossible desire of erasing the trauma and re-discovering the pre-traumatic 'cured' self – which was at the heart of this law reform exercise – is a lie that psychoanalysis exposes. One can never expunge or exorcise (individual or collective) trauma, it is 'an ever-persistent force that never dissipates' (Saketopoulou, 2023, p. 4) and can only be 'worked through', with much difficulty, by acknowledging the repressions and resistances of the psyche (Freud, 1914/1958). Some legal commentators have critiqued the new laws for the pretentious 'surface-level change of the imaginary [...] harbouring no aspirations for freedom at the structural and systemic level of the symbolic order itself' (Tundawala & Choudhuri, 2023). There was indeed 'no aspiration for freedom' at the level of the Symbolic, precisely because, as I have been arguing in this book, the Symbolic constitutes us from within. To desire one's freedom, the subject must first and forefront 'confront and defy the legislator within' (Aristodemou, 2014, p. 41). This is what the exercise of 'indigenising laws' did not even attempt.

The change in nomenclature from English to Sanskrit in and of itself is taken as a guarantee of 'Indiannness' (an enforced and constricted Indianness which represses plurality) reflects the same resistance to thought. With ease 'Indian' was replaced with 'Bhartiya', penal with 'Nyaya' and code with 'Sanhita'. The issue is not that the government failed to do a good job at decolonising the law, and of returning to the pre-colonial order. Rather the 'new' laws in retaining the colonial order *as* 'Indianised versions' are truly embracing the disavowed fact that the colonial and pre-colonial are united in their desire to inflict pain and suffering on the other. Therefore, *nyaya* (which means 'justice') did not replace *dand* (punishment); *dand* in itself became *nyaya*. To recall Upendra Baxi's remark on B.R. Ambedkar's dissection of the ancient Hindu laws, the 'classical lawless law of Hindu celebrates the 'Illegality of rights' [...] the terroristic 'sacred' law [...] aims to achieve its carceral political economy through unmitigated bloody-mindedness' (Baxi, 1993, p. 78). Thus, the decolonial, as a return to pre-colonial, will be nothing but always a reproduction of violence.

*

Psychoanalysis does not allow one to settle into a 'conclusion'. The task is always unfinished. The unconscious always exceeds the realm of knowledge. As a theory of reading the law as well as life, it offers no promise of resolution or successful accommodation, but nevertheless it brings us to confront the deadlocks of our desire (Žižek, 2006), as also the contradictions and repressions of our well-intentioned personal beliefs and political convictions.

Feminists have long cautioned us about over-reliance on the law for seeking justice. It has been argued that as law is based on a universal set of fixes, it erodes or homogenises multiple notions of justice (Menon, 2004). But this has not meant that feminists have abandoned law as a site for reform, as law cannot just be wished away. The pursuit of legal reforms through a discursive engagement with law is only seen as a partial but inevitable attempt to secure feminist justice. Diverging from this view of feminist engagement with law, in this work I have argued that feminists need to *re-claim* the law not merely as a discursive site but also a psychic site. We need a psychic theory of the law in order to even begin the work of transformatory change in socio-political order which is subject to the Law.

Working with the category of the 'legal unconscious' – the unconscious of the law and the unconscious of the subject of law – I have argued that we need to re-conceptualise the law and aspire for a 'feminine law' which accepts, rather than denies or resists, the inevitability of contradictions, its internal inconsistencies, its hold by the Symbolic Law. This requires a shift from the epistemological frame of 'law as reason' to law as the terrain of messy and contradictory reason-emotion continuums, where the emotion question is introduced into the domain of subjectivity as well as the analysis of law as subject. Such an epistemic shift to 'emotion' in terms of *subject's desire and the desire of the law,* this book has attempted to argue, would enable diverse, even conflicting, possibilities of justice. If we take the unconscious seriously, the subject of law will be destabilised; it will no longer remain the rational liberal subject-in-control; it would become imperative to acknowledge the legal subject in all her imperfections, emotional dimensions, bringing to fore the relationship between the conscious and unconscious aspects of human subjectivity. At the level of the structure and institutions of law, the unconscious will make us confront the emotional 'undertow' to law's rationality; how the law's rational structure is sustained by its own Law, the Law of the psychic order. This undertow is not hidden in some dark and deep abyssal zone, but manifests in the repetitions and clues writ large over the surface of the legal text. In fact, I have argued that the hyper-rationality of law is the impossible lid on its own unconscious.

We thus need to evolve a 'theory of readability' where psychoanalysis is employed as a critical methodology of reading the languages of law and the legal unconscious. *Avec* Goodrich, the hermeneutic intervention by psychoanalysis will not only provide 'an alternative technique for interpreting law' where legal texts and narratives are read 'in the symptomatic terms of their latent meanings' (Goodrich, 1997b, p. 1038). This hermeneutic technique, I argue, will also open up possibilities of reimagining both the law as well as feminism. A critical response to the postcolonial contemporaneity, constituted as it is by the retributive *jouissance* of law, denial of sexual agency, proliferation of dangerous group identities, requires a radical shift from the liberal imagination of the subject and the law. In our engagement with the law, we need to theoretically re-orient the concepts of power, sexuality, victimhood, consent, agency, masculinity, femininity, embracing a scandalous feminism (to return to Jacqueline Rose with whom I started this book) which has 'the courage of its contradictions' and the awareness that 'all certainties come to grief' (Rose, 2014, p. 269). This can be worked out only by acknowledging and working through the unconscious structure of our desires and our inner fascisms (Foucault, 1983, p. xi).

Feminism needs to embrace uncertainty in order to disrupt the psychic terrain of the L/law that remains entrenched in the rigid narratives of sexual difference, power and desire. We also need to accept and work to bring to light the devastating truths of our inner worlds which reside, again, not in the narratives of certainties of who we are and what we desire, but in the *ambivalence* of our psychic structures where the lines between hostility and vulnerability, love and hate are blurred. This feminism would compel us to see violence not merely as a simplistic ruthless acting out of male power but a desperate and melancholic 'male performative', 'a fraudulent boast' (Rose, 2018), performed and performable by men as well as women. This feminism would further caution us against any idealisation of the flaws of the divided self or of the experience and politics of traumatised subjects. For we may find, with Freud, that trauma leads not to openness and acceptance, 'but to dogma and delusion' and 'the most historically attested response to trauma is to repeat it' (Rose, 2014, p. 77). This feminism, in its quest for a compassionate law, will not be content with simplistic accounts of love and forgiveness but will struggle with the ambivalence of love where we are always at the risk of destroying, and being destroyed by, the one we are most attached to. Unless we acknowledge this side of our sociality which is based on 'festive cruelty' and 'sadistic delight', we will not be able to imagine new accounts of relationality and shake the foundations of the Symbolic.

Now, I am a little tired of my own verbosity in this book. But despite the fatigue from the weight of my own words, as I drew closer to 'conclusion', I repeatedly felt the urge to re-write it all over again, to begin afresh. To begin afresh, just like we want to begin afresh in our relationships, erasing the painful memories of betrayals, humiliations and our own violence unleashed onto those we love; but also to embrace 'scandalous feminism' more fully, let it run it through the text and the sub-text to its dark corners of unreason, contradiction and chaos. In resisting the tyranny of shoulds, did I slip into prescriptive scripts myself – offering the psychoanalytic method of reading as a medicine to treat the malaise inflicting the law and dominant forms of feminism? What lies beneath my refusal to let go of the discipline of law? Why didn't I let *in*discipline take over the inter-disciplinary territory I was charting for law, feminism and psychoanalysis? Why do I keep holding on to the law? Does this 'holding on' betray my own anxiety of losing self-sovereignty? Does it divulge my own desire for – being and remaining in – control? Am I in some way (how?) mirroring the subject of my critique? This is for the reader to say, for now it is time is to put *this* book on the couch.

References

Aristodemou, M. (2014). *Law, Psychoanalysis and Society: Taking the Unconscious Seriously*. Routledge.

Baxi, U. (1993). Emancipation as Justice: Babasaheb Ambedkar's Legacy and Vision. In K. I. Vibhute (Ed.), *Dr. Ambedkar and Empowerment, Constitutional Vicissitudes*. University of Poona.

Foucault, M. (1983). Preface. In G. Deleuze & F. Guattari, *Anti-Oedipus: Capitalism and Schizophrenia* (translated by R. Hurley, M. Seem & H. R. Lane) (pp. ix–xiv). Minneapolis, MN: University of Minnesota Press.

Freud, S. (1901/1960). The psychopathology of everyday life. In *The Standard Edition of the Complete Psychological Works of Sigmund Freud*, Vol. VI (translated by J. Stratchey). Hogarth Press.

Freud, S. (1913/1955a). Totem and Taboo. In *The Standard Edition of the Complete Psychological Works of Sigmund Freud*, Vol. XIII (translated by J. Stratchey). Hogarth Press.

Freud, S. (1913/1955b). The Claims of Psycho-Analysis To Scientific Interest. In *The Standard Edition of the Complete Psychological Works of Sigmund Freud*, Vol. XIII (translated by J. Stratchey). Hogarth Press.

Freud, S. (1914/1958). Remembering, repeating and working-through (Further recommendations on the technique of psycho-analysis II). In *The Standard Edition of the Complete Psychological Works of Sigmund Freud*, Vol. XII (translated by J. Stratchey). Hogarth Press.

Goodrich, P. (1997a). *Law and the Unconscious: A Legendre Reader*. Macmillan Press.

Goodrich, P. (1997b). Maladies of the Legal Soul: Psychoanalysis and Interpretation in Law. *Washington and Lee Law Review*, 54(3), 1038–1065.

Menon, N. (2004). *Recovering Subversion: Feminist Politics Beyond the Law*. New Delhi: Permanent Black.

Rose, J. (2014). *Women in Dark Times*. Bloomsbury.

Rose, J. (2018). I am a knife. *London Review of Books*, 40(4).

Saketopoulou, A. (2023). *Sexuality Beyond Consent: Risk, Race, Traumatophilia*. New York University Press.

Satish, M., Dash, P. P. & Pandey, A. (2024). Bharatiya Nyay Sanhita: Decolonising or Reinforcing Colonial Ideas? *The Wire*. https://thewire.in/law/bharatiya-nyay-sanhita-decolonising-or-reinforcing-colonial-ideas.

Shah, A. (2023). Speech of Honourable Minister of Home Affairs and Minister of Cooperation in Lok Sabha on 20-12-2023. In *Taxmann's Bharatiya Nyaya Sanhita 2023*. Taxmann Publications Pvt.

Tundawala, M. & Choudhuri, S. (2023). Does Today's India Need 'Decolonisation' Speak? *The Wire*. https://thewire.in/politics/does-todays-india-need-decolonisation-speak.

Uma, S. (2024). Why the Bharatiya Nyay Sanhita Is a Missed Opportunity for Gender Justice. *The Wire*. https://thewire.in/law/bharatiya-nyay-sanhita-women-gender-trans-queer-justice.

Žižek, S. (2006). *How to Read Lacan*. W.W. Norton & Company.

Index

Kolibri 360 GmbH
Ferdinand-Jühlke-Straße 7
99095 Erfurt, Deutschland
produktsicherheit@kolibri360.de